Qualifications and Credit Framework (QCF)

AQ2013

LEVEL 3 DIPLOMA IN ACCOUNTING

TEXT

Costs and Revenues

2014 Edition

For assessments from September 2014

Second edition June 2014
ISBN 9781 4727 0903 5

Previous edition
ISBN 9781 4727 0317 0

British Library Cataloguing-in-Publication Data
A catalogue record for this book is available from the British Library

Published by
BPP Learning Media Ltd
BPP House
Aldine Place
London
W12 8AA

www.bpp.com/learningmedia

Printed in the United Kingdom by Martins of Berwick
Sea View Works
Spittal
Berwick-Upon-Tweed
TD15 1RS

Your learning materials, published by BPP Learning Media Ltd, are printed on paper sourced from traceable sustainable sources.

The contents of this book are intended as a guide and not professional advice. Although every effort has been made to ensure that the contents of this book are correct at the time of going to press, BPP Learning Media makes no warranty that the information in this book is accurate or complete and accept no liability for any loss or damage suffered by any person acting or refraining from acting as a result of the material in this book.

CONTENTS

A NOTE ABOUT COPYRIGHT

Dear Customer

What does the little © mean and why does it matter?

Your market-leading BPP books, course materials and e-learning materials do not write and update themselves. People write them on their own behalf or as employees of an organisation that invests in this activity. Copyright law protects their livelihoods. It does so by creating rights over the use of the content.

Breach of copyright is a form of theft – as well being a criminal offence in some jurisdictions, it is potentially a serious breach of professional ethics.

With current technology, things might seem a bit hazy but, basically, without the express permission of BPP Learning Media:

- Photocopying our materials is a breach of copyright
- Scanning, ripcasting or conversion of our digital materials into different file formats, uploading them to facebook or emailing them to your friends is a breach of copyright

You can, of course, sell your books, in the form in which you have bought them – once you have finished with them. (Is this fair to your fellow students? We update for a reason). Please note the e-products are sold on a single user licence basis: we do not supply 'unlock' codes to people who have bought them secondhand.

And what about outside the UK? BPP Learning Media strives to make our materials available at prices students can afford by local printing arrangements, pricing policies and partnerships which are clearly listed on our website. A tiny minority ignore this and indulge in criminal activity by illegally photocopying our material or supporting organisations that do. If they act illegally and unethically in one area, can you really trust them?

BPP LEARNING MEDIA'S AAT MATERIALS

The AAT's assessments fall within the **Qualifications and Credit Framework** and most papers are assessed by way of an on demand **computer based assessment**. BPP Learning Media has invested heavily to ensure our materials are as relevant as possible for this method of assessment. In particular, our **suite of online resources** ensures that you are prepared for online testing by allowing you to practise numerous online tasks that are similar to the tasks you will encounter in the AAT's assessments.

Resources

The BPP range of resources comprises:

- **Texts**, covering all the knowledge and understanding needed by students, with numerous illustrations of 'how it works', practical examples and tasks for you to use to consolidate your learning. The majority of tasks within the texts have been written in an interactive style that reflects the style of the online tasks we anticipate the AAT will set. When you purchase a Text you are also granted free access to your Text content online.
- **Question Banks**, including additional learning questions plus the AAT's sample assessment(s) and a number of BPP full practice assessments. Full answers to all questions and assessments, prepared by BPP Learning Media Ltd, are included. Our question banks are provided free of charge in an online environment containing tasks similar to those you will encounter in the AAT's testing environment. This means you can become familiar with being tested in an online environment prior to completing the real assessment.
- **Passcards**, which are handy pocket-sized revision tools designed to fit in a handbag or briefcase to enable you to revise anywhere at anytime. All major points are covered in the Passcards which have been designed to assist you in consolidating knowledge.
- **Workbooks**, which have been designed to cover the units that are assessed by way of computer based project/case study. The workbooks contain many practical tasks to assist in the learning process and also a sample assessment or project to work through.
- **Lecturers' resources**, for units assessed by computer based assessments. These provide a further bank of tasks, answers and full practice assessments for classroom use, available separately only to lecturers whose colleges adopt BPP Learning Media material.

This Text for Costs and Revenues has been written specifically to ensure comprehensive yet concise coverage of the AAT's **AQ2013** learning outcomes and assessment criteria.

Each chapter contains:

- Clear, step by step explanation of the topic
- Logical progression and linking from one chapter to the next
- Numerous illustrations of 'how it works'
- Interactive tasks within the text of the chapter itself, with answers at the back of the book. The majority of these tasks have been written in the interactive form that students can expect to see in their real assessments
- Test your learning questions of varying complexity, again with answers supplied at the back of the book. The majority of these questions have been written in the interactive form that students can expect to see in their real assessments

The emphasis in all tasks and test questions is on the practical application of the skills acquired.

Supplements

From time to time we may need to publish supplementary materials to one of our titles. This can be for a variety of reasons, from a small change in the AAT unit guidance to new legislation coming into effect between editions.

You should check our supplements page regularly for anything that may affect your learning materials. All supplements are available free of charge on our supplements page on our website at:

http://www.bpp.com/about-bpp/aboutBPP/StudentInfo#q4

Customer feedback

If you have any comments about this book, please e-mail ianblackmore@bpp.com or write to Ian Blackmore, AAT Range Manager, BPP Learning Media Ltd, BPP House, Aldine Place, London W12 8AA.

Any feedback we receive is taken into consideration when we periodically update our materials, including comments on style, depth and coverage of AAT standards.

In addition, although our products pass through strict technical checking and quality control processes, unfortunately errors may occasionally slip through when producing material to tight deadlines.

When we learn of an error in a batch of our printed materials, either from internal review processes or from customers using our materials, we want to make sure customers are made aware of this as soon as possible and the appropriate action is taken to minimise the impact on student learning.

As a result, when we become aware of any such errors we will:

1) Include details of the error and, if necessary, PDF prints of any revised pages under the related subject heading on our 'supplements' page at: http://www.bpp.com/about-bpp/aboutBPP/StudentInfo#q4
2) Update the source files ahead of any further printing of the materials
3) Investigate the reason for the error and take appropriate action to minimise the risk of reoccurrence.

A NOTE ON TERMINOLOGY

The AAT AQ2013 standards and assessments use international terminology based on International Financial Reporting Standards (IFRSs). Although you may be familiar with UK terminology, you need to now know the equivalent international terminology for your assessments.

The following information is taken from an article on the AAT's website and compares IFRS terminology with UK GAAP terminology. It then goes on to describe the impact of IFRS terminology on students studying for each level of the AAT QCF qualification.

Note that since the article containing the information below was published, there have been changes made to some IFRSs. Therefore BPP Learning Media have updated the table and other information below to reflect these changes.

In particular, the primary performance statement under IFRSs which was formerly known as the 'income statement' or the 'statement of comprehensive income' is now called the 'statement of profit or loss' or the 'statement of profit or loss and other comprehensive income'.

What is the impact of IFRS terms on AAT assessments?

The list shown in the table that follows gives the 'translation' between UK GAAP and IFRS.

UK GAAP	IFRS
Final accounts	Financial statements
Trading and profit and loss account	**Statement of profit or loss (or statement of profit or loss and other comprehensive income)**
Turnover or Sales	Revenue or Sales Revenue
Sundry income	Other operating income
Interest payable	Finance costs
Sundry expenses	Other operating costs
Operating profit	Profit from operations
Net profit/loss	Profit/Loss for the year/period
Balance sheet	**Statement of financial position**
Fixed assets	Non-current assets
Net book value	Carrying amount

UK GAAP	IFRS
Tangible assets	Property, plant and equipment
Reducing balance depreciation	Diminishing balance depreciation
Depreciation/Depreciation expense(s)	Depreciation charge(s)
Stocks	Inventories
Trade debtors or Debtors	Trade receivables
Prepayments	Other receivables
Debtors and prepayments	Trade and other receivables
Cash at bank and in hand	Cash and cash equivalents
Trade creditors or Creditors	Trade payables
Accruals	Other payables
Creditors and accruals	Trade and other payables
Long-term liabilities	Non-current liabilities
Capital and reserves	Equity (limited companies)
Profit and loss balance	Retained earnings
Minority interest	Non-controlling interest
Cash flow statement	**Statement of cash flows**

This is certainly not a comprehensive list, which would run to several pages, but it does cover the main terms that you will come across in your studies and assessments. However, you won't need to know all of these in the early stages of your studies – some of the terms will not be used until you reach Level 4. For each level of the AAT qualification, the points to bear in mind are as follows:

Level 2 Certificate in Accounting

The IFRS terms do not impact greatly at this level. Make sure you are familiar with 'receivables' (also referred to as 'trade receivables'), 'payables' (also referred to as 'trade payables'), and 'inventories'. The terms sales ledger and purchases ledger – together with their control accounts – will continue to be used. Sometimes the control accounts might be called 'trade receivables control account' and 'trade payables control account'. The other term to be aware of is 'non-current asset' – this may be used in some assessments.

Level 3 Diploma in Accounting

At this level you need to be familiar with the term 'financial statements'. The financial statements comprise a 'statement of profit or loss' (previously known as an income statement), and a 'statement of financial position'. In the statement of profit or loss the term 'revenue' or 'sales revenue' takes the place of 'sales', and 'profit for the year' replaces 'net profit'. Other terms may be used in the statement of financial position – eg 'non-current assets' and 'carrying amount'. However, specialist limited company terms are not required at this level.

Level 4 Diploma in Accounting

At Level 4 a wider range of IFRS terms is needed, and in the case of Financial statements, are already in use – particularly those relating to limited companies. Note especially that a statement of profit or loss becomes a 'statement of profit or loss and other comprehensive income'.

Note: The information above was taken from an AAT article from the 'assessment news' area of the AAT website (www.aat.org.uk). However, it has been adapted by BPP Learning Media for changes in international terminology since the article was published and for any changes needed to reflect the move from AQ2010 to AQ2013.

ASSESSMENT STRATEGY

The assessment will cover all of the learning outcomes and assessment criteria of the QCF Unit Costs and Revenues. The assessment will comprise ten independent tasks. Students will normally be assessed by computer-based assessment.

Competency

For the purpose of assessment the competency level for AAT assessment is set at 70 per cent. The level descriptor below describes the ability and skills students at this level must successfully demonstrate to achieve competence.

<table>
<tr>
<td>QCF Level descriptor</td>
<td>
Summary
Achievement at level 3 reflects the ability to identify and use relevant understanding, methods and skills to complete tasks and address problems that, while well defined, have a measure of complexity. It includes taking responsibility for initiating and completing tasks and procedures as well as exercising autonomy and judgement within limited parameters. It also reflects awareness of different perspectives or approaches within an area of study or work.

Knowledge and understanding
■ Use factual, procedural and theoretical understanding to complete tasks and address problems that, while well defined, may be complex and non-routine.
■ Interpret and evaluate relevant information and ideas
■ Be aware of the nature of the area of study or work
■ Have awareness of different perspectives or approaches within the area of study or work

Application and action
■ Address problems that, while well defined, may be complex and non routine
■ Identify, select and use appropriate skills, methods and procedures
■ Use appropriate investigation to inform actions
■ Review how effective methods and actions have been

Autonomy and accountability
■ Take responsibility for initiating and completing tasks and procedures, including, where relevant, responsibility for supervising or guiding others
■ Exercise autonomy and judgement within limited parameters
</td>
</tr>
</table>

AAT UNIT GUIDE

Costs and Revenues (L3CSTR)

Introduction

This guidance note is written for the QCF Unit Cost and Revenues (2013 standards). The AAT unit for this will be assessed by one 150 minute computer based examination. Please read this document in conjunction with the standards for the unit. Some of the knowledge will be assessed indirectly through the demonstration of skills. Other aspects will be assessed by discursive testing.

The purpose of this unit is to ensure that students know and understand the role of costing in an organisation, and how organisations use cost and revenue information to aid management decision-making.

This unit builds on the knowledge and skills that students develop at Level 2 in the Basic Costing unit (BCST) and prepares them for the Level 4 Budgeting unit (BDGT). Together, these three units develop students with an underpinning understanding of cost and management accounting principles and the ability to apply relevant techniques.

Costs and Revenues also links into the wider development of students, by linking their growing knowledge and skills of cost and management accounting to those being developed in financial accounting. This is primarily through the connections to the Level 2 units Processing bookkeeping transactions (PBKT); Control accounts, journals and the banking system (CJBS); Computerised accounting (CPAG); and Work effectively in accounting and finance (WKAF). The unit also links to the Level 3 unit Accounts preparation (ACPR) and to the Level 4 units Financial performance (FPFM) and Internal control and accounting systems (ISYS).

There are tangential links to the remaining units in the Accounting Qualification.

The first five tasks are concerned with the knowledge and techniques required for dealing with direct costs and revenues; and with the treatment of overhead costs in the short term. This includes calculations and/or explanations relating to inventory control methods; direct labour costs, including overtime and bonuses; allocation and apportionment of indirect costs to responsibility centres; overhead absorption rates including under and over absorptions; and explanations and calculations for prime, marginal and absorption costs.

The second five tasks are concerned with the knowledge and techniques required for decision-making, using both short term and long term estimates of costs and revenues. This includes calculations and/or explanations relating to changes in unit costs/profit as activity levels change; segmented profit/loss by product; break-even (C-V-P) analysis; limiting factor decision making; job, batch, unit, process and service costing; reconciling budgeted and actual costs and revenues by means of flexible or fixed budgets; and capital investment appraisal techniques.

Learning objectives

The Cost and Revenues Unit involves students understanding the fundamental principles that underpin costing methodology and techniques. Students will develop an understanding of how costs are handled in organisations, and why different organisations treat costs in different ways. They will be able to recognise different approaches to cost accounting and make informed and reasoned judgements to guide management.

It also involves applying the principles of costing. Students will learn to identify why cost accounting is an important tool to an organisation, and be able to recognise different approaches and make informed reasoned judgements to inform management on the most effective costing techniques to aid decision making.

Learning outcomes

In total there are five learning outcomes that are assessed together.

These are:

- Understand the nature and role of costing systems within an organisation.
- Record and analyse cost information.
- Apportion costs according to organisational requirements.
- Analyse deviations from budget and report these to management.
- Be able to use information gathered from costing systems to assist decision-making.

QCF Unit	Learning Outcome	Assessment Criteria	Covered in Chapter
Costs and Revenues	Understand the nature and role of costing systems within an organisation	For detail see Delivery guidance.	**1,2,11**
	Record and analyse cost information	For detail see Delivery guidance.	**2,3,4**
	Apportion costs according to organisational requirements	For detail see Delivery guidance.	**5,11**
	Analyse deviations from budget and report these to management	For detail see Delivery guidance.	**9,10,13, 14**
	Be able to use information gathered from costing systems to assist decision-making	For detail see Delivery guidance.	**2,13,14**

Knowledge and understanding

1 Understand the nature and role of costing systems within an organisation

Students need to understand the different ways in which organisations record, analyse and report costs and revenues. Such costs and revenues are often treated differently from one company to the next, depending on the accepted practice within the business sector the organisation operates in, and on the specific measurement rules chosen by the individual organisation. Students are expected to have a basic appreciation of the treatment of costs in different sectors (eg a civil engineer would use job costing for an infrastructure project; whereas a petrol refinery would use process costing).

Effective internal reporting usually requires organisations to produce segmented reports. Students are, accordingly, expected to be able to produce basic profit and loss statements by product line.

Students should be able to comment on compliance with organisational policies, such as those for inventory control, and labour payment rates. They must be able to understand the significance of these different ways of dealing with cost and revenue information, and indirectly demonstrate knowledge by applying them in relevant circumstances.

Management needs accurate information, based on an understanding of cost behaviour. This information will be used for short-term decision making (eg break-even analysis techniques, and limiting factor decision making). It will equally be used for long-term decision-making (eg investment appraisal techniques); planning (eg forecasting changes in profitability as activity levels change); and control (eg through flexible budgeting and variance analysis).

Students need to understand the relationship between the various costing and accounting systems in an organisation. This includes the relationship between the materials costing system and the inventory control system; the relationship between the labour costing system and the payroll accounting system; and the relationship between the overheads costing system and the accounting system. This involves understanding and being able to deal with cost accounting journals for these areas.

They need to understand and be able to recognise and explain the difference between cost, profit and investment centres. They need to be able to identify which of these applies to different parts of an organisation. They also need to know and understand the principles behind cost objects and direct/indirect costs; and know the make up of the elements of cost (eg prime cost and production cost).

Students should be able to advise on the most appropriate costing principles and methods to use within an organisation. They should understand the circumstances in which marginal costing is more appropriate (eg short term decision making), and those in which absorption costing is more appropriate or is a requirement (eg statutory financial reporting).

Students need to know and understand the principles of marginal (variable) and absorption (full absorption) costing. They should understand the causal effects on reported profits, and closing inventories in any one accounting period due to the choice of costing principle; but that over the life of an organisation there is no effect on overall reported profits.

They should understand the difference between product costs and period costs. Students should be able to indirectly demonstrate knowledge, through the application of skills, by making calculations of product costs and reported profits using both principles.

2 Record and analyse cost information

Students must be able to record inventories in inventory records, and deal with labour cost calculations (for basic pay, overtime and bonuses) in payroll calculation sheets and in other methods of presentation.

Students must be able to interpret and explain the processes set out above.

Students should know and understand the reasons behind, and the implications of, classifying the costs of inventory at different stages. This includes understanding the recording of different stages of processed inventory in the accounting records, and that equivalent unit calculations (see below) are made in this context.

They must be able to identify and explain the principles behind First in First out (FIFO), Last in First out (LIFO) and Weighted Average Cost (AVCO) methods of inventory control and valuation.

Although inventory control is no longer explicitly stated in the revised standards its understanding and application is implied; Students should be able to undertake calculations for FIFO, LIFO and AVCO methods of inventory control and valuation, including analysis of the closing balance. Calculation tasks based on LIFO are now specifically included for internal management accounting purposes; although excluded under IAS for external reporting. They should be able to advise management what the effects on reported profits and inventory values are of using each method in different circumstances, such as when reorder costs are increasing or decreasing.

They should know, understand be able to analyse the different methods that organisations use to control inventories, such as inventory buffers, lead times, minimum/maximum order quantities and the Economic Order Quantity (EOQ). Calculations may be required for all of these, including EOQ, and they need to know the formulae for these methods.

They need to be able to identify how particular costs would be classified, based upon their short term cost behaviour, and the implications of cost behaviour for cost recording, reporting and analysis. Cost classifications are made up of fixed, variable, semi-variable and step-fixed costs.

They should appreciate that such a classification of costs holds only in the short term, and that in the long term (by definition) all costs are variable. Students should be able to undertake calculations based on cost behaviour (fixed, variable, semi-variable and step-fixed costs), including using the high/low method.

They should be able to undertake calculations using Job, Batch, Unit, Process and Service costing systems.

Note: Calculation tasks will now be set on Job, Batch and Unit based systems.

An understanding is required of appropriate organisational costing systems – and students should be aware that the choice of system depends on the business sector of the organisation; for example, a shipbuilder is likely to use job costing whereas a chemical manufacturer is likely to use process costing. Process and job costing systems represent the extreme ends of a continuum, and many organisations need a combination of these two elements (as in batch costing).

Process costing will be examined to the following extent:

- Students should be able to explain and prepare calculations for normal loss; abnormal loss; and abnormal gain.
- There will be no more than two processes. The associated T accounts (eg the scrap account) will not be required – just the process account itself.
- Process accounts will be required, covering the terms under the first bullet point, where there is no closing work in progress. This will include scrap sales revenue.
- Unit cost calculations for equivalent units where there is closing or opening work in progress, but not both and not including process losses.

Neither by-products nor joint products will be examined.

3 Apportion costs according to organisational requirements

Students need to be able to identify, explain and make calculations for both the direct and step down bases of allocation and apportionment of overheads. They should appreciate, and be able to explain, the difference between allocations and apportionments.

They should be able to allocate costs to responsibility centres where these have entirely incurred the relevant cost. They should be able to make primary apportionments to responsibility centres where these have shared the benefits of the relevant cost.

They should then be able to make secondary apportionments from cost centres to profit/investment centres using either the direct or step down methods.

Students should be able to undertake calculations on an appropriate basis leading to final budgeted overhead absorption rates, and must be able to identify, interpret and make calculations of under and over recovery (absorption) of overheads.

They must know and understand different bases of absorption. These are confined to machine hours, direct labour hours, and direct labour % add on methods (a variant of the direct labour hours basis) for manufacturers; and to

appropriate volume bases (eg miles travelled for a bus company) for service sector organisations. They should be able to choose the most appropriate basis for a particular organisation, and to justify their choice of basis.

They should understand the significance of under and over recoveries and how they are recorded in the organisation's statement of profit or loss (income statement). Students should recognise the arbitrary nature of these methods under traditional costing systems, and the need to review and perhaps change them as the organisation changes over time (eg as a company adds more automation, it may be appropriate to change from a labour hour to a machine hour basis of absorption).

Students should be able to consult with staff in operational departments as well as with specialist accounting and management personnel. This may be examined by a brief 'report', memo or email as set out below.

4 Analyse deviations from budget and report these to management

Students should be able to identify and calculate variances for:

- Direct materials
- Direct labour
- Fixed overheads
- Sales revenue

The sub-division of these variances into price and usage elements will not be examined.

They should be able to reconcile the budgeted and actual costs and revenues, using the variances set out above.

'Budget costs and revenues' refers to both fixed and flexed budgets. Students are expected to be competent in using either approach, and in identifying the causes of variances from both. Flexed budgets will not involve semi-variable cost calculations. Students will not be asked to calculate the subdivisions, but will be expected to answer discursive tasks that require knowledge of their subdivision.

Students should be able to explain the meaning and significance of the above variances. This includes being able to explain the likely causes and effects of each, and should be able to advise management of ways of addressing significant deviations from budget; for example, an adverse material variance may be resolved by reducing the amount of materials wasted or buying it at a cheaper price.

Students should be able to prepare reports in an appropriate format and present these to management within the required timescales. Students may be asked in any task to produce a written report, memo, or e-mail to advise of their findings.

5 Be able to use information gathered from costing systems to assist decision-making

Students should be able to identify and explain relevant (avoidable) and irrelevant (unavoidable) costs in the context of short-term decision making. They should be able to categorise costs as direct or indirect, and as relevant or irrelevant. They should appreciate that in the long term all costs are relevant (avoidable).

They should be able to identify and explain the principles underpinning break-even (CVP) analysis. This includes identification, explanations and calculations of break-even units; break-even revenue; margin of safety units; margin of safety revenue; margin of safety %; target profit units; and target profit revenues.

Students should be able to identify and explain the principles underpinning limiting factor decision making for a single limiting factor. Knowledge of linear programming for multiple limiting factors is not required.

Students should be able to undertake calculations for payback, net present cost, net present value and internal rate of return. Calculations for discounted payback and accounting rate of return are not required.

Note: tasks requiring students to make basic internal rate of return calculations will now be set.

Tasks requiring students to explain the principles of discounted cash flow will no longer be set. Discursive tasks will be concerned with interpreting the meaning of investment appraisal criteria (including their own results) rather than discussing the underpinning principles.

Students must be able to identify, explain and understand the effects of changes in activity levels on unit product and service costs, revenues and profits. This requires an understanding of cost behaviour as set out in the cost classifications above.

Students need to be able to identify, explain and make calculations based upon different types of short term cost behaviour. They should be able to produce short term forecasts based on short term cost behaviour classifications, and long term forecasts based on all costs being purely variable.

chapter 1: INTRODUCTION TO COST ACCOUNTING

chapter coverage

In this opening chapter we will consider the overall purposes of cost or management accounting together with an introduction to the key concepts and terms that will be used throughout this Text. We will also consider the main methods of costing that will be used in many areas of the syllabus for this unit. Don't worry too much about understanding every word in this chapter. You will pick it up as you read further chapters of this Text. The topics that we shall cover are:

- Financial accounting and management accounting
- Summary of financial and management accounting
- Overview of a costing system
- Cost, profit and investment centres
- Classification of costs
- The unit cost card
- Methods of costing
- Revenue

FINANCIAL ACCOUNTING AND MANAGEMENT ACCOUNTING

The accounting function of a business will be concerned with providing information for both management accounting and financial accounting purposes. However the type of information required, the timing of the information and the format of the information will be different for each.

Financial accounting

FINANCIAL ACCOUNTING is predominantly concerned with the collection and classification of historic data in order to prepare the annual, or sometimes six monthly, financial statements of the business. These financial statements are prepared for users outside of the business such as:

- the current shareholders
- prospective investors
- providers of loan capital
- receivables and payables (also called debtors and creditors)
- the government

Financial statements can be used by those external to the organisation to judge the performance of the business as a whole and to judge how successfully the directors of a company have carried out their stewardship function.

The financial statements must be prepared according to both legal requirements and the extensive requirements of accounting standards and must be presented in statutory formats. If the organisation is a company the financial statements must usually also be audited by an external auditor.

Management accounting

In contrast MANAGEMENT ACCOUNTING, as the name implies, is all about providing the management of an organisation with the information that it needs to carry out its functions properly. The three main functions of management are:

- Planning
- Control
- Decision making

Therefore the purpose of management accounting information is to be relevant to these three functions.

This will require the provision of both historic information and estimates of future figures in a format that is useful to the relevant members of the management team. Most importantly, the information must be provided regularly and on a timely basis, particularly for the purposes of control and can be one-off reports or information for decision making purposes.

SUMMARY OF FINANCIAL AND MANAGEMENT ACCOUNTING

	Financial accounting	Management accounting
Users	External to the organisation	Internal management
Timing	Annual	When required
Type of information	Historic	Historic and future
Format	Specified by law	To be useful

The key here is that the type of management information provided must be useful, relevant and timely. Without these qualities it will not be possible for management to carry out their functions of planning, control and decision making.

OVERVIEW OF A COSTING SYSTEM

One of the key concerns that management will have will be how much the products that it produces, or the services that it provides, cost. This information will be vital for many purposes including the following:

- Setting the selling price
- Determining the quantities of production and sales
- Continuing or discontinuing a product
- Controlling costs
- Controlling production processes
- Appraising managers

Organisations record, analyse and report costs and revenues for management purposes in a variety of ways. This depends on the business sector and measurement practices of the organisation.

For instance an oil refinery will use PROCESS COSTING to account for its inventory whereas a bridge building organisation will adopt JOB COSTING. These terms are explained later in the Text.

Manufacturing industries will typically look at costs by function classifying costs into production, sales, administration and so on. This helps management understand the costs and revenues by the main areas of activity.

A retail organisation is likely to record costs and revenues by its shops which are PROFIT CENTRES.

In some organisations the management accountant will report costs and revenues to a Board and have to present a report. In other organisations, things may be more informal and a quick memo or email will be enough.

Types of cost

Costs in both manufacturing and service industries are traditionally split between:

- Material costs
- Labour costs
- Overheads (or expenses)

These costs in turn can be described as DIRECT COSTS or INDIRECT COSTS. This analysis depends upon whether the cost in question can be directly attributed to a unit of production or unit of service. The first stage in the cost allocation process then is to determine the cost units of the business.

Task 1

Which of the following costs are direct costs of a special type of bicycle? (**Hint**: remember that direct costs are costs which are incurred on one specific product.)

A Component parts of the special bicycle

B Supervisor wages (the supervisor supervises several different types of bicycle being made)

C Electricity for heating and lighting

D Paint which is just used on the special bicycle

E Wages for staff who assemble the special bicycles only

In a manufacturing business the COST UNIT may be each unit of production or each batch of production. In a service business the identification of the cost unit may not be quite so straightforward but, for example, in a transport business the cost unit might be each lorry mile travelled or, in a restaurant, it might be each meal served. Later in this chapter we look at how a COST UNIT is made up.

Any material cost or labour cost or expense that can be directly related to the cost unit is a DIRECT COST of that cost unit. However many costs of the business

cannot be directly attributed to a cost unit and these INDIRECT COSTS are initially taken to a cost centre.

A COST CENTRE is an area of the business, maybe a department such as the factory or canteen, for which costs are incurred that cannot be directly attributed to the cost units. These costs are known as INDIRECT COSTS or overheads.

There are two types of cost centre – those that are directly involved in the production or provision of the cost unit, such as the factory, and these are known as production cost centres. There are also cost centres that, while not actually producing the cost unit, do provide a service to the production cost centres such as the canteen. These are known as service cost centres.

A COST OBJECT is any activity for which a separate measurement of costs is desired. If the users of management information wish to know the cost of something, this something is called a cost object. Examples include the cost of a product, the cost of operating a department and the cost of a service.

COST, PROFIT AND INVESTMENT CENTRES

RESPONSIBILITY CENTRES are areas of the business for which costs or revenues are gathered and compared to budgets for control purposes. There are a variety of different types of responsibility centre depending upon the type of cost and/or revenue that the centre deals with.

Responsibility centres are known as such due to the fact that each area of the business designated as such has a manager who is responsible for the activities of that area.

RESPONSIBILITY ACCOUNTING is a method of budgeting and comparing actual costs to budgets for each of the responsibility centres.

Types of responsibility centres

A COST CENTRE (as we have already discussed) is an area of the business for which costs can be ascertained. This may be the entire factory or a smaller area such as a single machine. The manager responsible for a cost centre has authority regarding the costs incurred by his/her area of responsibility and should be held responsible for controlling the costs.

A PROFIT CENTRE is an area of the business for which both revenues and costs can be ascertained and therefore a profit or loss for a period can be determined. Often profit centres are larger areas of the business such as an entire division or geographical sales area. The manager of the profit centre has authority over both costs and income and is responsible for the profit and thereby variances for both costs and revenues.

An INVESTMENT CENTRE is similar to a profit centre, the difference being that the manager of an investment centre is responsible not only for the profit that is earned by the area of the business but also the net assets of the area of the business. Investment centres will often be entire divisions. The manager of an investment centre not only has authority over the costs and income of the centre but also over its assets and liabilities. A measure called 'return on capital employed' is calculated to determine how well the manager of an investment centre is performing.

Allocation and apportionment of overheads

The overheads of both the production and the service cost centres are part of the necessary cost of producing the COST UNITS and therefore in some costing systems they are included in the overall cost of the cost unit. We will look at this in detail later in the Text so this is just a short overview. The way in which overheads end up in cost units is achieved by the following process:

- Allocation of overheads that relate to just one cost centre, such as the depreciation of the factory machinery being allocated to the factory cost centre.
- Apportionment of overheads that relate to a number of cost centres to each relevant cost centre on some fair basis, such as the apportionment of the rent of the building to each cost centre in the building on the basis of floor space occupied.
- Re-apportionment of service cost centre costs to the production cost centres to ensure that all overheads are now included within the production cost centre costs.
- Absorption of all of the overheads of each production cost centre into the cost of cost units on some fair basis such as the number of labour hours or machine hours that each cost unit uses.

We can summarise this process in a diagram:

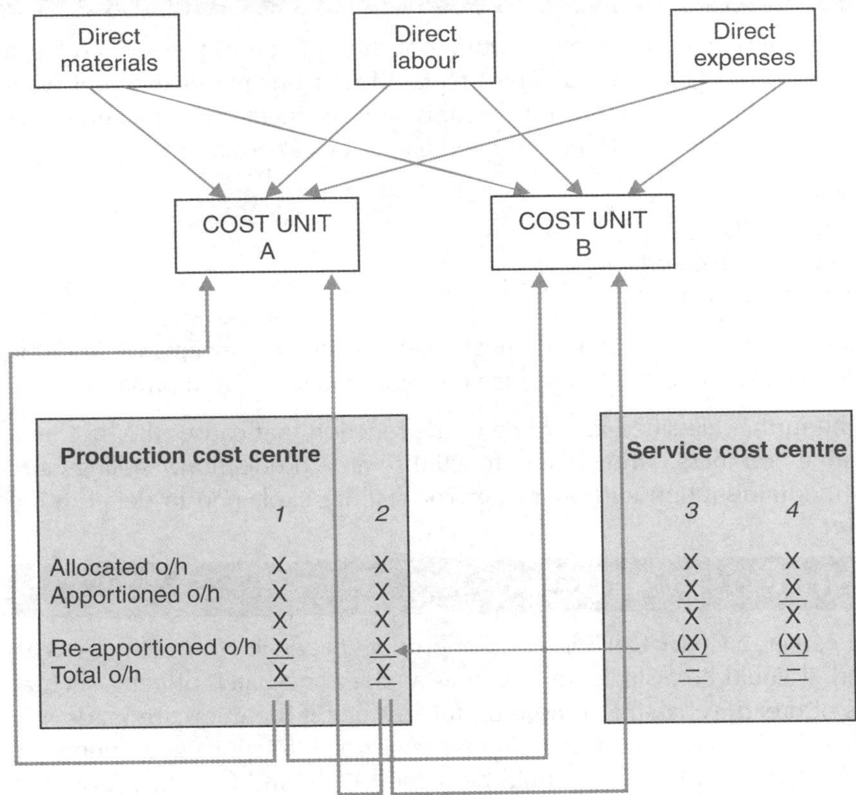

CLASSIFICATION OF COSTS

In order to be able to correctly deal with all of these different types of cost you must be able to recognise that different types of cost behave in different ways when the levels of activity in the organisation change. This is known as classification of costs by behaviour and the main classifications are:

- Variable costs
- Fixed costs
- Semi-variable costs
- Step-fixed costs

Each of these will be illustrated in the next chapter and the concepts will then be used in later chapters in order to produce relevant management information.

Costs can be further classified according to the function that causes the cost. In a manufacturing business, the main functions are production, selling and distribution, administration and financing. This will be explained in detail in the next chapter.

THE UNIT COST CARD

As we said earlier, a COST UNIT is a unit of product or service to which costs can be attached. It could be a single item such as a table, or a batch of items such as 200 loaves of bread. A batch is a more useful cost unit if the items are made in a batch and/or the individual cost of an item is very small: fractions of a penny, for example. For a hotel, a cost unit would be a guest night and for a taxi service, a passenger mile.

The cost of a cost unit is an important piece of costing information that will be used in many different ways. The cost is built up on a COST CARD, which groups the costs using the categories that we have just looked at.

COST CARD	
	£
Direct materials	X
Direct labour	X
Direct expenses	X
Prime cost	X
Production overheads	X
Production cost	X
Non-production overheads	
– selling and distribution	X
– administration	X
– finance	X
Total cost	X

The cost card has two subtotals:

- PRIME COST is a term used for the total of the direct costs.
- PRODUCTION COST is the total of the manufacturing costs. It is this cost that would be used for reporting purposes, in other words for the valuation of inventory in the statement of financial position and the cost of goods sold in the statement of profit or loss. In cost accounting the non-production overheads are included to give the full cost, shown as total cost here, so that the business can ensure that all costs are covered by the selling price and that a profit is being made.

There are a number of different ways in which the values of materials, labour and overheads on the cost card are found. For a one-off job made to a customer's individual specifications, all the costs can be identified with that particular job. This method is known as JOB COSTING. If the product is made in batches of identical items, the costs of producing a batch would be found, which is called BATCH COSTING. The cost of an individual item within a batch can be found, if this is meaningful, by dividing the batch cost in total by the number of items in the batch. The next few chapters detail how materials, labour and overhead costs are recorded. Later on we look at job and batch costing in a little more detail together with a further costing system known as process costing.

The way in which a production overhead cost per cost unit is found is known as ABSORPTION COSTING. This technique aims to attach an appropriate amount of each type of overhead, such as lighting, heating, power, depreciation and maintenance, to the products made. It is dealt with in detail in a later chapter.

METHODS OF COSTING

We have seen in outline how the cost of a COST UNIT is calculated. Some of these principles should also be familiar from your previous studies. We will now move onto the different methods of calculating a cost per unit that a business may use. The method chosen will depend upon the type of business and the policy of management. There are three main methods of calculating a cost per unit. We look at absorption costing and marginal costing in later chapters. Activity based costing is beyond the scope of our syllabus:

- **Absorption costing** – under this costing method a 'full' production cost per unit is calculated by including in the cost of the cost unit a proportion of the production overheads from each of the production and service cost centres. This is done by allocating, apportioning and absorbing the overheads.

- **Activity based costing** – this is a method of absorption costing that uses more sophisticated methods of allocating overheads to cost units than the normal methods of overhead allocation and apportionment.
- **Variable or marginal costing** – under this method only the variable costs (or marginal costs) of production are included in the cost per cost unit. The fixed overheads are treated as period costs and not as part of the cost unit. The fixed overheads are charged to the statement of profit or loss as an expense for the period.

REVENUE

The emphasis in this chapter has been on the costs incurred by a business as this will be of prime importance to management. However, they will of course also be interested in the revenue earned by the business, and therefore revenue cannot be ignored. In particular management will be concerned to ensure that enough units are sold at the right price in order to cover all costs and therefore make a profit. We will cover this in the remainder of the unit.

CHAPTER OVERVIEW

- Financial accounting is concerned with providing historic information to parties external to the organisation in the form of annual financial statements.
- Management accounting is concerned with providing relevant, useful and timely information to management based upon actual costs and revenues and forecast figures in order that management can carry out its main functions of planning, control and decision making.
- Direct costs are costs that can be related directly to a cost unit whereas indirect costs are initially allocated or apportioned to a cost centre.
- Responsibility centres are used to compare actual costs and revenues to budgets. The main responsibility centres are cost, profit and investment centres.
- Cost units collect overhead costs by way of allocation, apportionment and absorption of costs.
- Costs are often classified according to their behaviour as activity levels change – the main classifications are variable costs, fixed costs, step-fixed costs and semi-variable costs.
- Costs can also be classified according to the function that causes the cost.
- The unit cost card collects direct and indirect costs and groups them into a prime cost and a production cost.
- There are three main methods of costing – absorption costing, marginal costing and activity based costing (ABC). (You don't need to know about ABC.)
- Absorption costing is where the production overheads are included in full in the cost of each cost unit.
- Under marginal costing only variable overheads are included in the cost of cost units with the fixed overheads being charged to the statement of profit or loss as a period cost.

Keywords

Financial accounting – the provision of financial statements for parties external to the organisation based upon historical data

Management (cost) accounting – the provision of both actual figures and forecast figures to enable management to carry out their prime functions of planning, control and decision making

Process costing – a costing system where the unit cost is determined by averaging the periodic costs of the process over the expected good output from the process

Job costing – costing system that allocates costs to individual 'one-off' jobs for customers

Cost unit – the individual product or service for which costs are to be gathered

Direct costs – costs that can be directly attributed to cost units

Responsibility centres – areas of the business for which costs or revenues are gathered and compared to budgets for control purposes

Responsibility accounting – a method of budgeting and comparing actual costs to budgets for each of the responsibility centres.

Cost centre – an area of the business for which costs are to be gathered

Profit centre – is an area of the business for which both revenues and costs can be ascertained and therefore a profit or loss for a period can be determined

Investment centre – is similar to a profit centre, the difference being that the manager of an investment centre is responsible not only for the profit that is earned by the area of the business but also the net assets of the area of the business

Indirect costs – costs that cannot be attributed directly to a cost unit but are initially attributed to a cost centre

Variable costs – costs that increase/decrease directly in line with any changes in activity level

Fixed costs – costs that remain constant as activity levels change

Step-fixed costs – costs that are fixed over a relatively small range and then increase in steps

Semi-variable costs – costs that have both a fixed element and variable element

Cost card – document which groups the costs of a product or service in order to arrive at a total cost

Absorption costing – a costing method that includes all production overheads within the cost of the cost units

Keywords cont'd

Marginal costing – a costing method that includes only variable costs within the cost of the cost units whereas fixed costs are written off as period costs

Prime cost – the total of direct costs

Production cost – the total of manufacturing costs

TEST YOUR LEARNING

Test 1

Complete the following sentences:

(a) The three main functions of management are

[ ],

[ ] and [ ].

(b) Direct cost are costs that can be directly attributed to a

[ ] [ ].

(c) Indirect costs are initially allocated and apportioned to

[ ] [ ].

Test 2

A cost unit is

A The cost per hour of operating a machine
B The cost per unit of electricity consumed
C A unit of product or service in relation to which costs are ascertained
D A measure of work output in a standard hour

Test 3

A cost centre is

A A unit of product or service in relation to which costs are ascertained

B An amount of expenditure attributable to an activity

C A production or service location, function, activity or item of equipment for which costs are accumulated

D A centre for which an individual budget is drawn up

Test 4

Which of the following items might be a suitable cost unit within the accounts payable department of a company?

(i) Postage cost
(ii) Invoice processed
(iii) Supplier account

A Item (i) only
B Item (ii) only
C Item (iii) only
D Items (ii) and (iii) only

Test 5

Prime cost is

A all costs incurred in manufacturing a product
B the total of direct costs
C the material cost of a product
D the cost of operating a department

Test 6

Which of the following costs are part of the prime cost for a manufacturing company?

A Cost of transporting raw materials from the supplier's premises
B Wages of factory workers engaged in machine maintenance
C Depreciation of lorries used for deliveries to customers
D Cost of indirect production materials

Test 7

Which of the following are direct expenses?

(i) The cost of special designs, drawing or layouts
(ii) The hire of tools or equipment for a particular job
(iii) Salesman's wages
(iv) Rent, rates and insurance of a factory

A (i) and (ii)
B (i) and (iii)
C (i) and (iv)
D (iii) and (iv)

Test 8

Which of the following are indirect costs?

(i) The depreciation of maintenance equipment
(ii) The overtime premium incurred at the specific request of a customer
(iii) The hire of a tool for a specific job

A Item (i) only
B Items (i) and (ii) only
C Items (ii) and (iii) only
D All of them

chapter 2: COST CLASSIFICATION AND COST BEHAVIOUR

chapter coverage

In this chapter of the Text we will be looking in more depth at some of the topics introduced in the first chapter. The topics to be covered are:

- Classification of costs
- Capital and revenue expenditure
- Classification of costs by function
- Direct and indirect cost elements
- Cost behaviour: fixed and variable costs
- Calculating the fixed and variable elements of semi-variable costs

CLASSIFICATION OF COSTS

A business will incur many different types of cost from day to day. For cost accounting purposes it is useful to group or classify these costs. There are, however, a number of different ways of doing this.

CAPITAL AND REVENUE EXPENDITURE

The expenses of a business can be categorised as either capital or revenue.

CAPITAL EXPENDITURE includes

- the purchase of non-current assets
- the improvement of the earning capability of non-current assets

NON-CURRENT ASSETS Non-current assets are assets that are used in the business for more than one accounting period to provide benefits. These benefits are (we hope!) the profits earned from using the non-current assets in the business. Plant and machinery, land and buildings, office equipment and motor vehicles are all examples of non-current assets that play their part in earning profits by being used within the business rather than being bought to make profit on their resale.

REVENUE EXPENDITURE includes

- the purchase of goods for resale
- the maintenance of the existing earning capacity of non-current assets
- expenditure incurred in conducting the business

Capital expenditure is shown as a non-current asset in the statement of financial position, while revenue expenditure is charged as a cost in the statement of profit or loss. In costing terms, capital expenditure would not be included in the cost of a product: only revenue expenses are included. It is therefore important to distinguish correctly between capital and revenue items, as this could hit profit quite hard given the relatively large figures involved where non-current assets are concerned. It would also mean that the statement of financial position did not show the correct cost of assets used by the business. For costing purposes it would mean that the amounts included in the calculations of PRODUCT COSTS (costs of a finished product built up from its cost elements) would be inaccurate.

Some tricky items you might come across when deciding between capital and revenue categories often involve changes to non-current assets:

	Capital	Revenue
Extension to a building	✓	
Repairs to a building or machine		✓
Legal costs of buying a new factory	✓	
Installation of new machinery	✓	
Redecorating offices		✓

Task 1

Explain why an extension to a building is treated as capital expenditure, but a repair to a building is treated as revenue expenditure.

CLASSIFICATION OF COSTS BY FUNCTION

Revenue expenditure can be further classified according to the function that causes the cost. The main functions within a manufacturing business will give rise to the following cost categories:

- **Production costs.** Materials and labour used to make the products, maintenance costs of the machinery and supervision of the workforce are examples of costs caused by the production function of a business.
- **Selling and distribution costs.** Advertising, delivery costs and sales staff salaries would be caused by the selling and distribution function.
- **Administration costs.** The administration function gives rise to management, secretarial and accounting costs in coordinating the other functions of the business.
- **Financing costs.** The financing function gives rise to all the expenses associated with raising money to finance the business, such as a loan or overdraft.

The distinction between these categories is not always clear, particularly when we are talking about administration costs, as there are no rules or regulations to follow: just common sense. What's more, these are not the only possible functions within a business. Large companies often have a research and development function, or a training function; it depends on the type of business.

Task 2

Look at the list of costs below and decide whether each one would be classified as a production cost, a selling and distribution cost or an administration cost.

(a) Factory rent
(b) Managing Director's salary
(c) Sales Director's salary
(d) Depreciation of office equipment
(e) Depreciation of plant and machinery
(f) Petrol for delivery vans
(g) Factory heating and lighting

DIRECT AND INDIRECT COST ELEMENTS

A different way of classifying revenue expenses looks at the three major cost elements.

- Materials
- Labour
- Expenses

Each category is then sub-divided into

- DIRECT COSTS: costs that can be directly identified with a particular unit of production or service provided
- INDIRECT COSTS: costs that cannot be directly identified with a unit of production or service

It is usually easy to identify the amount of a direct expense that is spent on one unit, but it is more difficult to do so with indirect costs as they are not spent directly on one unit: they are usually spent in relation to a number of units.

The resulting six cost elements, and examples of these costs are shown in the table below.

Direct materials	Materials that are incorporated into the finished product (eg wood used in the construction of a table).
Indirect materials	Materials that are used in the production process but not incorporated into the product (eg machine lubricants and spare parts). Insignificant costs that are attributable to each unit are sometimes included in indirect materials for convenience (eg nails and glue).
Direct labour	Wages paid to those workers who make products in a manufacturing business (eg machine operators) or perform the service in a service business (eg hairdressers in a hair salon).
Indirect labour	Wages and salaries of the other staff, such as supervisors, storekeepers and maintenance workers.
Direct expenses	Expenses that are identifiable with each unit of production, such as patent royalties payable to the inventor of a new product or process.
Indirect expenses	Expenses that are not spent on individual units of production (eg rent and rates, electricity and telephone).

In costing, the three types of indirect cost are often lumped together and called overheads.

OVERHEADS = indirect materials + indirect labour + indirect expenses.

Task 3

A building contractor employs a painter to paint the exterior and interior of the buildings they have built. Explain whether this is a direct or an indirect cost.

COST BEHAVIOUR: FIXED AND VARIABLE COSTS

Costs can also be classified by their BEHAVIOUR, ie how the total cost is affected by a change in production level or activity level. Costs behave in different ways when the levels of activity in the organisation change. This is known as classification of costs by behaviour and the main classifications are:

- Variable costs
- Fixed costs
- Semi-variable costs
- Stepped costs or step-fixed costs

These classifications only apply in the short term as in the long term all costs are variable. Each of these will be illustrated in this chapter and the concepts will then be used in later chapters in order to produce relevant management information. Management must understand how costs behave when making short-term decisions for instance calculating a break-even profit or level of activity. This is covered in Chapter 13. Management will also use what they know about the behaviour of costs in the organisation to forecast future profitability when they are setting budgets. Variance analysis uses information on how costs and revenues behave to compare fixed and flexible budgets against actual costs and revenues thereby calculating variances. We look at these topics in Chapters 9 and 10. Finally, long-term decision making uses knowledge of cash flows to predict future costs and revenues. This is covered in Chapter 14.

Variable costs

VARIABLE COSTS are costs that vary directly in line with changes in the level of activity. Direct materials are often viewed as variable costs. For example if 1kg of a material is needed for each cost unit then 100,000 kg will be required for 100,000 units of production and 500,000 kg for 500,000 units of production.

The total variable cost can be expressed as:

Total variable cost = Variable cost per unit × number of units

A graph can be used to illustrate the total variable cost as activity levels change:

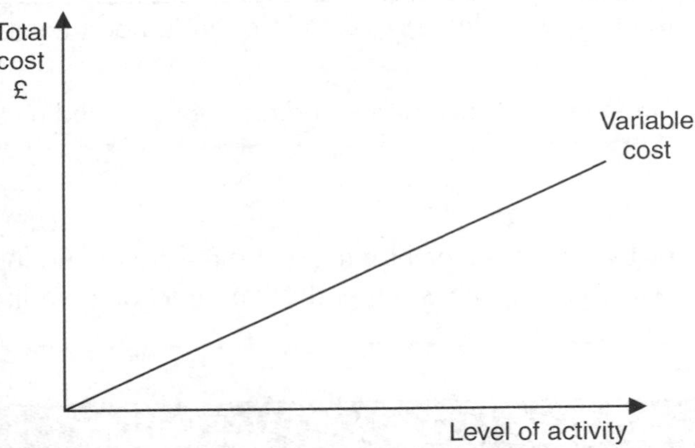

Direct costs such as materials costs may not always be true variable costs. For example, if a supplier offers a bulk purchasing discount for purchases above a certain quantity, then the cost per unit will fall if orders are placed for more than this quantity. As a general rule, as the direct cost is spent directly on each unit of production, this will be the same amount for each unit so a graph of unit cost against level of output will be horizontal.

Graph of variable cost per unit

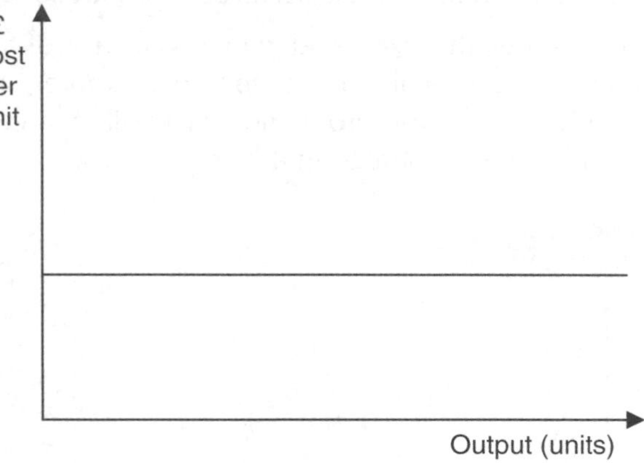

Some indirect costs may also vary in line with output, for example maintenance costs of a machine will increase if it is used more.

Fixed costs

FIXED COSTS are not affected by changes in production level. They remain the same in total whether no units or many units are produced. They are incurred in relation to a period of time rather than production level, and are often referred to as PERIOD COSTS. This is the case with the salary of a supervisor, the rent of a factory or straight-line depreciation of plant and machinery.

A graph of fixed costs against output level would produce a horizontal line.

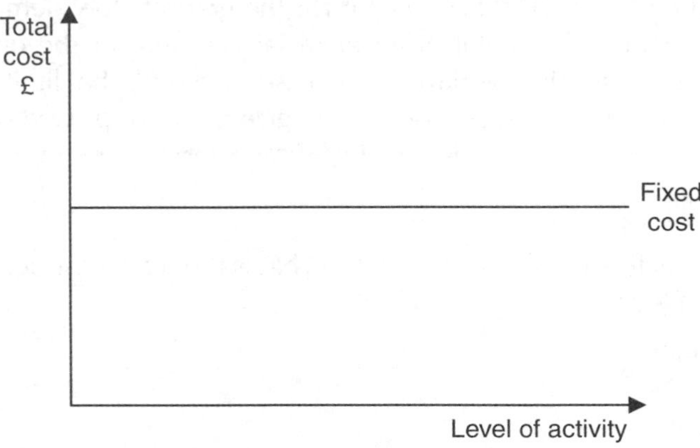

In practical terms fixed costs are only truly fixed over the RELEVANT RANGE. For example the rent of the factory will only remain constant provided that the level of activity is within the production capacity of the factory. If production levels increase above the capacity of the current factory then more factory space must be rented thus increasing the rent cost for this level of production.

As the activity level increases the fixed cost remains fixed in total but the fixed cost per unit will fall as the total cost is split over more units. This gives management an incentive to increase production as it will mean that each unit is cheaper to produce. This is demonstrated in the graph below.

Graph of fixed cost per unit

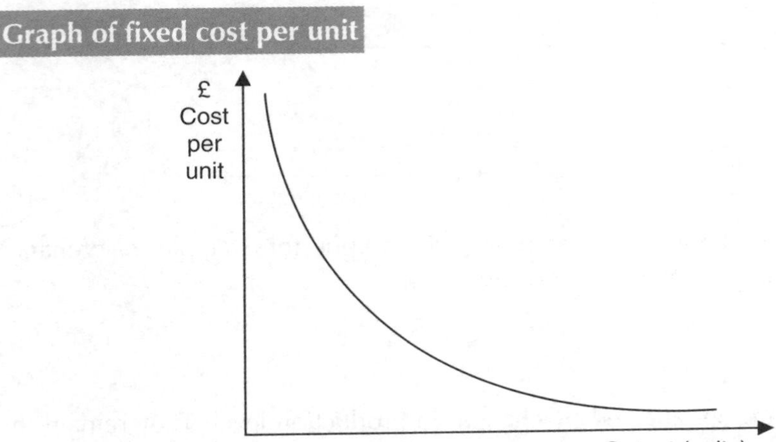

There are problems with calculating a fixed cost per unit. Some of these will become apparent later in the Text, but one arises because many fixed costs are only fixed over a certain range of output. If the business decides to expand beyond a certain level, there will be a sudden jump in the cost to a new fixed amount. Such costs are STEP-FIXED COSTS; the graph below demonstrates how they got their name. The rental of an extra factory unit, or the employment of another supervisor as the workforce increases beyond the limit that can be managed efficiently by one supervisor would give rise to step-fixed costs.

Task 4

A business incurs fixed costs of £100,000. What is the fixed cost per unit if production levels are:

(a) 20,000 units
(b) 40,000 units
(c) 80,000 units

Step-fixed costs

STEP-FIXED COSTS are costs that are fixed over a relatively small range of activity levels but then increase in steps when certain levels of activity are reached. For example, if one production supervisor is required for each 30,000 units of a product that is made then 3 supervisors are required for production of 90,000 units, 4 for production of 120,000 units, 5 for production up to 150,000 units and so on.

Step-fixed costs can be illustrated on a graph:

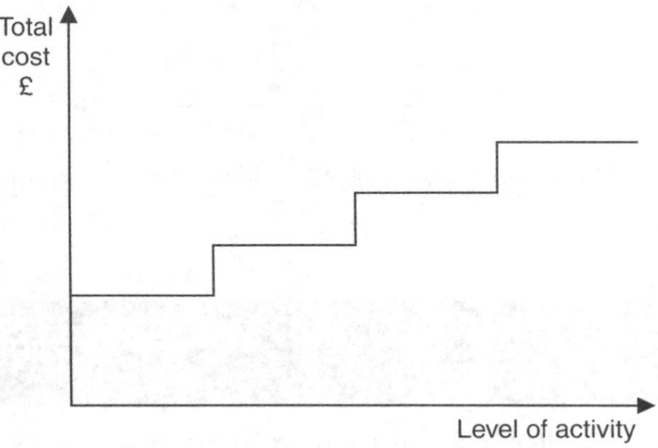

Step-fixed costs are really a fixed cost with a relatively short relevant range.

Task 5

What is meant by the relevant range of a fixed cost?

Semi-variable costs

SEMI-VARIABLE COSTS are costs that have a fixed element and also a variable element. For example, the telephone bill includes a fixed element being the fixed line rental for the period and a variable element that will increase as the number of calls increase.

The total of a semi-variable cost can be expressed as:

Total cost = Fixed element + (variable cost per unit × number of units)

A semi-variable cost can be illustrated on a graph as follows:

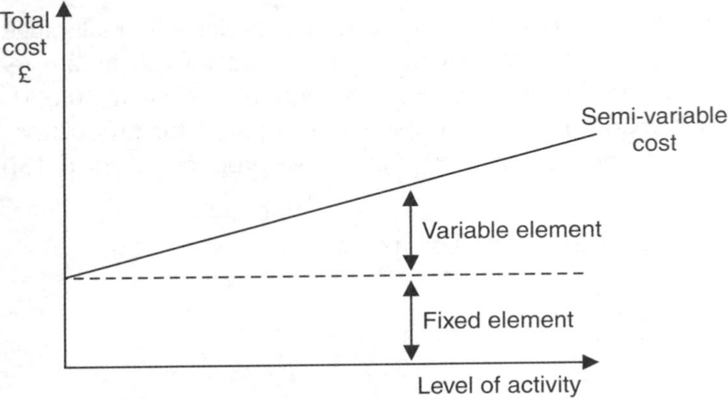

The calculation of the fixed and variable elements of a semi-variable cost is covered below.

CALCULATING THE FIXED AND VARIABLE ELEMENTS OF SEMI-VARIABLE COSTS

The HIGH-LOW TECHNIQUE can be used to estimate the fixed and variable parts of a semi-variable cost. It requires several observations of the costs incurred at different output levels, such as would be recorded over a number of accounting periods. This data can then be used to predict costs that would be incurred at other output levels.

HOW IT WORKS

Over the last five years, Stormbreak Ltd has recorded the following costs:

Year	*Output (units)*	*Total cost*
		£
20X1	32,000	505,000
20X2	37,000	580,000
20X3	48,000	745,000
20X4	53,000	820,000
20X5	51,000	790,000

Stormbreak Ltd wants to estimate the cost for 20X6, when they expect to produce 52,000 units.

This problem can be tackled by following four steps.

Step 1 Identify the high and low output and associated costs.

Look carefully at the information given and identify the highest and lowest output levels. Write these down, along with the total costs at those levels. (Don't be put off by any other information, such as the year, or the order in which the data is given; even if the cost column is given first, it is the highest and lowest output that matter.)

Output (units)		*Total cost*
		£
Highest	53,000	820,000
Lowest	32,000	505,000

Step 2 Deduct the lowest output/costs from the highest output/costs.

Output (units)		*Total cost*
		£
Highest	53,000	820,000
Lowest	32,000	505,000
Increase	21,000	315,000

This tells us that an increase of 21,000 units has led to an increase in costs of £315,000. This is due to the variable costs only, and gives us the figures we need for the next step.

Step 3 Calculate the variable cost per unit.

$$\text{Variable cost per unit} = \frac{\text{High cost} - \text{low cost}}{\text{High output} - \text{low output}}$$

$$= \frac{£315{,}000}{21{,}000}$$

$$= £15$$

Step 4 Find the fixed costs at one of the output levels used in the above calculations.

Choose either the highest or the lowest output level. Both will give the same result. Calculate the variable cost by taking the cost per unit from Step 3 multiplied by the number of units of output. Deduct this from the total cost at the same level of output and you will be left with the fixed cost.

At 53,000 units:

	£
Total cost	820,000
Less: variable cost (53,000 × £15)	795,000
= fixed cost	25,000

At 32,000 units (as a check):

	£
Total cost	505,000
Less: variable cost (32,000 ×£15)	480,000
= fixed cost	25,000

Now we are in a position to answer the actual question asked, which is 'What are the expected costs when output is 52,000 units?' All we need to do is build up the total cost from the fixed and variable elements at this level of output.

	£
Fixed cost	25,000
Add: variable cost (52,000 × £15)	780,000
= total cost	805,000

Task 6

How would each of the following costs be classified according to their behaviour?

(a) Stores department costs which include £5,000 of insurance premium and an average of £100 cost per materials receipt or issue

(b) Machinery depreciation based upon machine hours used

(c) Salary costs of lecturers in a training college where one lecturer is required for every 200 students enrolled

(d) Buildings insurance for a building housing the stores, the factory and the canteen

(e) Production workers' wages who are paid per unit produced with a guaranteed weekly minimum wage of £250

HOW IT WORKS

The use of cost behaviour principles in product costing is illustrated in the following example.

Cameron Ltd produces one product which requires the following inputs:

Direct materials	1 kg @ £3.50 per kg
Direct labour	1 hour @ £6.00 per hour
Rent	£4,000 per quarter
Leased machines	£1,500 for every 4,000 units of production
Maintenance costs	£1,000 per quarter plus £1.00 per unit

What is the total cost of production and the cost per unit for each of the following production levels for the coming quarter:

(a) 4,000 units
(b) 10,000 units
(c) 16,000 units?

Direct materials – these are a variable cost therefore the total cost is found by multiplying the number of units by the unit cost:

£3.50 × 4,000 units	=	£14,000
£3.50 × 10,000 units	=	£35,000
£3.50 × 16,000 units	=	£56,000

Direct labour – another variable cost:

£6.00 × 4,000 units	=	£24,000
£6.00 × 10,000 units	=	£60,000
£6.00 × 16,000 units	=	£96,000

Rent – this is a fixed cost and therefore provided we are still operating within the relevant range, it will remain at £4,000 whatever the production level

Leased machines – this is a stepped cost and the number of machines leased will depend upon the quantity of production

4,000 units	=	1 machine	=	£1,500
10,000 units	=	3 machines	=	£4,500
16,000 units	=	4 machines	=	£6,000

Maintenance costs – this is a semi-variable cost with a fixed element of £1,000. The total cost for each activity level is:

4,000 units	=	£1,000 + (4,000 × £1.00)	=	£5,000
10,000 units	=	£1,000 + (10,000 × £1.00)	=	£11,000
16,000 units	=	£1,000 + (16,000 × £1.00)	=	£17,000

	Production level – units		
	4,000	*10,000*	*16,000*
	£	£	£
Direct materials (variable)	14,000	35,000	56,000
Direct labour (variable)	24,000	60,000	96,000
Rent (fixed)	4,000	4,000	4,000
Leased machines (stepped)	1,500	4,500	6,000
Maintenance costs	5,000	11,000	17,000
Total cost	48,500	114,500	179,000
Cost per unit	£12.13	£11.45	£11.19

The cost per unit is decreasing as the production quantity increases. This is due to the fact that the fixed cost and the fixed element of the semi-variable cost are being spread over a larger number of units.

Suppose now that the supplier of the materials offers a bulk purchasing discount of 6% for all purchases if an order is placed for more than 8,000 kgs. What is the direct materials cost in total and per unit at each level of production?

4,000 units

Total cost	4,000 × £3.50	=	£14,000
Cost per unit	£14,000/4,000	=	£3.50

10,000 units

Total cost	10,000 × (£3.50 × 94%)	=	£32,900
Cost per unit	£32,900/10,000	=	£3.29

16,000 units

Total cost	16,000 × (£3.50 × 94%)	=	£52,640
Cost per unit	£52,640/16,000	=	£3.29

The direct materials are now not a true variable cost as the cost per unit falls once production is in excess of 8,000 units.

This has been a simple example of producing flexible budgets for different levels of activity. This will be dealt with in more detail in a later chapter of this Text.

Task 7

A salesman receives a fixed salary of £800 per month plus commission of £20 for each sale confirmed in the month. What is the salesman's monthly salary for the month if his confirmed sales are:

(a) 4 sales
(b) 8 sales
(c) 15 sales

Task 8

Sunny Ltd has recorded the following total costs over the past six months:

Month	*Production volume (units)*	*Total cost £*
January	3,500	47,000
February	2,900	41,000
March	3,300	45,000
April	3,700	49,000
May	4,200	54,000
June	4,000	52,000

Estimate Sunny Ltd's fixed costs using the high/low technique.

Task 9

The costs of operating the maintenance department of a computer manufacturer for the last four months have been as follows.

Month	Cost £	Production volume (units)
1	110,000	7,000
2	115,000	8,000
3	111,000	7,700
4	97,000	6,000

Calculate the costs that should be expected in month five when output is expected to be 7,500 units.

Cost behaviour and levels of activity

Knowledge of cost behaviour is essential when a business is planning its production levels and costs for the coming period. Estimates of the numbers of units of product that can be made and sold can never be accurate, and it is often helpful to look at a range of options.

HOW IT WORKS

Cloudy Ltd makes pencils and operates from a factory that costs £40,000 per annum to rent. The production line is largely mechanised and the depreciation of the machinery amounts to £15,000 per annum. These costs are fixed over the range of output levels under consideration.

The variable costs per box of 100 pencils are:

- raw materials and packaging, £1.20
- labour, £1.60
- expenses, £0.20

An overseer is employed to supervise the production line and inspect samples of the product. If production exceeds 500,000 boxes per annum another overseer has to be employed on a salary of £18,000 per annum.

Cloudy Ltd produced 400,000 boxes of pencils last year, but hopes to increase this to 600,000 next year as they have had enquiries from new customers. However, there is a threat of industrial action by one of their major raw material suppliers, and if they can't source their raw materials from elsewhere, they will have to cut production by 50% to 200,000 boxes.

To analyse the effect of these possible activity levels on costs, a budgeted production schedule can be drawn up. Variable costs can be found by multiplying the units of output by the variable cost per unit. Fixed costs remain the same at each output level. The amount included for the overseer's salary will be one salary for 200,000 and 400,000 units, but two salaries if production is 600,000 units. This is a step-fixed cost.

The estimated costs for the three possible production levels are as follows:

BUDGETED PRODUCTION COSTS

Units	*200,000*	*400,000*	*600,000*
	£	£	£
Costs			
Variable (units × (£1.20 + £1.60+ £0.20))	600,000	1,200,000	1,800,000
Fixed (£40,000+£15,000)	55,000	55,000	55,000
Step-fixed	18,000	18,000	36,000
Total production cost	673,000	1,273,000	1,891,000
Cost per unit	£3.37	£3.18	£3.15

Tutor's Note

It is important to note that when we talk about different types of cost behaviour, we are usually referring to the short-term. Over longer periods of time, however, say a number of years, all costs will tend to vary in response to large changes in activity level. Costs traditionally classified as fixed will become step costs as no cost can remain unchanged forever. And so as the time span increases, step costs become variable costs, varying with the passing of time. For example, when considered over many years, rent will appear as a variable cost, varying in the long term with large changes in the level of activity. So, in the long run, all costs are variable.

CHAPTER OVERVIEW

- Costs are either capital or revenue in nature. Revenue expenditure is included in the cost of a product, but capital expenditure is not. Capital expenditure is converted to revenue expenditure in the form of depreciation.
- Revenue costs can be classified by several methods
  - By function: production, selling and distribution, administration and finance
  - By element

	Materials
Direct	Labour
	Expenses
	Materials
Indirect	Labour
	Expenses

  - By nature or cost behaviour: fixed, variable, step-fixed, semi-variable
  - But in the long run, all costs are variable
- At different production levels:
  - Variable costs will change in line with the quantity produced, but fixed costs will remain the same
  - The variable cost per unit will be the same, but the fixed cost per unit will fall as the quantity produced increases
- The high-low technique can be used to find the variable and fixed elements of a semi-variable cost by identifying the costs at the highest and lowest levels of output.

Keywords

Capital expenditure – purchases of non-current assets or the improvement of the earning capability of non-current assets

Non-current assets – assets used in the business for a period longer than one accounting period to bring benefits

Revenue expenditure

- purchase of goods for resale
- maintenance of the existing earning capacity of non-current assets
- expenditure incurred in conducting the business

Direct costs – can be directly identified with a unit of production or service

Indirect costs – cannot be directly identified with a unit of production or service

Overheads – indirect costs (ie indirect materials, labour and expenses)

Cost behaviour – the way a cost changes as production quantity or activity level changes

Variable costs – vary according to the level of production

Fixed costs – costs that do not vary with changes in production level

Period costs – costs which relates to a time period rather than the output of products or services

Product cost – a cost of a finished product made up from its cost elements

Relevant range – the relevant range of a fixed cost is the range of activity within which the cost does not change

Step-fixed costs – costs that are fixed over a certain range, but when output increases beyond a certain level, there will be a sudden jump in cost to a higher fixed amount

Semi-variable (or semi-fixed, or mixed) costs – costs that have both a fixed element and a variable element

High-low technique – a method for estimating the fixed and variable parts of a semi-variable cost

TEST YOUR LEARNING

Test 1

Study the list below and decide which items are capital and which are revenue. Tick the appropriate box.

	Capital ✓	Revenue ✓
A new telephone system		
Depreciation of vehicles		
Salesperson's car		
Road fund licence for delivery van		
Telephone bill		
Computer software costing £10,000		
Repairs to the Managing Director's company car after an accident		

Test 2

Complete the following sketch graphs:

(a) Fixed costs

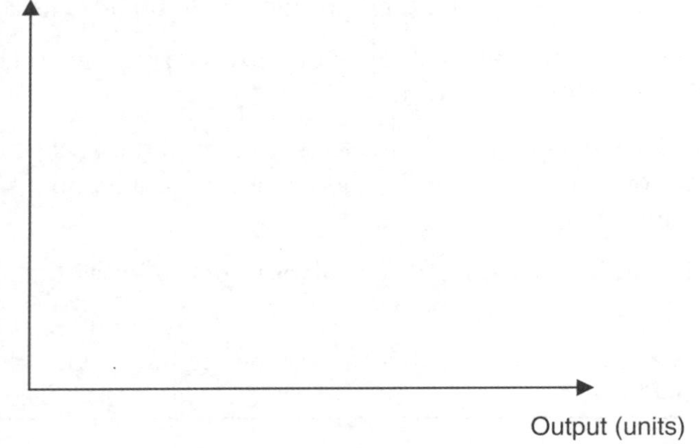

(b) Fixed cost per unit

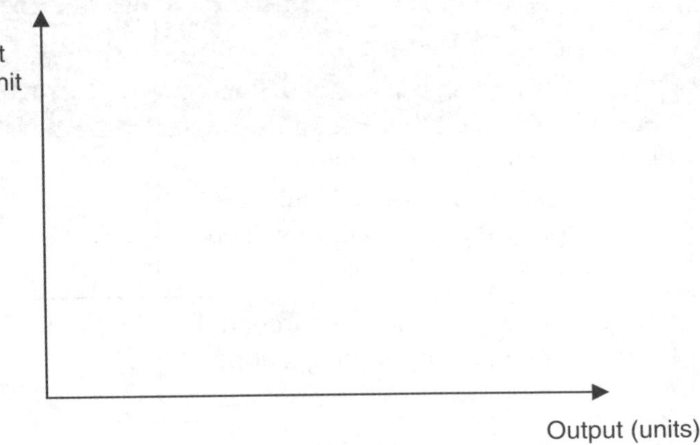

Test 3

Look at the following sketch graph and then decide which of the suggested costs could account for that shape of graph. (Tick the correct answers.)

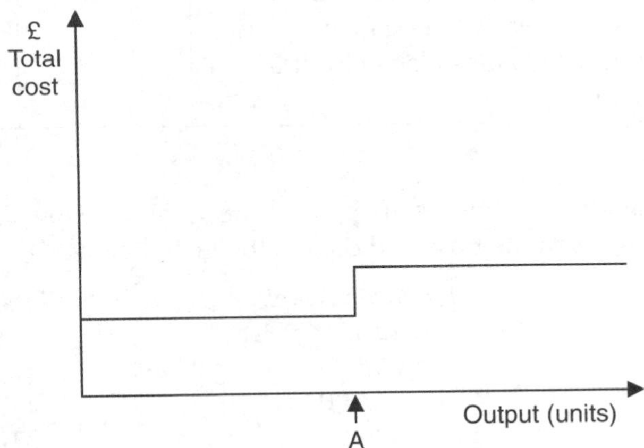

		Cost behaviour	
		Does fit the graph shape	Does *not* fit the graph shape
(a)	Plastic used in the manufacture of moulded plastic furniture. A bulk-buying discount is given at point A on the graph		
(b)	Straight-line depreciation of a freehold factory. A new factory is bought at point A		
(c)	Rent of a warehouse. A further warehouse is rented at point A		
(d)	Electricity costs that have a standing charge and a cost per unit of power used. At point A the level of production reaches the point where a nightshift is required, which uses electricity at a cheaper rate		

Test 4

Use the high-low technique to predict the costs at a production level of 12,000 units, given the observed data in the table below.

Year	*Production level (units)*	*Total cost* £
20X2	9,000	22,500
20X3	6,500	17,500
20X4	13,500	31,500
20X5	10,300	25,100
20X6	12,600	29,700

Test 5

Draw up a cost card using the following information. All costs given are per cabinet.

To make a filing cabinet, metal sheeting to the value of £3.80 is cut, formed, welded and painted by machine. A group of machines are monitored, the labour cost of which has been worked out at £0.30. Metal fixtures costing £1.80 are attached manually, and the cabinets are then assembled and packaged. The labour cost of assembly and packaging is £6.70, and the packaging materials cost £0.90. The power used by the factory gives a cost of £0.20, and delivery costs and advertising works out at £3.00.

Test 6

Variable costs are conventionally deemed to

A be constant per unit of output
B vary per unit of output as production volume changes
C be constant in total when production volume changes
D vary, in total, from period to period when production is constant

Test 7

The following is a graph of cost against level of activity:

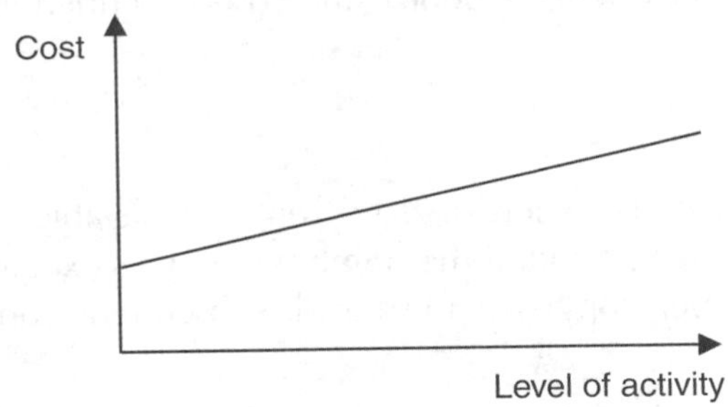

To which one of the following costs does the graph correspond?

A Electricity bills made up of a standing charge and a variable charge

B Bonus payment to employees when production reaches a certain level

C Salesperson's commissions payable per unit up to a maximum amount of commission

D Bulk discounts on purchases, the discount being given on all units purchased

The following information relates to Tests 8, 9 and 10.

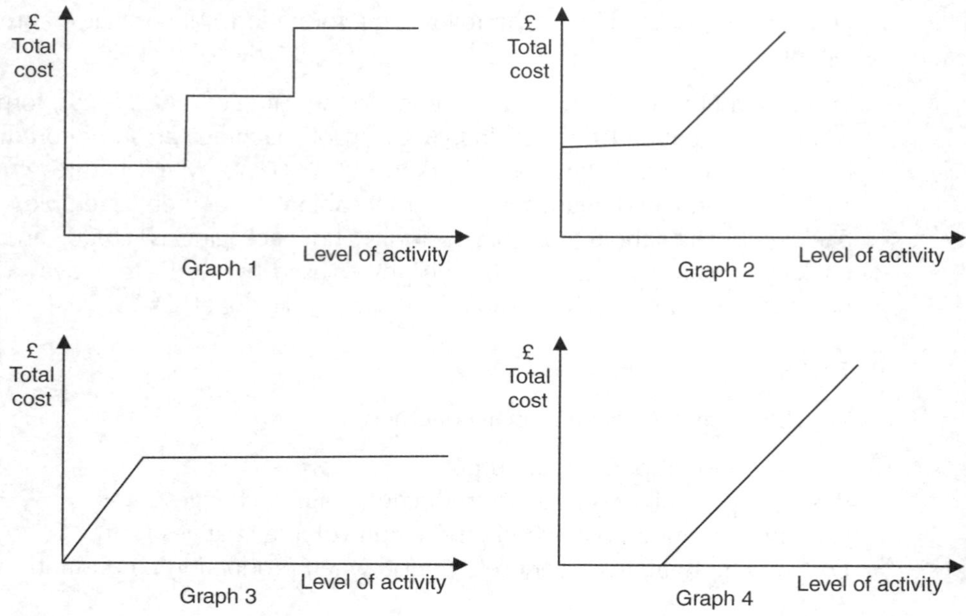

Which one of the above graphs depicts the costs described in Tests 8, 9 and 10?

Test 8

Photocopier rental costs, where a fixed rental is payable up to a certain number of copies each period. If the number of copies exceeds this amount, a constant charge per copy is made for all subsequent copies during that period.

A Graph 1
B Graph 2
C Graph 3
D Graph 4

Test 9

Supervisor salary costs, where one supervisor is needed for every five employees added to the staff.

A Graph 1
B Graph 2
C Graph 3
D Graph 4

Test 10

Vehicle hire costs, where a constant rate is charged per mile travelled, up to a maximum monthly payment regardless of the miles travelled.

A Graph 1
B Graph 2
C Graph 3
D Graph 4

Test 11

A production worker is paid a salary of £650 per month, plus an extra 5 pence for each unit produced during the month. This labour cost is best described as:

A A variable cost
B A fixed cost
C A step-fixed cost
D A semi-variable cost

chapter 3: MATERIAL COSTS AND INVENTORY VALUATION

chapter coverage

This chapter looks at inventories. The topics to be covered are:

- Materials
- Inventory
- Inventory valuation
- FIFO
- LIFO
- AVCO
- Cost bookkeeping for materials
- Inventory costs
- Inventory control
- Inventory counting (stocktaking)

MATERIALS

You should be familiar with what materials are from your earlier studies. We will just recap here. The term 'materials' encompasses:

- Raw materials and components that are incorporated into products made by a manufacturing business
- Goods bought for resale by a retail or wholesale business
- Goods bought for consumption by a business

Raw materials and components used by a manufacturer would be classified as direct costs for costing purposes. Examples are fabric in a tailoring company, paper in a printing company and electrical components in a manufacturer of electrical goods.

A retailer, such as a shop, and a wholesaler, which acts as a 'middle man' between the manufacturer and the retailer, would buy the products of the manufacturing companies. So, the clothing, printed matter and electrical goods produced by the manufacturers would be the materials of the retailer and wholesaler.

All businesses will buy some sort of goods for consumption, which are generally classified as indirect materials and included in overheads. In a manufacturing business, machine spares and lubricants would be production overheads, whilst office stationery would be a non-production overhead.

Task 1

List the raw materials that would be used to make a pair of shoes.

INVENTORY

You should also remember what inventories are from earlier units. There are three types of inventory held by the business:

- **Raw materials** and components for incorporation into products, and consumable stores
- **Finished goods** ready for sale and goods purchased for resale
- **Work in progress (WIP)** which are goods (and services) that are only partially completed

WIP arises as an inevitable consequence of certain businesses. If your business is making spoons for example, there may be several stages in the production process: stamping out the shape, removing the rough edges, polishing and packaging. At any point along the way, an unfinished spoon will be described as WIP until it is finished. Some businesses will keep WIP for a considerable time, such as makers of whisky which needs to be matured over a number of years.

Most businesses will choose to keep inventories of materials and finished goods ready for when they are needed.

- Raw materials inventories will be kept by a manufacturer so that materials are available for transfer to the production line when they are needed. Production would have to stop if there were no raw materials, with several serious knock-on effects, such as labour being unable to work but still being paid, delay in producing the products and consequent dissatisfaction of customers. This would make the products more expensive for the business to make. Goodwill might also be lost, meaning that customers would consider other suppliers in future.
- Finished products will be kept in inventory by a manufacturer so that demand from customers can be met and to avoid problems such as loss of goodwill.
- Goods for resale, which are the finished goods of manufacturers that have been bought for selling by retailers and wholesalers, are stocked so that changes in demand from day to day can be catered for. A shop would not be the same without an inventory of goods for the customer to look at and choose from!
- Consumable stores are needed, again so that there is no disruption of production or the administrative function of the business. For example, an inventory of printer cartridges is needed so that printing of plans and diagrams (a production use of the printer), quotes for customers (sales), letters and reports (administration) would not have to wait until more cartridges could be obtained.

INVENTORY VALUATION

The stores ledger accounts or inventory record cards record the value of materials purchased, and this information can be obtained from the purchase order and invoice. When goods are issued from stores or a warehouse, a value will need to be recorded on the stores ledger accounts and on the costing details for the job or department that is going to bear that cost. The question is how do we value these issues if prices are changing regularly? Furthermore, how are the remaining inventories on hand valued? This is not just a costing problem; it is also something that is needed for the preparation of the financial accounts.

Some items can be specifically priced from an invoice as they are individual items, but for most materials that are bought in quantity and added to an existing inventory, this is not possible, so one of the following methods can be used to estimate the cost.

FIFO (first in, first out)

This method assumes that the first items bought will be the first items issued to production departments. So, as items are issued (from the warehouse or stores), the earliest invoice prices are used up first, working forwards through to the latest prices. The inventory on hand will always represent the later prices. This method is most appropriate in businesses where the oldest items are actually issued first, which is the case with perishable goods such as food. Even so, this is a very popular method in many types of business.

Say, for example, ABC Ltd's inventory consisted of four deliveries of raw material in the last month:

	Units		
1 September	1,000	at	£2.00
8 September	500	at	£2.50
15 September	500	at	£3.00
22 September	1,000	at	£3.50

If on 23 September 1,500 units were issued to production, 1,000 of these units would be priced at £2 (the cost of the 1,000 oldest units in inventory), and 500 at £2.50 (the cost of the next oldest 500). 1,000 units of closing inventory would be valued at £3.50 (the cost of the 1,000 most recent units received) and 500 units at £3.00 (the cost of the next most recent 500).

LIFO (last in, first out)

This method assumes that the most recent purchases are issued first, as might be the case if new deliveries were piled on top of existing inventories, and goods issued were picked from the top of the pile. Issues are valued at the latest prices, working back through the records. This will tend to value inventory on hand at earlier prices. In the example above it will be 1,000 units of issues which will be valued at £3.50, and the other 500 units issued will be valued at £3.00. 1,000 units of closing inventory will be valued at £2.00, and 500 at £2.50.

AVCO (average cost)

With this method, a weighted average cost is calculated each time a new delivery is received. The weighting is provided by the number of units at each price brought into the calculation. The general formula is

$$\text{Average price per unit} = \frac{\text{Total value of existing inventory} + \text{Total value of units added to inventory}}{\text{Units of existing inventory} + \text{units added to inventory}}$$

AVCO would be most appropriate if the inventories were to be mixed when they are stored, for example chemicals stored in a vat.

HOW IT WORKS: FIFO, LIFO AND AVCO

ABC Ltd recorded the following transactions during May:

TRANSACTIONS DURING MAY 20X3

	Quantity	*Unit cost*	*Total cost*	*Sales price per unit on date of transaction*
	Units	£	£	£
Opening balance, 1 May	100	2.00	200	
Receipts, 3 May	400	2.10	840	2.11
Issues, 4 May	200			2.11
Receipts, 9 May	300	2.12	636	2.15
Issues, 11 May	400			2.20
Receipts, 18 May	100	2.40	240	2.35
Issues, 20 May	100			2.80
Closing balance, 31 May	200			2.83
			1,916	

FIFO

FIFO assumes that materials are issued out of inventory in the order in which they were delivered into inventory: issues are priced at the cost of the earliest delivery remaining in inventory.

Using FIFO, the cost of issues and the closing inventory value in the example would be as follows.

Date of issue	*Quantity issued*	*Value*		
	Units		£	£
4 May	200	100 o/s at £2	200	
		100 at £2.10	210	
				410
11 May	400	300 at £2.10	630	
		100 at £2.12	212	
				842
20 May	100	100 at £2.12		212
Cost of issues				1,464
Closing inventory value	200	100 at £2.12	212	
		100 at £2.40	240	
				452
				1,916

The cost of materials issued plus the value of closing inventory equals the cost of purchases plus the value of opening inventory (£1,916).

Value of closing inventory. This represents the latest items to be bought, 100 @ £2.12 + 100 @ £2.40

The market price of purchased materials is rising dramatically. In a period of inflation, there is a tendency with FIFO for materials to be issued at a cost lower than the current market value, although closing inventories tend to be valued at a cost approximating to current market value.

The format for the FIFO Inventory record card is as follows:

Inventory Record Card									
	Purchases			Sales			Balance	
Date	Quantity	Cost	Total cost	Quantity	Cost	Total cost	Quantity	Total cost
		£	£		£	£		£
Balance at 1 May							100	200
3 May	400	2.10	840				500	1,040
4 May				100 100	2.00 2.10	200 210	300	630
9 May	300	2.12	636				600	1,266
11 May				300 100	2.10 2.12	630 212	200	424
18 May	100	2.40	240				300	664
20 May				100	2.12	212	200	452

LIFO

LIFO assumes that materials are issued out of inventory in the reverse order to which they were delivered: the most recent deliveries are issued before earlier ones, and are priced accordingly.

Using LIFO, the cost of issues and the closing inventory value in the example above would be as follows.

Date of issue	*Quantity issued*	*Valuation*		
	Units		£	£
4 May	200	200 at £2.10		420
11 May	400	300 at £2.12	636	
		100 at £2.10	210	
				846
20 May	100	100 at £2.40		240
Cost of issues				1,506
Closing inventory value	200	100 at £2.10	210	
		100 at £2.00	200	
				410
				1,916

Notes

(a) The cost of materials issued plus the value of closing inventory equals the cost of purchases plus the value of opening inventory (£1,916).

(b) In a period of inflation there is a tendency with LIFO for the following to occur.

(i) Materials are issued at a price which approximates to current market value.

(ii) Closing inventories become undervalued when compared to market value.

The format of the LIFO inventory record card is as follows:

Inventory Record Card									
	Purchases			Sales			Balance	
Date	Quantity	Cost	Total cost	Quantity	Cost	Total cost	Quantity	Total cost
		£	£		£	£		£
Balance at 1 May							100	200
3 May	400	2.10	840				500	1,040
4 May				200	2.10	420	300	620
9 May	300	2.12	636				600	1,256
11 May				300 100	2.12 2.10	636 210	200	410
18 May	100	2.40	240				300	650
20 May				100	2.40	240	200	410

AVCO

The average costing method or cumulative weighted average pricing method calculates a **weighted average price** for all units in inventory. Issues are priced at this average cost, and the balance of inventory remaining would have the same unit valuation. The average price is determined by dividing the total cost by the total number of units.

A new weighted average price is calculated whenever a new delivery of materials into store is received. This is the key feature of cumulative weighted average pricing.

In our example, issue costs and closing inventory values would be as follows:

Date	*Received* Units	*Issued* Units	*Balance* Units	*Total inventory value* £	*Unit cost* £	£
Opening inventory			100	200	2.00	
3 May	400			840	2.10	
			* 500	1,040	2.08	
4 May		200		(416)	2.08	416
			300	624	2.08	
9 May	300			636	2.12	
			* 600	1,260	2.10	
11 May		400		(840)	2.10	840
			200	420	2.10	
18 May	100			240	2.40	
			* 300	660	2.20	
20 May		100		(220)	2.20	220
						1,476
Closing inventory value			200	440	2.20	440
						1,916

* A new inventory value per unit is calculated whenever a new receipt of materials occurs.

Notes

(a) The cost of materials issued plus the value of closing inventory equals the cost of purchases plus the value of opening inventory (£1,916).

(b) In a period of inflation, using the cumulative weighted average pricing system, the value of material issues will rise gradually, but will tend to lag a little behind the current market value at the date of issue. Closing inventory values will also be a little below current market value. The value of closing inventory is calculated using the latest average inventory value per unit.

The format of the AVCO Inventory record card is as follows:

Inventory Record Card								
	Purchases			Sales			Balance	
Date	Quantity	Cost	Total cost	Quantity	Cost	Total cost	Quantity	Total cost
		£	£		£	£		£
Balance at 1 May							100	200
3 May	400	2.10	840				500	1,040
4 May				200	2.08	416	300	624
9 May	300	2.12	636				600	1,260
11 May				400	2.10	840	200	420
18 May	100	2.40	240				300	660
20 May				100	2.20	220	200	440

Task 2

The inventory record of a raw material has the following details for a week:

Day	Cost (£ per unit)	Receipts (units)	Issues (units)
2	260	18	
3	270	12	
4			10
6			14

The first-in first-out (FIFO) method is used for pricing issues. There was no raw material at the start of Day 1.

(a) Which was the value of the inventory on Day 5?

A £5,200
B £5,220
C £5,320
D £5,400

(b) Complete the stores ledger account below using the figures calculated in the FIFO example above. (You can invent GRN and Requisition Note numbers.)

STORES LEDGER ACCOUNT												
Inventory item		Doggy bed					Maximun		200			
Code		D49802					Minimum		20			
Day	Receipts				Issues				Balance			
	GRN	Qty	Unit price £	£	Req No	Qty	Unit price £	£	Qty	Unit price £	£	

Which valuation method should be used?

Reviewing the results obtained from each of the three methods used in the example above, we can compare the different answers.

	FIFO	*LIFO*	*AVCO*
	£	£	£
Sales*	1,582	1,582	1,582
Issues	1,464	1,506	1,476
Closing inventory	452	410	440
Profit	118	76	106

*£((200 × 2.11) +(400 × 2.20) +(100 × 2.80))

If costs are increasing, FIFO will give a higher profit than LIFO as issues, which form cost of sales, are at the earlier, lower prices. Where costs are falling, LIFO will give the higher profit as issues will be priced at later, lower prices. Closing inventories are higher under FIFO. AVCO, as you might imagine, falls somewhere between the other two methods. In the long term, over the life of the business, any such differences will disappear: all costs will eventually be charged against profit.

The choice of method is left to the management of the business, and this method should be used consistently from period to period. However, it is important to note that LIFO is not permitted for external financial reporting under IAS.

COST BOOKKEEPING FOR MATERIALS

We must now consider how the materials movements that have been recorded in the inventory record card are recorded in the costing bookkeeping accounts.

HOW IT WORKS

Given below is the stores ledger account for inventory item BB24 which is a material used in the manufacture of a number of products made by Gilchrist Chemicals.

STORES LEDGER ACCOUNT

Inventory item	BB24	Maximun	400
Code	BB2416C	Minimum	50

Date	Receipts				Issues				Balance		
	GRN	Qty	Unit price £	£	Req No	Qty	Unit price £	£	Qty	Unit price £	£
1 May									100	4.00	400
5 May	6612	200	4.20	840					200	4.20	840
10 May					4172	100	4.00	400	300		1,240
						40	4.20	168			
						140		568	140		568
									160		672
15 May					4181	100	4.20	420	100		420
									60		252
21 May	6629	300	4.50	1,350					300		1,350
28 May									360		1,602
					4195	60	4.20	252	60		252
31 May									300		1,350

The materials movements are recorded in the MATERIALS CONTROL ACCOUNT at their valuation from the inventory control account. We will start with the opening balance, a debit entry in the account, as it is an asset, the opening inventory.

Materials control account

		£		£
1 May	Opening balance	400		

Next each of the purchases in the period are entered as debits in the materials control account with the credit entry being to payables or cash depending upon whether the purchase was on credit or not.

Materials control account

		£		£
1 May	Opening balance	400		
5 May	Bank/payables	840		
21 May	Bank/payables	1,350		

Then the issues to production should be recorded. They are entered as a credit entry in the materials control account and a debit entry in the WORK IN PROGRESS CONTROL ACCOUNT. The work in progress control account is the account in which we are going to gather together all of the direct costs of production during the period, starting here with the materials cost.

Materials control account

		£		£
1 May	Opening balance	400	10 May WIP	568
5 May	Bank/payables	840	15 May WIP	420
21 May	Bank/payables	1,350	28 May WIP	252

Work in progress control account

		£		£
10 May	Materials control	568		
15 May	Materials control	420		
28 May	Materials control	252		

Finally the materials control account can be balanced to show the closing balance at 31 May.

Materials control account

		£		£
1 May	Opening balance	400	10 May WIP	568
5 May	Bank/payables	840	15 May WIP	420
21 May	Bank/payables	1,350	28 May WIP	252
			31 May Closing balance	1,350
		2,590		2,590

HOW IT WORKS

Using the stores ledger accounts from the previous example for inventory item BB24 for Gilchrist Chemicals we will now **code** the ledger account entries to be made, rather than actually enter them into the ledger accounts. The codes for the cost ledger accounts are as follows:

1003	Materials control account
2005	Work in progress control account
3001	Payables control account (also called creditors control account)

We will assume that all purchases are made on credit.

The first purchase was made on 5 May – the entries for this purchase would be coded as follows:

		DEBIT	*CREDIT*
		£	£
5 May	1003	840	
5 May	3001		840

This is a debit in the materials control account and a credit to the payables control account.

The first issue is on 10 May:

		DEBIT	*CREDIT*
		£	£
10 May	2005	568	
10 May	1003		568

A debit to work in progress and a credit to the materials control account.

The entries continue for the rest of the month:

		DEBIT £	CREDIT £
15 May	2005	420	
15 May	1003		420
21 May	1003	1,350	
21 May	3001		1,350
28 May	2005	252	
28 May	1003		252

This is a good method of testing your knowledge of the accounting entries for materials purchases and issues without the need for writing up ledger accounts.

Task 3

Shrier Ltd receives £1,250 of raw materials on credit from its supplier. It issues £750 to production. The relevant codes are as follows:

Raw materials	500
Work in progress	600
Payables	700
Cash	800

Complete the journal below to record these transactions.

Journal

Debit	£	*Credit*	£
1.			
2.			

Direct materials and indirect materials

We saw earlier in the Text that materials, labour and expenses can be classified as either direct or indirect depending upon whether or not they relate to a specific unit of product or service. The importance of this distinction is that the direct materials are part of the cost of the units produced which is being gathered together in the work in progress control account, whereas the indirect materials are overheads which must be recorded separately in a PRODUCTION OVERHEAD CONTROL ACCOUNT.

HOW IT WORKS

During the month of June Gilchrist Chemicals made total purchases of materials of £71,400. Direct materials valued at £69,200 were issued to the factory for production and indirect materials for machine maintenance during the month were £3,600. At the beginning of June the total inventory valuation was £7,300.

The materials control account is initially debited with the opening inventory valuation and the purchases for the month.

Materials control account

		£			£
1 Jun	Opening balance	7,300			
30 Jun	Purchases	71,400			

The issues from stores must now be entered on the credit side of the materials control account. The direct materials are debited to the work in progress control account whilst the indirect materials are debited to the production overhead control account.

Materials control account

		£			£
1 June	Opening balance	7,300	30 June	Direct materials – WIP	69,200
30 June	Purchases	71,400	30 June	Indirect materials – Production o/h control	3,600

Work in progress control account

		£			£
30 June	Materials control	69,200			

Production overhead control

		£			£
30 June	Materials control	3,600			

Finally, the materials control account can be balanced to find the closing inventory value. However, we will not balance the other two accounts yet as there are more entries to be made to them in the next two chapters.

Materials control account

		£			£
1 June	Opening balance	7,300	30 June	Direct materials – WIP	69,200
30 June	Purchases	71,400	30 June	Indirect materials – Production o/h Control	3,600
			30 June	Closing balance	5,900
		78,700			78,700

INVENTORY COSTS

There are many different costs that can occur if a business keeps inventory. These need to be controlled and kept to a minimum.

Holding costs

Costs associated with high inventory levels. Examples of these are given below.

- Storage costs such as warehouse rent, storekeeper's wages, depreciation and other costs of storage equipment
- Cost of capital tied up: the price paid to buy or make the inventory stored cannot be used for alternative purposes such as earning interest in a deposit account. This opportunity to invest is being lost and the interest thus foregone is therefore a cost to be brought into consideration
- Insurance
- Obsolescence and deterioration: if inventory is kept for some time it may become out-of-date or damaged. These inventories may need to be sold at a reduced price or scrapped, and there may also be costs involved in disposing of them
- Security

Ordering costs

Ordering costs are more significant if inventory levels are kept low and more orders have to be placed. Examples include the following:

- Administrative costs of placing an order: involving the purchasing department, accounts and goods receiving
- Transport inwards

INVENTORY CONTROL

INVENTORY CONTROL is the regulation of inventory levels so that the costs associated with inventory are kept to a minimum. There are two main aspects to this.

(1) Minimisation of the amount of inventory held whilst still being able to deliver the goods on time to the user department or customer and subject to avoiding excessive ordering costs. This requires regular measurement of the amount of inventory held in relation to the level of inventory needed before an order needs to be placed. The minimum inventory level is called 'BUFFER INVENTORY, as it acts as the buffer for the time between placing an order and receiving the inventory (the LEAD TIME). Control limits of maximum and minimum inventory levels will be set and an optimal amount to order when inventories need replenishing will be calculated for each inventory line.

(2) Minimisation of inventory losses and discrepancies. This involves counting the inventory on a regular basis and comparing the physical quantities with the inventory records – inventory record cards and/or stores ledger accounts. Discrepancies revealed by this exercise would then be investigated and action taken where necessary to prevent further problems. Security is an important aspect of safeguarding inventory.

Reordering inventory

Small businesses may be able to review their inventory levels on an informal basis and order what they judge to be the right quantity at the right time. Slightly more sophisticated than this is the **two-bin system**. This works on the basis that two bins are kept for each inventory line. Inventory is used from bin 1 until it is empty. At this point an order is placed for more inventory and inventory is now taken from bin 2. The new delivery, which should arrive just before bin 2 is empty, is placed in bin 1. An order is placed for more inventory for bin 2 when that is empty, and then the process begins again.

More sophisticated methods rely on a manual or computerised PERPETUAL INVENTORY SYSTEM. Earlier on we looked at inventory ledger accounts which are used in such a system. These records noted various details which would be used in deciding when inventory should be ordered, and the appropriate quantity. Various formulae exist to help the business arrive at these figures.

REORDER LEVEL is the inventory level that should trigger the placing of an order:

Reorder level = buffer inventory + (maximum usage × maximum lead time)

The rationale behind this formula is that an order will be placed as the amount in inventory falls to the maximum quantity that is expected to be used in the time between placing the order and receiving the goods (buffer inventory). Therefore inventory should never fall to zero.

HOW IT WORKS

Kite & Co sell 2,000 of their best selling inventory line, the 'Aerobat', each year. They buy them in from a supplier at a cost of £13 each, and the costs of placing the order, delivery and receiving the goods into inventory has been calculated as £250 per order. Kite & Co have also calculated that it costs £4 to hold one unit in inventory for one year. Details of usage and lead time are tabulated below. There is no buffer inventory.

	Lead time (days)	*Usage (sales per day)*
Minimum	1	2
Average	3	8
Maximum	6	12

For Kite & Co the reorder level is 12 × 6 = 72 'Aerobats'. As soon as the inventory of Aerobats falls to 72 units, more will need to be ordered, but how many should be ordered?

Task 4

Burrows Ltd keeps inventory of a fast-moving item, the mand. There is a time lag of 3 weeks whenever an order for mands is placed. The company plans to use 5,000 mands per week and keeps a buffer inventory of two weeks' budgeted usage.

At what level of inventory should mands be reordered?

ECONOMIC ORDER QUANTITY (EOQ) is the amount to order each time to minimise total inventory holding costs.

$$EOQ = \sqrt{\frac{2cd}{h}}$$

where c is the cost of placing an order
d is the annual demand
h is the cost of holding one unit in inventory for one year

This formula aims to keep the costs to a minimum by finding the balance between order costs and the holding costs. If relatively few orders are placed each year, the ordering costs will be low, but this means holding larger quantities of goods and holding costs will be high. If more orders are placed for a smaller quantity of goods each time, ordering costs would rise, but holding costs would fall.

For Kite & Co the economic order quantity is:

$$EOQ = \sqrt{\frac{2 \times £250 \times 2,000}{£4}} = \sqrt{250,000} = 500 \text{ units}$$

So, each time inventory is needed, 500 units will be ordered. This means that 4 orders will be placed each year to satisfy annual demand of 2,000 units.

Practical issues when ordering inventory

In theory, the reorder level and EOQ should govern the ordering of inventory. However, for practical reasons, other information often has to be taken into account.

We have seen that MINIMUM INVENTORY LEVEL or BUFFER INVENTORY is the level below which inventory should not be allowed to fall as a general rule. It gives a buffer against unexpected demand or a problem with receiving an order in time, and aims to prevent stock-outs (running out of inventory). One way of calculating this is given below.

> Buffer inventory = reorder level – (average usage × average lead time) or minimum inventory level

For Kite & Co:

Minimum inventory level	= 72 – (8 × 3)
	= 48

Kite & Co should hold a buffer inventory of 48 units. If they don't they may risk having a stockout.

MAXIMUM INVENTORY LEVEL is the level above which inventory cannot be allowed to rise. This is often due to a lack of storage space, so the space available will determine the maximum inventory level. Alternatively, a formula can be used which assumes that the maximum amount that will be held in inventory will arise when the minimum demand occurs in the minimum possible lead time. This will mean that when a new delivery is received there will still be a relatively large quantity of unused inventory remaining.

> Maximum inventory level = Reorder level + reorder quantity – (minimum usage × minimum lead time)

For Kite & Co:

Maximum inventory level	= 72 + 500 – (2 × 1)
	= 570

The maximum inventory Kite & Co should need to accommodate is 570. If their storage space cannot hold this quantity they may need to adjust their reorder policy.

Task 5

Kite & Co only have room for 520 'Aerobats' in inventory at any particular time. Use the formula for maximum inventory above to calculate a reorder quantity that would ensure this.

INVENTORY COUNTING (STOCKTAKING)

The second aspect of inventory control is the minimisation of inventory discrepancies. A major part of this is INVENTORY COUNTING: the counting of physical quantities of inventory. It is sometimes called an 'inventory count'.

Periodic inventory counting is usually carried out once per year with all inventory being counted on a particular day. Many businesses will use this method to actually establish an inventory figure for their annual accounts as they do not keep a perpetual inventory.

Continuous inventory counting occurs on a year-round basis. A number of items are checked each week so that each inventory line will have been checked over the period of one year, whilst valuable or high-turnover items are checked more often. This method is run alongside a perpetual inventory system as updated inventory records are needed for checking. It also means that the inventory value shown in the records can be used in the financial accounts without the disruption that is often caused by a periodic inventory count.

Inventory discrepancies

An inventory list will be completed by a inventory checker, detailing the items checked and the quantities found in the stores. This is then compared with the BIN CARD and stores ledger account. Differences may be due to a number of factors, but all of these should be investigated and the system tightened up where necessary, as suggested in the examples below.

- Clerical errors on the inventory records. Regular inventory checks by someone independent of the record-keeping department will help to prevent this. The error in the records will need rectifying
- Theft. Only authorised members of the stores department should be allowed in the stores. Inventory numbers should be amended on the records to take account of the missing items
- Breakages. Correct storage and handling can reduce this. Again, the inventory records should be amended

- Documentation incorrectly completed. If GRNs or MATERIALS REQUISITIONS etc have the wrong figures on them, the accounting records will be wrong. More careful counting of the inventory involved and its recording on the document is required. The supervisor of the relevant department should check these amounts also

A stores credit note will be used to update the accounting records for a reduction in inventory following the investigation of a inventory discrepancy. A stores debit note is used for an increase in inventory. An example of a stores credit note is shown below.

STORES CREDIT NOTE

Quantity	Inventory code	Description	£

Date: ________________

Authorised by: ________________

Task 6

Distinguish between perpetual inventory and continuous inventory counting.

Task 7

What are the possible consequences of a failure of control over ordering and receipt of materials?

CHAPTER OVERVIEW

- The valuation of inventory normally requires an assumption to be made regarding the valuation method – this will be FIFO, LIFO or AVCO.
- Inventory movements are recorded in the materials control account.
- Direct materials issued to production are debited to the work in progress control account and indirect materials issued are debited to the production overhead control account.
- When a business holds inventories it will incur two main types of costs – the holding costs of that inventory and the ordering costs – the purpose of inventory control is to balance these two costs in order to minimise the overall cost of holding the inventory.
- The reorder level for inventory is calculated to ensure that the inventory levels should never fall below zero during the lead time.
- The economic order quantity is the amount that should be ordered when each order is placed to ensure the minimisation of the overall cost of holding inventory.
- Often a business will set a minimum inventory level or buffer inventory level below which the inventory level should not be allowed to fall.
- In order to control the inventory that is held, businesses will regularly count their inventories and compare the physical quantity with the inventory records – any discrepancies should be investigated and corrected.

Keywords

Inventory – goods held by the business as a current asset made up of raw materials, work in progress and finished goods

Perpetual inventory – a continuously updated inventory record system showing receipts, issues and the resulting balances of individual inventory lines

Bin cards – are usually maintained in the stores department and are in terms of quantity

Stores ledger accounts – are kept in the costing department and show values as well

Materials requisition – a request for materials by the production department sent to the stores

FIFO (first in, first out) – assumes that the earliest purchases or production are used first. Inventory on hand is valued at the latest prices, issues at earlier prices

Keywords cont'd

LIFO (last in, first out) – assumes that the latest purchases are used first. Inventory on hand is valued at earlier prices and issues are at the latest prices at the time of the issue.

AVCO (average cost) – a weighted average cost is calculated each time a delivery is received. Subsequent issues and inventory on hand are valued at this cost.

Holding costs – costs of holding inventory, such as storage costs, cost of capital tied up, insurance, obsolescence and security

Ordering costs – costs of ordering materials, such as administrative costs and transport inwards

Inventory control – the regulation of inventory levels so that the costs associated with inventory are kept to a minimum

Reorder level – the inventory level that triggers the placing of an order

Lead time – time taken from an order being placed to the goods arriving

Economic order quantity (EOQ) – the amount to order each time in order to minimise inventory holding costs

Minimum inventory level or buffer inventory – the level below which inventory should not be allowed to fall as a general rule

Maximum inventory level – the level above which inventory cannot be allowed to rise

Material control account – cost ledger account where inventory movements are recorded

Work in progress control account – cost ledger account where all the direct costs of production are gathered

Production overhead control account – cost ledger account for all production overheads

TEST YOUR LEARNING

Test 1

Using the:

(a) FIFO

(b) LIFO

(c) AVCO methods

Calculate the cost of materials issues and the value of closing inventory using the information below. Enter your answer into the inventory record cards below.

January 3	Balance	100 kg	Valued @ £8.80 per kg
January 16	GRN 423	400 kg	Invoiced @ £9 per kg
January 27	Materials requisition 577	250 kg	
February 5	Materials requisition 582	180 kg	
February 9	GRN 439	400 kg	Invoiced @ £9.30 per kg
February 17	Materials requisition 589	420 kg	
February 25	GRN 446	500 kg	Invoiced @ £9.35 per kg

(a) **FIFO**

Inventory Record Card								
	Purchases			Requisitions			Balance	
Date	Quantity (kg)	Cost £	Total cost £	Quantity (kg)	Cost £	Total cost £	Quantity (kg)	Total cost £
3 Jan								
16 Jan								
27 Jan								
5 Feb								
9 Feb								
17 Feb								
25 Feb								

(b) **LIFO**

Inventory Record Card								
	Purchases			Requisitions			Balance	
Date	Quantity (kg)	Cost £	Total cost £	Quantity (kg)	Cost £	Total cost £	Quantity (kg)	Total cost £
3 Jan								
16 Jan								
27 Jan								
5 Feb								
9 Feb								
17 Feb								
25 Feb								

(c) **AVCO**

Inventory Record Card								
	Purchases			Requisitions			Balance	
Date	Quantity (kg)	Cost £	Total cost £	Quantity (kg)	Cost £	Total cost £	Quantity (kg)	Total cost £
3 Jan								
16 Jan								
27 Jan								
5 Feb								
9 Feb								
17 Feb								
25 Feb								

Test 2

What are the advantages and disadvantages of the LIFO method of valuing materials?

Test 3

On 1 March a business has £12,400 of materials inventories. During March there were £167,200 of purchases and issues to production totalling £160,400. There were also £8,300 of indirect materials issued to the factory.

Write up the cost ledger accounts to reflect the month's transactions.

Test 4

Give three examples each of holding costs and ordering costs. Explain what would happen to these costs if inventory usage remained the same, but the reorder quantity increased.

Test 5

Eagle Printing Company Limited print posters for which they buy paper on rolls. Each roll costs £12. Each week, 15 rolls are used; the company operates every week of the year. Each time an order for more rolls of paper is placed, it costs the company £50, and the estimated cost of storing one roll is £19.65 per annum.

You are required to calculate the economic order quantity.

Test 6

Kestrel Limited experiences a lead time of 4-8 days for orders of paint. Paint usage is between 150 and 200 litres per day. What would be a suitable reorder level?

Test 7

XYZ Co had an opening inventory value of £880 (275 units valued at £3.20 each) on 1 April.

The following receipts and issues were recorded during April.

8 April	Receipts	600 units	£3.00 per unit
15 April	Receipts	400 units	£3.40 per unit
30 April	Issues	900 units	

Using the FIFO method, the total value of the **issues** on 30 April is £ [ ]

Test 8

2,400 units of component C, valued at a price of £6 each, were in inventory on 1 March. The following receipts and issues were recorded during March.

3 March	Received	4,000 units @ £6.20 per unit
12 March	Received	2,000 units @ £6.86 per unit
23 March	Issued	5,100 units

Using the weighted average price method of inventory valuation, the total value of the components remaining in inventory on 23 March was £ [ ]

Test 9

2,400 units of component C, valued at a price of £6 each, were in inventory on 1 March. The following receipts and issues were recorded during March.

3 March	Received	4,000 units @ £6.20 per unit
12 March	Received	2,000 units @ £6.86 per unit
23 March	Issued	5,100 units

Using the FIFO method of inventory valuation, the total value of the components **issued** on 23 March was £ [ ] (to the nearest £)

chapter 4: LABOUR COSTS AND EXPENSES

chapter coverage

This chapter looks at two other major costs: labour and expenses. It looks in particular, at how labour costs are calculated and documented. The topics to be covered are:

- Labour costs
- Remuneration methods
- Recording labour costs
- The wages control account

LABOUR COSTS

You should be familiar with labour costs from your workplace or previous studies. As a reminder these include the gross pay of the employee, employer's national insurance, training costs and benefits such as company cars. All employees will give rise to labour costs; office workers in administration departments, canteen staff, maintenance staff and supervisory staff are examples of **indirect labour**. **Direct labour** costs arise from the employees that work directly on the goods produced by a manufacturing business, or employees that provide the service in a service business. We will run through the two main types of remuneration briefly as these are also covered in earlier studies. This chapter concerns itself with the calculation of costs in payroll calculation sheets and other ways of presenting labour costs for management and other users.

REMUNERATION METHODS

We will briefly go through the main remuneration methods which have been covered in your earlier studies.

Time rate (or day rate)

A TIME RATE means that a basic amount is paid per hour worked.

> Wages = hours worked × basic rate of pay per hour

Workers will be paid so much per hour no matter how much they produce so there is no incentive to improve performance. A plus point for a time rate system is that workers will not feel that they have to rush, so quality can take priority.

If the hours worked exceed a pre-set maximum, OVERTIME is often paid at a higher rate. You may have heard the expression 'time and a half', which refers to overtime being paid at 1 ½ × basic rate.

HOW IT WORKS

Finch Limited pays overtime at time and a third for all complete hours worked over 35 hours per week. Peter is paid a basic wage of £6 per hour. During the week ending 24 March he worked a total of 39 hours. Work out Peter's total pay for the week.

	£
Basic (35 × £6)	210
Overtime (4 × £6 × 1 1/3)	32
Total pay for the week	242

The overtime pay in this illustration is £32. This comprises two elements.

(a) The basic element is the basic pay rate × additional hours worked, in this case 4 hours × £6 = £24.

(b) The OVERTIME PREMIUM is the extra paid on top of the basic rate for the additional hours worked. In this case the hourly premium is £6 × 1/3 = £2. The total overtime premium is therefore 4 hours × £2 = £8

In the assessment the layout you should use is as follows:

	£
Pay at basic rate: 39 hours @ £6	234
Overtime premium: 4 hours @ £6/3	8
	242

This analysis is necessary as most (but not all) businesses treat the basic pay as a direct cost, but the overtime premium as an indirect cost for costing purposes. This way, all units produced are costed at the basic labour cost, irrespective of whether they were produced during normal working hours or at the weekend, for example, when overtime was being paid. There are, however, two situations we look at here where overtime premiums are included in the direct cost.

- If the overtime is worked at the request of the customer so that his/her order can be completed within a certain time, the overtime premium will be a direct cost of that particular order.
- If overtime is normally worked in the production department, an average direct labour hourly rate can be calculated which will include the overtime premium that is generally incurred.

Task 1

Julie is paid £10 per hour for a 37-hour week as an assembly worker. She is paid overtime at time and a half. Calculate the direct and indirect labour cost incurred if Julie works for 41 hours in a particular week.

Piecework

With PIECEWORK, an amount is paid for each unit or task successfully completed, acting as an incentive to produce more. This method of remuneration can only be used in certain situations ie when there are specific, measurable tasks to be done which are not affected by other employees' performances.

DIFFERENTIAL PIECEWORK offers higher rates as production increases. For example, 5p per unit is paid for production of up to 2,000 units per week, rising to 7p per unit for 2001 to 3000 units, and so on.

Task 2

Darren paints vases in a pottery. He is paid 50p for every vase painted up to a total of 400 in one week. Thereafter, he receives an extra 20p per additional vase up to 100 additional vases; his rate further increases by 20p for each 50 further vases. One week he paints 530 vases. What will his gross pay be in that week?

Bonus systems

A BONUS SYSTEM involves the payment of a bonus if output is better than expected. This will be in addition to the normal time rate. The trigger for the payment of a bonus depends on the type of system that operates.

- A time-saved bonus is paid if the employee performs a task in a shorter time than the standard time allowed.
- A discretionary bonus is paid if the employer judges that the employee deserves one.
- A group bonus scheme pays a bonus to all workers who contributed to a successful job.
- A profit-sharing scheme involves the payment of a proportion of the business's profits to employees, the proportion paid often reflecting level of responsibility.

This system can operate at all levels in any business, and can give an incentive for workers to produce more with the security of their basic time rate. As with piecework, though, a bonus system can be complex to calculate and will need quality control checks.

Salary

Employees on a monthly SALARY are paid one twelfth of their agreed annual salary each month. Overtime, bonuses and commissions on sales, for example, can be paid on top of this. Salaries tend to relate to indirect labour, such as office staff and supervisors. In the service sector, though, many salaried staff such as solicitors and accountants are a direct cost of providing the service.

HOW IT WORKS

Java Bananas imports bananas and distributes its products throughout the UK using its own fleet of delivery vehicles.

Arran handles the bananas, preparing them for loading and is paid on the following basis:

	£ per hand
Value	0.20
Fairtrade	0.24
Organic	0.30

In the week ending 24 November, Arran handled 290 value, 480 fair-trade and 395 organic.

Barry is a mechanic for the delivery vehicles, who earns £9 per hour for a 40-hour week. He is paid overtime at time and a quarter, and earns a bonus of £5 for each job on which he makes a time saving of 5% or more on the standard time. In the week-ending 24 November he works a total of 43 hours and qualifies for bonus payments in respect of five jobs performed.

Colin works in the sales office. His contract of employment specifies a 35-hour week and an annual salary of £15,000. Any hours worked in excess of the contractual weekly amount are paid at his basic rate. In the month of November he works a total of 15 hours' overtime.

The gross pay of each employee for the appropriate period is calculated as follows.

Arran: piecework

Week ending 24 November

Gross pay = (290 × £0.20) + (480 × £0.24) + (395 × £0.30)

= £ 291.70

Barry: time rate with overtime and time-saved bonus

Week ending 24 November

	£
Basic rate pay (43 hours × £9)	387.00
Overtime premium (3 hours × £9 × 0.25)	6.75
Bonus (5 jobs × £5)	25.00
Gross pay	418.75

Colin: salary with overtime

	£
Basic salary (£15,000 / 12)	1,250.00
Overtime $\dfrac{£15,000}{35 \text{ hours} \times 52 \text{ weeks}} \times 15$ hours	123.63
Gross pay	1,373.63

In this case, we had to work out a basic hourly rate by dividing the annual salary by the total number of hours worked in a year under the contract. This was then used to work out how much Colin could be paid for overtime.

RECORDING LABOUR COSTS

Information on labour hours worked and rates of pay is needed by two departments. The payroll department needs to know so that the amount that each employee has earned can be worked out. The costing department needs to know so that the labour cost of each task or unit of product can be calculated.

The human resources or personnel department will maintain records of each employee's contract of employment and basic rate of pay. They will issue the payroll department with a list of employees and rates of pay. Computerised payroll systems will often have access to a database containing pay rates, piecework rates etc.

The time worked by each employee is recorded on various types of document, depending upon the nature of the job.

Attendance time records

Sometimes, all that needs to be recorded is the attendance of the employee at the place of work. This can be achieved by using one of the following:

- **Attendance record.** Essentially a calendar for an individual; a tick in the box recording the presence of the employee at work on that day. If absent, the reason (sickness, holiday etc) can be indicated.
- **Signing-in book.** This book will have a page for each employee, and is signed by the employee when entering or leaving the building, or when a break is taken. This allows a more accurate calculation of time worked.
- **Clock cards.** Each employee has a card which is entered in a time recording clock as work is commenced and finished. The time is recorded on the CLOCK CARD which is then used for pay calculations. Computerised systems perform the same function by means of a plastic swipe card. The time is recorded by the computer rather than on the card.

A typical clock card would look like this:

Name			Week ending		
	Hours	**Rate £**	**Amount £**	**Deductions**	**£**
Basic Overtime				Income tax NI Other	
				Total deductions	
Total Less: deductions Net pay due					
Time	**Day**		**Basic time**	**Overtime**	
The time recording clock will stamp this part of the card				Payroll clerks will work out the hours worked and then the pay due	
Signature					

Job costing

Where an employee works on more than one job in a day or a week, more detailed analysis of time worked needs to be recorded so that the jobs can be costed. Note that attendance time records will also, generally, be kept for payroll purposes.

- TIMESHEETS are used to record the time spent by an employee on each job that they have worked on. Timesheets are passed to the costing department daily (DAILY TIMESHEETS), or weekly if there are few job changes in a week (WEEKLY TIMESHEETS). Timesheets are often used in the service sector, for example accountants will fill in a weekly timesheet showing the number of hours and the clients for whom they have performed accounting services during that week.

- JOB CARDS are prepared for each job or an operation on a larger job. The job card will describe the task to be performed. The employee will fill in the start and finish times of the job, and time out for any breaks. The card will be completed in the accounting department where the cost of that job can be calculated.

JOB CARD			
Job No 824 **Date**			
Time allowed 2 hours **Start time** **Finish time**			
Job description	**Hours**	**Rate**	**Cost £**
Apply dark oak varnish to the exterior surfaces			
Employee number .... Employee signature .... Supervisor's signature			

- **Route cards** are similar to job cards, but they detail all the operations to be carried out on a job, rather than just one, and will follow the job through to completion. As each operation is completed, the relevant employee will enter the time spent on it. The full cost of the job will gradually build up on the route card.

Job costing systems will be considered in more detail later in this Text.

Piecework

A **piecework ticket** (or **operation card**) is used to record the number of units produced in a piecework system. Piecework tickets are very similar to job cards, and are used for each operation to be performed on a batch of units. The worker will record the number of units completed, the number of rejects, and the number of good units; they will only be paid for good production. A supervisor and an inspector will be required to sign the ticket to validate the quantities.

Payroll calculation sheets

The payroll department nowadays are likely to use a payroll computer package but some may still use pre-printed payroll calculation sheets to work out gross and net pay for employees. Remember that gross pay less PAYE and employee NIC is the net pay paid to the employee. However the total cost of employing someone is gross pay plus employer's NIC, also paid over to HMRC. Employers may also have to account for tax (NIC), on benefits they give to employees. We have an example here which shows the gross pay and employer's NIC.

Payroll Calculation Sheet

Employee ______________________

Pay Period: ______________________

Department: ______________________

Approved Pay Rate (per Agreement)

Hourly:	£	Monthly Salary:	£
Overtime:	£	Pay Period Salary:	£

Personal Services	Hours Worked		Rate of Pay		TOTAL
Salaried Employee	Not Applicable	×	Not Applicable	=	£
Hourly Employee		×	£	=	£
Overtime		×	£	=	£
Total Gross Salary				=	£

Benefits (employer's contribution)		Amount Paid
Pension	%	£
Health Insurance (less dependents)	£ / month	£
Total Fringe Benefits		£

National insurance (employer's contribution)		Amount Paid
N.I.C. =	%	£
Total Social Security Benefits		£

Timesheets

You may be asked to complete a timesheet in the assessment. This will normally take the form of a timesheet that has been filled in with hours worked and you will be expected to complete it with calculations of pay and overtime or bonus payments. Let's look at an example here.

HOW IT WORKS

Rubble Industries pay their employees basic and overtime pay under the following arrangement:

For a basic seven-hour shift every day from Monday to Friday – basic pay.

For any overtime in excess of the basic seven hours, on any day from Monday to Friday – the extra hours are paid at time-and-a-half (basic pay plus an overtime premium equal to half of basic pay).

For three contracted hours each Saturday morning – basic pay.

For any hours in excess of three hours on Saturday – the extra hours are paid at double time (basic pay plus an overtime premium equal to basic pay).

For any hours worked on Sunday – paid at double time (basic pay plus an overtime premium equal to basic pay).

Complete the columns headed Basic pay, Overtime premium and Total pay.

(**Notes**: Zero figures should be entered in cells where appropriate, Overtime pay is the premium amount paid for the extra hours worked).

Employee's weekly timesheet for week ending 5 April

Employee: F. Flintstone			**Profit Centre:** Stone carving			
Employee number: P450			**Basic pay per hour:** £12.00			
	Hours spent on production	**Hours worked on indirect work**	**Notes**	**Basic pay £**	**Overtime premium £**	**Total pay £**
Monday	5	2	10am-12am Polishing rock drill			
Tuesday	3	4	9am-1pm HR awareness course			
Wednesday	8					
Thursday	7					
Friday	6	1	3-4pm health and safety training			
Saturday	4					
Sunday	1					
Total	**34**	**7**				

The hours recorded in the timesheet can be used to calculate F. Flintstone's pay for the week.

Employee's weekly timesheet for week ending 5 April

Employee: F Flintstone				**Profit Centre:** Stone carving		
Employee number: P450				**Basic pay per hour:** £12.00		
	Hours spent on production	**Hours worked on indirect work**	**Notes**	**Basic pay £**	**Overtime premium £**	**Total pay £**
Monday	5	2	10am-12am Polishing rock drill	84	–	84
Tuesday	3	4	9am-1pm HR awareness course	84	–	84
Wednesday	8			96	6	102
Thursday	7			84	–	84
Friday	6	1	3-4pm health and safety training	84	–	84
Saturday	4			48	12	60
Sunday	1			12	12	24
Total	**34**	7		492	30	522

THE WAGES CONTROL ACCOUNT

The source documents above will be used to compile the PAYROLL. This is a record showing each employee's gross pay, net pay and deductions such as PAYE, National Insurance and pensions. There is also usually an analysis, which is used for cost accounting purposes. The payroll analysis can analyse gross pay by department, class of labour, product, and be broken down into various constituents such as direct, indirect and idle time. Idle time is time when employees are at work and being paid but they are not producing goods or services. This is normally treated as an indirect labour cost.

A wages control account is used to record the payroll costs. Obviously, the amount debited as the wages expense will be the gross pay, as this will be the cost to the business and the cost that needs to be used for costing purposes. However, the constituents of gross pay will be posted separately to the wages control account.

- Net pay is posted from the cash book.
- Deductions are debited with the credit entries being recorded in payables accounts until the amounts are due to be paid to the HMRC/ pension scheme etc.

The credits to the wages control account are:

- Direct labour (debited to WIP)
- Indirect production labour (debited to a production overheads account)
- Administration labour (debited to a non-production overheads account)

HOW IT WORKS

Gilchrist Chemicals has on its payroll records the following details for the month of June.

	£
Net pay	100,000
PAYE and NIC deductions	25,000
Contributions to company welfare scheme	15,000
Gross pay	140,000

The payroll analysis shows that £110,000 relates to direct labour, and £30,000 is for indirect labour.

These details are recorded in the wages control account as follows.

Wages control account

	£		£
Bank	100,000	WIP	110,000
HM Revenue & Customs	25,000	Production O/H	30,000
Welfare scheme Contributions	15,000		
	140,000		140,000

The other sides of the entries are added to the materials entries in the work in progress control account and the production overheads control account.

Work in progress control account

		£		£
30 June	Materials control	69,200		
30 June	Wages control	110,000		

Production overhead control

		£		£
30 June	Materials control	3,600		
30 June	Wages control	30,000		

You will notice that the wages control account has no balance carried down as it simply shares out the total gross wage cost between direct and indirect labour costs. The other two accounts will not yet be balanced as there would be overhead expenses still to enter.

Task 3

The following wages summary relates to the month of June 20X9. Write up the journal entries relating to the wages control account.

Wages summary

	£
Gross wages	47,300
Net wages	30,700
PAYE and NIC deductions	16,600

The payroll analysis shows £38,050 relates to direct labour and £9,250 relates to indirect labour.

CHAPTER OVERVIEW

- Remuneration methods generally fall into one of the following categories:
  - time rate
  - piecework
  - bonus system
  - salary
- Employees record their attendance times on attendance records, signing-in books or clock cards.
- Job costing requires more detailed records of time spent on each job, and this is recorded on a timesheet, a job card or a route card.
- Piecework is recorded on a piecework ticket (or operation card).
- The wages control account records payroll costs. These may also be charged to the work in progress control account and production overhead control account in a manufacturing business.

Keywords

Time rate – a basic amount per hour is paid

Overtime – a higher rate of pay if hours worked in a week exceed a pre-set limit

Overtime premium – the additional cost of overtime hours above the basic rate

Piecework – an amount is paid for each unit or task successfully completed

Differential piecework – the piecework rate increases for additional units over and above a pre-set quantity

Bonus system – the payment of an amount in addition to the time rate or salary if a target is exceeded

Salary – the payment of a set amount at agreed intervals, usually weekly or monthly

Clock card – a card for each employee that records the start and finish times of periods of work

Timesheet – a form completed by an employee detailing the time spent on each client's work each day, or week

Payroll calculation sheets – used to work out gross and net pay, NIC and taxes due

Job card – details the task to be performed on a particular job, and follows the job round; each employee records the time spent on their operation on the job

Cost centre – a section of the business to which overheads can be charged

Payroll – record showing each employee's gross pay, net pay and deductions

TEST YOUR LEARNING

Test 1

Cockerel Breakfast Cereals Limited pays a time rate of £7 per hour for a 35 hour week. Overtime is paid at time and a half for time worked in excess of 7 hours on weekdays, and double time for any work done at the weekend.

Calculate the gross pay of the employees whose clock card information is summarised below.

	Hours worked			
	J Sparrow	K Finch	M Swallow	B Cuckoo
Monday	7	7	7.25	7
Tuesday	7	8	7	7
Wednesday	7.5	7	7.5	7
Thursday	8	8	7.5	7.5
Friday	7	7.5	7.5	7
Saturday	3		2	2

Test 2

John Gosse is a direct worker who operates a lathe. During one week he works 40 hours, 35 of which are paid at a time rate of £10 per hour, the remainder being overtime which is paid at a premium of £4 per hour. Calculate the direct and indirect labour cost.

Test 3

Explain how a business can remunerate employees so as to give them an incentive to produce more. What are the drawbacks of such schemes?

Test 4

Alpha Industries pay their employees basic and overtime pay under the following arrangement:

For a basic six-hour shift every day from Monday to Friday – basic pay.

For any overtime in excess of the basic six hours, on any day from Monday to Friday – the extra hours are paid at time-and-a-half (basic pay plus an overtime premium equal to half of basic pay).

For four contracted hours each Saturday morning – basic pay.

For any hours in excess of four hours on Saturday – the extra hours are paid at double time (basic pay plus an overtime premium equal to basic pay).

For any hours worked on Sunday – paid at double time (basic pay plus an overtime premium equal to basic pay).

Complete the columns headed Basic pay, Overtime premium and Total pay. (**Notes**: Zero figures should be entered in cells where appropriate; Overtime pay is the premium amount paid for the extra hours worked.)

Employee's weekly timesheet for week ending 5 April

Employee: M. Rooney			**Profit Centre:** Widget carving			
Employee number: A450			**Basic pay per hour:** £10.00			
	Hours spent on production	**Hours worked on indirect work**	**Notes**	**Basic pay £**	**Overtime premium £**	**Total pay £**
Monday	6	2	10am-12am Machine calibration			
Tuesday	2	4	9am-1pm HR awareness course			
Wednesday	8					
Thursday	6					
Friday	6	1	3pm-4pm Customer care training			
Saturday	6					
Sunday	3					
Total	**37**	**7**				

Test 5

X Co has recorded the following wages costs for direct production workers for November.

Basic pay	£70,800
Overtime premium	£2,000
Gross wages	£72,800

The overtime was not worked for any specific job.

The accounting entries for these wages would be:

A	DEBIT	Work-in-progress account	72,800	
	CREDIT	Wages control account		72,800
B	DEBIT	Wages control account	72,800	
	CREDIT	Work-in-progress account		72,800
C	DEBIT	Wages control account	72,800	
	CREDIT	Overhead control account		2,000
	CREDIT	Wages control account		70,800
D	DEBIT	Work-in-progress account	70,800	
	DEBIT	Overhead control account	2,000	
	CREDIT	Wages control account		72,800

chapter 5: ACCOUNTING FOR OVERHEADS

chapter coverage

Finding the indirect cost of output is not as straightforward as finding the direct cost. This chapter examines ways in which this can be done. The topics that are to be covered are:

- Overheads
- Under-and over-absorption of overheads
- Accounting for overhead absorption
- Non-production overheads

OVERHEADS

From previous chapters, we know that OVERHEADS is the collective term for indirect materials, indirect labour and indirect expenses. Overheads tend to be grouped as to their function:

- **Production (or factory) overheads** include indirect materials, indirect factory wages, factory rent and rates, and power and light used in the factory
- Non-production overheads:
  - **Administration overheads** include office rent and rates, office salaries, indirect office materials and depreciation of office equipment that is used for administration (rather than the main activity of the business)
  - **Selling and distribution overheads** include delivery costs, salaries of sales staff and depreciation of delivery vehicles
  - **Finance overheads** are bank interest and charges

In most cost accounting systems the aim will be to find the full production cost of the cost units. This means that a method has to be found for including the **production overheads** in the cost of each cost unit. Be clear that we are only dealing with production overheads at this stage. Non-production overheads will be dealt with later in the chapter.

If you study the examples of production overheads above, you will appreciate the problem that the cost accountant has. None of these costs are directly attributable to a cost unit, but unless they are included in the cost of producing cost units, production costs will be underestimated which may lead, for example, to selling prices being set too low.

ABSORPTION COSTING (sometimes called full costing) is one way of finding an appropriate amount of overhead per cost unit so that the total cost of producing a product or job can be found. We will look at this briefly here as you will need to understand how overheads are absorbed before we look at under- and over-absorption. Absorption costing uses three stages to attach overhead costs to units of activity. By the final stage, which is absorption, an overhead absorption rate is calculated which is used to absorb overheads into cost units. In this way, all cost units have an additional overhead charged to them. This overhead absorption rate (OAR) is calculated in advance based on budgeted overheads and budgeted levels of activity. We will study absorption costing and a similar system, marginal costing, in the next chapter.

OAR = Budgeted overheads/budgeted activity level

THE ARBITRARY NATURE OF OVERHEAD APPORTIONMENT

One of the major criticisms of absorption costing is the difficulty of achieving a totally fair overhead cost in each cost unit. Even if the bases for apportionment and absorption are carefully considered, a precise result is not possible.

Task 1

ACD Co has budgeted overheads for the year of £75,000. It has budgeted to make 15,000 units using 15,000 labour hours. Calculate the overhead absorption rate (OAR) per labour hour.

UNDER- AND OVER-ABSORPTION OF OVERHEADS

The overhead cost of output is found using the **budgeted** overhead costs for the period and the **budgeted** activity level. The calculations are performed in advance of the costs actually being incurred, partly because of the nature of overheads: they are often incurred in relation to time periods. Predicting overhead costs is also needed so that selling prices can be set in advance and to enable control of costs by investigating variances between actual overheads and budgeted figures.

But using budgeted figures means that the actual overhead cost is unlikely to be the same as the overheads absorbed into production, as we are relying on two estimates:

- Overhead costs
- Activity levels

These will inevitably differ from the actual values that are experienced during the period. Consequently, at the end of the period when the statement of profit or loss is drawn up, the profit figure will be wrong as the overhead charge will be the absorbed amount (which was based on estimates) rather than the actual amount. The error in the profit figure results from one of two possibilities.

(1) If more overheads are absorbed than have actually been incurred, this is known as OVER-ABSORPTION.

(2) If fewer overheads are absorbed than have actually been incurred, this is known as UNDER-ABSORPTION.

The amount over- or under-absorbed is adjusted for in the statement of profit or loss after the production cost has been charged. Under-absorption means that too little overhead has been charged in the production cost, so a deduction is made from profit. Over-absorption means that too much overhead has been charged, so there is a compensating addition to profit.

The organisation needs to review the bases of calculation of the OAR as the activity changes over time. For instance, if an organisation becomes more automated and requires fewer workers, it would seem appropriate to change from calculating overheads based on labour hours to those based on machine hours.

HOW IT WORKS

Cowslip Limited budget to make and sell 10,000 units of their product in each of the next three months. They will be sold for £20 each and direct costs per unit are £6. Budgeted overheads are £15,000 per month, which is recovered using a rate per machine hour basis. Each unit requires three hours of machine time, the budgeted machine hours being 30,000. Actual overheads over the next three months are:

	£
February	15,000
March	14,000
April	16,000

All other actual costs, revenues and quantities are as budgeted (ie only the overheads incurred differ from budget).

The overhead absorption rate will be $= \frac{\text{Overheads}}{\text{Machine hours}}$

$= \frac{£15{,}000}{10{,}000 \text{ units} \times 3\text{h per unit}}$

$=$ £0.50 per machine hour

First, **in February**, the actual and budgeted overheads are the same at £15,000.

Statement of profit or loss for February

	£
Sales (10,000 × £20)	200,000
Less: production cost of sales	
direct costs (10,000 × £6)	(60,000)
overheads (30,000 hrs × £0.50)	(15,000)
Profit	125,000

A comparison of actual overheads and absorbed overheads will show that the two are the same:

	£
Actual overheads	15,000
Absorbed overheads (10,000 units × 3hrs × £0.50)	15,000
Under/over absorption	Nil

In March, however, actual overheads are lower than budget, at £14,000. The production cost charged in the statement of profit or loss will still be the same, as the same number of machine hours have been used. But we can't leave profit at the same level as before: the overheads are £1,000 less than were budgeted for, so we should have a profit of £1,000 more. By including 30,000 machine hours at a cost of £0.50 per hour in the statement of profit or loss, we have absorbed more overheads than were actually incurred, which is an over absorption.

	£
Actual overheads	14,000
Absorbed overheads (30,000h × £0.50)	15,000
Over absorption	1,000

This is credited to the statement of profit or loss.

Statement of profit or loss for March

	£
Sales (10,000 × £20)	200,000
Less: production cost of sales	
direct costs	(60,000)
overheads	(15,000)
	125,000
Add: over absorption of overheads	1,000
Profit	126,000

In April actual overheads are £16,000

	£
Actual overheads	16,000
Absorbed overheads (30,000h × £0.50)	15,000
Under absorption	1,000

The under-absorbed overheads will be debited to the statement of profit or loss. Under-absorption means that not enough overheads have been charged against profits, so we deduct the under absorption from profit to make up for this.

Statement of profit or loss for April

	£
Sales	200,000
Less: production cost of sales	
direct costs	(60,000)
overheads	(15,000)
	125,000
Less: under absorption of overheads	(1,000)
Profit	124,000

Note be very careful to calculate the under or over absorption based on actual v absorbed costs; budgeted costs are not brought into this calculation. This is particularly relevant when the actual amounts of both overheads and activity are different from budget.

Let's say that **in May**, the number of units produced and sold by Cowslip Limited is 12,000, machine hours amounted to 38,000 and overheads actually incurred amount to £16,500. So this time both overheads and activity level are different from budget.
Calculate the overhead under- or over-absorbed as before, being careful to pick up the correct figures.

	£
Actual overheads	16,500
Absorbed overheads (38,000h × £0.50)	19,000
Over absorption	2,500

The profit calculation will take account of the over-absorption.

Statement of profit or loss for May

	£
Sales (12,000 × £20)	240,000
Less: production cost of sales	
direct costs (12,000 × £6)	(72,000)
overheads absorbed (38,000h × £0.50)	(19,000)
	149,000
Add: over absorption of overheads	2,500
Profit	151,500

Task 2

Tulip Limited planned to make 30,000 units, each of which was expected to require two hours of direct labour. Budgeted overheads were £54,000. Actual production was 28,000 units, requiring a total of 55,000 direct labour hours. Actual overheads were £47,000.

Calculate:

(a) the overhead absorption rate based on direct labour hours; and

(b) the under- or over-absorption, stating whether this would be an addition to, or a deduction from, profit.

ACCOUNTING FOR OVERHEAD ABSORPTION

We have seen how the statement of profit or loss is adjusted for any eventual under- or over-absorption. Now we must take a step back and see how the amount of overhead to be absorbed is actually included in the cost ledger accounts. The accounting is straightforward and logical. The absorbed overhead is part of the production cost of the cost units and therefore it is **debited** to the work-in-progress control account together with the direct materials, direct labour and any direct expenses incurred, to give the total production cost for the period. The **credit entry** is to the production overhead control account which will have been debited with the actual overhead incurred. Any balance on the production overhead control account is the transfer to the statement of profit or loss as under or over-absorbed overhead.

HOW IT WORKS

We will return to the cost ledger accounts of Gilchrist Chemicals where neither the work in progress control account nor the production overhead control account were yet completed for the month of June. Gilchrist has incurred other expenses of £16,500 for royalties and £38,900 of indirect expenses. These are debited in the control accounts and credited to the bank account as shown. We are now going to look at how overheads are accounted for.

Work in progress control account

		£			£
30 June	Materials control	69,200			
30 June	Wages control	110,000			
30 June	Bank	16,500			

Production overhead control

		£		£
30 June	Materials control	3,600		
30 June	Wages control	30,000		
30 June	Bank	38,900		

The debits in the production overhead control account are the actual overheads incurred during the month. You are now told that the amount of overhead to be absorbed into production based upon the overhead absorption rate is £75,000.

This must be debited to the work in progress control account and credited to the production overhead control account.

Work in progress control account

		£		£
30 June	Materials Control	69,200		
30 June	Wages control	110,000		
30 June	Bank	16,500		
30 June	Prod'n overhead control	75,000		

Production overhead control

		£		£
30 June	Materials Control	3,600	30 June WIP	75,000
30 June	Wages control	30,000		
30 June	Bank	38,900		

If we balance the production overhead control account we will find any under or over absorbed overhead to transfer to the statement of profit or loss.

Production overhead control

		£		£
30 June	Materials control	3,600	30 June WIP	75,000
30 June	Wages control	30,000		
30 June	Bank	38,900		
30 June	St of profit or loss	2,500		
		75,000		75,000

The overheads actually incurred total £72,500 (£3,600 + £30,000 + £38,900) whereas the overhead absorbed was £75,000. This is an over absorption of overhead, which is debited in the production overhead control account and credited to the statement of profit or loss, thereby increasing profit. If the balance had been on the credit side of the production overhead control account this would have been an under absorption which would then have been debited or charged to the statement of profit or loss.

We will now finish the cost accounting process by considering the work in progress control account. The total on this account of £270,700 is the total production cost for the period. We are now told that during the period finished products with a production cost of £250,000 have been transferred to the warehouse ready for sale. The accounting entries reflect this with £250,000 being credited to work in progress and debited to a finished goods account.

Work in progress control account

		£			£
30 June	Materials control	69,200	30 June	Finished goods	250,000
30 June	Wages control	110,000			
30 June	Bank	16,500	30 June	Closing balance	20,700
30 June	Production o/h	75,000			
		270,700			270,700

Finished goods account

		£			£
30 June	WIP	250,000			

The closing balance on the work in progress control account is the amount of work in progress at the end of the month, cost units that have been started but not yet completed in the month.

NON-PRODUCTION OVERHEADS

So far we have concentrated on how we find the production cost of output, and how production overheads are incorporated into that cost. As far as financial accounting is concerned, this is where the cost of the product should stop. In the financial statements, other overheads will be charged as expenses in the statement of profit or loss. But for internal purposes, the business will need to know the full cost of producing each unit, including selling and distribution, administration, finance and research and development costs etc. They need to know if each product is making a profit and some businesses, such as solicitors and builders, set their prices by adding a certain percentage to full cost.

Some non-production overheads can be specifically allocated to a particular product, for example advertising for one type of product, and refrigerated distribution required only for one product. Sales value is a reasonable basis for the absorption of selling, distribution and marketing costs. It is difficult to find a reasonable basis for the absorption of other non-production overheads, so a percentage of production cost is used as the basis, which can be represented by the formula below.

$$\text{Percentage of production cost} = \frac{\text{Non-production overheads}}{\text{Production cost of output}} \times 100\%$$

Of course, this calculation will use budgeted figures, as with all overhead absorption.

HOW IT WORKS

Non-production overheads are expected to be £4,000. The production cost of the budgeted 24,000 units is £32,000. What is the overhead absorption rate for non-production overheads?

$$\text{Overhead absorption rate} = \frac{\pounds4{,}000}{\pounds32{,}000} \times 100\%$$

$$= 12.5\% \text{ of production cost}$$

CHAPTER OVERVIEW

- Overhead absorption rates are based on budgeted values for activity levels and overheads incurred. This results in under- and over-absorption of overheads which is adjusted for in the statement of profit or loss.
  - under-absorption is a deduction in the statement of profit or loss which reduces profit.
  - over-absorption is an addition in the statement of profit or loss which increases profit.
- Non-production overheads are charged to cost units to help with price-setting purposes.

Keywords

Overheads – indirect labour, indirect materials and indirect expenses

Absorption costing – a way of finding an appropriate amount of overhead per cost unit so that the total cost of producing a product or job can be found

Overhead absorption rate – the rate at which overheads are charged to cost units calculated by dividing budgeted overheads by the budgeted level of activity

Over-absorption – more overheads are absorbed into production than have actually been incurred

Under-absorption – fewer overheads are absorbed into production than were actually incurred

TEST YOUR LEARNING

Test 1

Calculate the under- or over-absorption of overheads in each of the three cases below, and state how this would be adjusted for in the statement of profit or loss.

(a) An overhead absorption rate of £3 per unit, based on expected production levels of 500 units. Actual overheads turn out to be £1,600, and actual production is 650 units.

(b) The budget is set at 1,000 units, with £9,000 overheads recovered on the basis of 600 direct labour hours. At the end of the period, overheads amounted to £8,600, production achieved was only 950 units and 590 direct labour hours had been worked. Overheads are absorbed on the basis of labour hours.

(c) 3,000 units of product X are to be made. Overheads are to be absorbed at a rate of £5 per machine hour. Actual production was the same as planned in the budget, incurring overheads of £3,500, and using 552 machine hours.

Test 2

Which of the following statements about overhead absorption rates are true?

(i) They are predetermined in advance for each period
(ii) They are used to charge overheads to products
(iii) They are based on actual data for each period
(iv) They are used to control overhead costs

A (i) and (ii) only
B (i), (ii) and (iv) only
C (ii), (iii) and (iv) only
D (iii) and (iv) only

Test 3

Over-absorbed overheads occur when

A absorbed overheads exceed actual overheads
B absorbed overheads exceed budgeted overheads
C actual overheads exceed budgeted overheads
D budgeted overheads exceed absorbed overheads

Test 4

A company absorbs overheads on machine hours which were budgeted at 11,250 with overheads of £258,750. Actual results were 10,980 hours with overheads of £254,692.

Overheads were

A under-absorbed by £2,152
B over-absorbed by £4,058
C under-absorbed by £4,058
D over-absorbed by £2,152

The following information relates to Tests 5 and 6

Budgeted labour hours	8,500
Budgeted overheads	£148,750
Actual labour hours	7,928
Actual overheads	£146,200

Test 5

Based on the data given above, what is the labour hour overhead absorption rate?

A £17.20 per hour
B £17.50 per hour
C £18.44 per hour
D £18.76 per hour

Test 6

Based on the data given above, what is the amount of under-/over-absorbed overhead?

A £2,550 under-absorbed overhead
B £2,550 over-absorbed overhead
C £7,460 over-absorbed overhead
D £7,460 under-absorbed overhead

chapter 6: ABSORPTION COSTING

chapter coverage

Finding the indirect cost of output is not as straightforward as finding the direct cost. This chapter examines ways in which this can be done. The topic to be covered is:

- Absorption costing

ABSORPTION COSTING

From previous chapters, we know that OVERHEADS is the collective term for indirect materials, indirect labour and indirect expenses. Overheads tend to be grouped as to their function.

In most cost accounting systems the aim will be to find the full production cost of the cost units. This means that a method has to be found of including the **production overheads** in the cost of each cost unit. Be clear that we are only dealing with production overheads at this stage.

If you study the examples of production overheads above, you will appreciate the problem that the cost accountant has. None of these costs are directly attributable to a cost unit, but unless they are included in the cost of producing cost units production costs will be underestimated which may lead, for example, to selling prices being set too low.

ABSORPTION COSTING (sometimes called full costing) is one way of finding an appropriate amount of overhead per cost unit so that the total cost of producing a product or job can be found.

The first stage in the process is that all of the production overheads must be shared out amongst the relevant cost centres. Some cost centres will be PRODUCTION COST CENTRES such as the assembly department or finishing department where the cost units are actually produced. However, production overheads will also be incurred by SERVICE COST CENTRES that are areas of the business that support the production of the cost units such as stores, canteen, maintenance etc.

Once all of the overheads have been allocated or apportioned to each of the relevant production and service cost centres **the next stage** is to take the service cost centre overhead totals and share these amongst the production cost centres in some fair manner. Now all of the production overheads are included in the production cost centres.

The final stage is to absorb the production cost centre overheads into the units produced during the period.

This process is summarised in the diagram below.

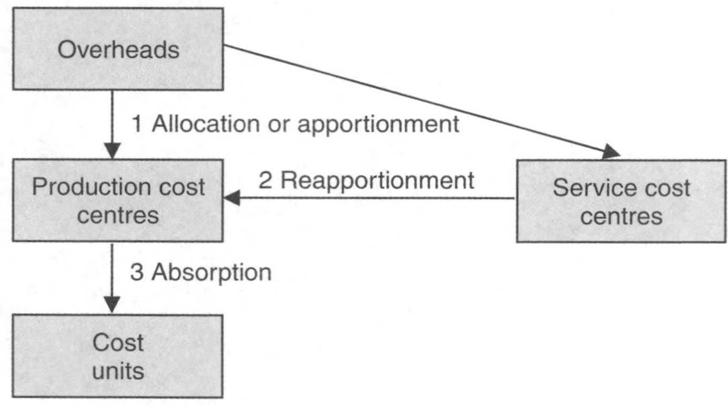

Stage 1: allocation and apportionment

ALLOCATION of overheads is the charging of an overhead to a single responsibility centre that has incurred the whole of that overhead. For example, the cost of a supervisor could be allocated to the department supervised and the depreciation of the warehouse could be allocated to the warehouse directly. Remember that a responsibility centre is a function or department of an organisation that is headed by a manager who has direct responsibility for its performance. They include cost centres, profit centres and investment centres.

APPORTIONMENT of overheads is the charging of a proportion of an overhead to each responsibility centre that incurs part of the overhead. Rent of a business premises might need to be shared between the various departments making up the business, for example. Apportionment should be done so that the share charged to a cost centre reflects its usage of that overhead. This means that each type of overhead needs to be considered separately to find a suitable basis. Examples of commonly used methods are given in the table below.

Overhead	Suitable basis for apportionment
Buildings costs such as rent, rates, repairs, insurance, heating, lighting and depreciation	Floor area or volume of space occupied by the cost centre
Canteen costs	Number of employees using the cost centre
Equipment costs such as insurance and depreciation	Cost or net book value of equipment
Maintenance costs	Amount of usage of maintenance department

In the assessment, you will need to show you know the difference between the allocation and apportionment of costs. (You could be asked to explain the difference between allocations and apportionments.) The assessment will state that overheads are allocated or apportioned 'on the most appropriate basis'.

Task 1

Rose Ceramics Limited rents office premises and owns a factory and a warehouse. There are four cost centres in the factory, the factory offices are the fifth cost centre, and the warehouse forms a sixth.

On 25 January, several invoices were received for overheads. For each of these decide:

(a) Whether the cost would be allocated or apportioned
(b) The cost centre(s) to be charged
(c) A suitable basis if apportionment is required

Overhead	(a) Allocate or apportion?	(b) Cost centre(s) charged?	(c) Basis of apportionment
Factory light & heat			
Rent			
Factory rates			
Office stationery			
Cleaning of workers' overalls			
Roof repair to warehouse			

HOW IT WORKS: OVERHEAD APPORTIONMENT

Bluebell Electronics Limited produces electronic equipment for the broadcasting industry. Certain components are made in the Components shop; others are bought-in and are kept in the Stores, along with various raw materials; the equipment is assembled in the Assembly department. The Maintenance department is responsible for the upkeep of the machines. The company is preparing its budget for the forthcoming period and forecasts overheads of £51,950 as follows.

	Total	*Components shop*	*Assembly dept.*	*Stores*	*Maintenance*
	£	£	£	£	£
Indirect wages	19,050	4,700	10,300	1,900	2,150
Indirect materials	15,400	9,400	2,500		3,500
Supervisor's wages	2,500				
Rent and rates	6,300				
Heat and light	3,200				
Buildings insurance	500				
Depreciation of machinery	5,000				
	51,950				

Additional information:

Floor area (sq metres)	500	250	150	50	50
Net book value of machinery	£50,000	£40,000	£5,000	£2,000	£3,000
Supervisor's time in the department (hours per week)	40	30	10		
Number of employees	17	9	4	2	2

How are these costs distributed to the four cost centres?

- Indirect wages and indirect materials have been incurred by each department individually, and have already been allocated. Bluebell Electronics will have been able to identify these costs separately from clock cards and materials requisitions.
- Supervisor's wages can be apportioned on the basis of the time spent in each cost centre, a 30:10 split between components shop and assembly.
- Rent and rates, heat and light and buildings insurance can be apportioned on the basis of floor area as details of volume occupied are not available; we can assume that all departments are housed in the same building and that the ceiling is at a uniform height. The split will be 250:150:50:50. You can apportion each cost given separately, or save time by doing all three costs together, as shown below.

- Depreciation of machinery will be based on the net book value of the machinery, giving a 40:5:2:3 split.

The final overhead apportionments for each cost centre can now be built up.

	Total	*Components shop*	*Assembly dept.*	*Stores*	*Maintenance*
	£	£	£	£	£
Indirect wages	19,050	4,700	10,300	1,900	2,150
Indirect materials	15,400	9,400	2,500		3,500
Supervisor's wages	2,500				
30:10					
30/40 × 2,500		**1,875**			
10/40 × 2,500			**625**		
Rent and rates	6,300				
Heat and light	3,200				
Buildings insurance	500				
250:150:50:50	10,000				
250/500 × 10,000		**5,000**			
150/500 × 10,000			**3,000**		
50/500 × £10,000				**1,000**	
50/500 × £10,000					**1,000**
Depreciation of machinery					
40:5:2:3	5,000				
40/50 × £5,000		**4,000**			
5/50 × £5,000			**500**		
2/50 × £5,000				**200**	
3/50 × £5,000					**300**
Total	51,950	24,975	16,925	3,100	6,950

Stage 2: reapportionment

The initial allocation or apportionment will be to production and service cost centres. The next step is to REAPPORTION the overheads of the service cost centres to production cost centres. This is achieved by considering the relative amount of use made of the service department by the production departments. So, if production department A (PA) has twice as many workers using the canteen as production department B (PB), canteen costs could be split between PA and PB in the ratio 2:1. The only complication that can arise is when service cost centres reciprocate, ie they perform services for other service cost centres as well as production cost centres.

Thus, when reapportionment is carried out more costs will be given to the service departments that we are trying to empty of their costs.

There are various methods which can be used for the reallocation of service department costs; the two required for this unit are:

- **Direct apportionment** which is suitable if the service cost centres only provide services for production cost centres. Service cost centre costs are only reapportioned to production cost centres.
- **The step-down method** which is appropriate if some service centres perform services for other service centres. Reapportionment is performed in a particular order so that, once the costs of a service cost centre have been reapportioned, no further costs are allocated to it.

HOW IT WORKS: REAPPORTIONMENT

If we continue with the example of Bluebell Electronics Limited, we can look at each method individually and see how the reapportionment is achieved.

Direct reapportionment

Suppose the Maintenance and Stores departments do no work for each other. This enables us to use the direct method as all the service department costs are incurred in servicing the production departments. All we have to do is find a suitable basis for reapportioning each service cost centre's costs. For Stores, the number or value of materials requisitions could be used. For Maintenance, we could use the number of hours worked or the value of machinery.

Budgeted use of service cost centres.

	By the Components shop	By the Assembly department
Number of materials requisitions from Stores	750	200
Maintenance hours required	300	120

The final apportionment to production cost centres will be as follows.

	Total	*Components shop*	*Assembly dept*	*Stores*	*Maintenance*
	£	£	£	£	£
Overheads	51,950	24,975	16,925	3,100	6,950
Reapportion maintenance 300 : 120 (W1) (hours required as above)		**4,964**	**1,986**		**(6,950)**
Reapportion stores 750 : 200 (W2) (materials requisitions as above)		**2,447**	**653**	**(3,100)**	
	51,950	32,386	19,564	–	–

The total overheads of £51,950 have been apportioned to the two production cost centres, and the figures are now ready for the third stage of the process of finding the overhead cost per unit or absorption.

Workings

		£
1	£6,950 × 300/(300 + 120) =	4,964
	£6,950 × 120/(300 + 120) =	1,986
		6,950

		£
2	£3,100 × 750/(750 + 200) =	2,447
	£3,100 × 200/(750 + 200) =	653
		3,100

Task 2

Jaques Ltd has three cost centres, A, B and C (which is a service centre, providing equal services to A and B). Overheads incurred in May are as follows:

	To be apportioned	
Electricity	£15,000	3:2:1
Rent	£12,000	6:3:1
Supervision	£5,000	1:1:0
Licence for Service Centre C	£2,000	n/a

Using direct reapportionment calculate the total overheads for A and B.

Cost centre		A	B	C	Total
	Basis used	£	£	£	£
Electricity					15,000
Rent					12,000
Supervision					5,000
Licence					2,000
Reapportion C				( )	
Total				0	34,000

The step-down method

This time, let's assume that Maintenance makes use of Stores by requisitioning spare parts for machinery and other materials, but Stores does not use the services of Maintenance at all.

Budgeted use of service cost centres.

	By the Components shop	By the Assembly department	By Maintenance
Number of materials requisitions from Stores	750	200	50
Maintenance hours required	300	120	

The step-down method is appropriate in this case, which means that we must give some thought to which department is reapportioned first. If we empty Maintenance first, when we reapportion Stores' costs we will put some costs back into Maintenance, as a charge for the services provided by Stores. Therefore, it is more efficient to do Stores first, and then Maintenance, as no further reapportionment will be necessary.

	Total	*Components shop*	*Assembly dept*	*Stores*	*Maintenance*
	£	£	£	£	£
Overheads	51,950	24,975	16,925	3,100	6,950
Reapportion stores first 750 : 200 : 50 (W1) (materials requisitions)		**2,325**	**620**	**(3,100)**	**155**
					7,105
Reapportion maintenance next 300 : 120 (W2) (maintenance hours)		**5,075**	**2,030**		(7,105)
	51,950	32,375	19,575	–	–

Notes

1. Stores are reapportioned first as some costs will go to Maintenance too.
2. Maintenance costs are reapportioned **after** Stores costs are added in.

Workings

		£
1	£3,100 × 750/(750 + 200 + 50) =	2,325
	£3,100 × 200/(750 + 200 + 50) =	620
	£3,100 × 50/(750 + 200 + 50) =	155
		3,100
2	£7,105 × 300/(300 + 120) =	5,075
	£7,105 × 120/(300 + 120) =	2,030
		7,105

Stage 3: Absorption

Overhead absorption is the way that overheads are charged to output. This is also known as **overhead recovery**. An OVERHEAD ABSORPTION RATE or **overhead recovery rate** is calculated so that each time a cost unit passes through the production cost centre, it is charged with a certain amount of overheads. The aim is for all the overheads incurred over a particular time to be absorbed into cost units made in that period.

The overhead absorption rate is calculated in advance based on the budgeted overheads and the budgeted level of activity. Activity can be expressed in a number of ways: hours worked, machine hours used, costs incurred or units produced, and any of these can be used to calculate the absorption rate. In this unit you will be tested on machine hours or direct labour hours or direct labour hour percentage for manufacturing businesses and any appropriate volume basis for service organisations eg miles travelled for a bus company. You must be able to justify your choice of basis for absorption.

Whichever basis of absorption you choose, will have an effect on how the overheads are charged to output. If hours worked are used, then each time an hour is worked, production will be charged with a portion of the overheads; if machine hours are the basis, then for each hour a machine is used, production will be charged with a portion of overheads.

$$\text{Rate per direct labour hour} = \frac{\text{Budgeted overheads}}{\text{Budgeted direct labour hours}}$$

$$\text{Rate per machine hour} = \frac{\text{Budgeted overheads}}{\text{Budgeted machine hours}}$$

HOW IT WORKS: ABSORPTION

Bluebell Electronics makes two products, the Videobooster and the Blastbox. It is trying to decide on an appropriate basis for the absorption of overheads. The following budgeted information is provided.

Production units	*Videobooster 4,000*		*Blastbox 6,000*	
	Components shop	*Assembly*	*Components shop*	*Assembly*
	£	£	£	£
Direct labour:				
hours per unit	1.25	0.5	2	1
total hours	5,000	2,000	12,000	6,000
Machine hours				
per unit	2	1	0.3	0.2
total hours	8,000	4,000	1,800	1,200

Calculate:

(a) separate departmental overhead absorption rates using first labour hours and then machine hours as the absorption basis

(b) the overhead absorbed by each product under each of the overhead absorption bases.

Note. The final apportionment of overheads to the two production cost centres was: Components shop, £32,375; and Assembly, £19,575.

(a) Departmental absorption rates

		Components	*Assembly*
Rate per direct labour hour			
$\frac{\text{Overheads}}{\text{Direct labour hours}}$	=	$\frac{£32,375}{5,000 + 12,000}$	$\frac{£19,575}{2,000 + 6,000}$
	=	£1.90 per direct labour hour	£2.45 per direct labour hour
Rate per machine hour			
$\frac{\text{Overheads}}{\text{Machine hours}}$	=	$\frac{£32,375}{8,000 + 1,800}$	$\frac{£19,575}{4,000 + 1,200}$
	=	£3.30 per machine hour	£3.76 per machine hour

(b) The overhead absorbed by each product

Rate per direct labour hour

	Videobooster		Blastbox	
		£		£
Components shop	£1.90 × 1.25h	2.38	£1.90 × 2h	3.80
Assembly	£2.45 × 0.5h	1.23	£2.45 × 1h	2.45
Total absorbed per unit		3.61		6.25

Rate per machine hour

	Videobooster		Blastbox	
		£		£
Components shop	£3.30 × 2h	6.60	£3.30 × 0.3h	0.99
Assembly	£3.76 × 1h	3.76	£3.76 × 0.2h	0.75
Total absorbed per unit		10.36		1.74

Which absorption rate should you use?

As you can see from the example above, the type of absorption rate used can have a huge effect on the cost of a product; the amount of overhead absorbed into the Blastbox varied from £1.74 to £6.25! It is therefore important to consider very carefully which rate is appropriate for each department. The way in which the cost is incurred can guide us towards the best method.

- A rate per direct labour hour would be appropriate if the department is labour intensive and most of the overheads relate to labour (this may apply to Bluebell's Assembly department).
- A rate per machine hour is a fair method if the department is largely mechanised, with relatively little labour input (perhaps Bluebell's Component shop).

The methods chosen for each department should be reviewed on a regular basis. This is because production methods or products might change, and the existing overhead absorption method may no longer be the best one. For example, as a company adds more automation, it may be appropriate to change from a labour hour to a machine hour basis.

HOW IT WORKS

If we use the labour hour basis for absorption of Bluebell's assembly department and the machine hour basis for the components shop, the overheads charged to each product will now be

	VideoBooster	*Blastbox*
Components shop	6.60	0.99
Assembly	1.23	2.45
Total	£7.83	£3.44

Task 3

Cactus Limited has 2 production departments, X and Z, which make several different products. Budgeted overheads apportioned to each department are estimated at X £20,000 and Z £40,000. Total labour hours for the budgeted period are expected to be X 4,000 and Z 16,000. Budgeted machine hours are X 12,000 and Z 100

Calculate:

(a) Separate departmental absorption rates based on labour hours
(b) Separate departmental absorption rates based on machine hours
(c) Comment on your results

Why do we bother with predetermined OARs?

Many overheads are not known until the end of a period. If we waited until the end of a period, this would cause delays in invoicing, inventory valuation and so on. This is why we calculate an OAR based on budgeted figures. It gives us a way of taking account of overheads before we actually know what they are.

What basis of absorption would be used in a service sector organisation?

If you get a service sector organisation in your assessment you will need to use an appropriate **volume** basis. For example, the number of miles travelled for a bus company.

CHAPTER OVERVIEW

- Absorption costing is a method used to charge an appropriate amount of production overheads to cost units.
- Some overheads can be allocated to a cost centre, others have to be apportioned or split between a number of cost centres.
- A fair basis for the apportionment of each type of overhead has to be found.
- Service cost centre overheads must be reapportioned to the production cost centres – reapportionment of service cost centre costs is achieved using an appropriate method depending upon whether one service cost centre provides services for another cost centre.
- The production cost centre costs must then be absorbed into the cost of units of production.
- A fair basis for the absorption of production cost centre overheads must be used – this is usually based upon direct labour hours or machine hours.

Keywords

Overheads – indirect labour, indirect materials and indirect expenses

Absorption costing – a way of finding an appropriate amount of overhead per cost unit so that the total cost of producing a product or job can be found

Production cost centres – a cost centre that actually produces cost units

Service cost centres – a cost centre that is not directly involved with production, but with supporting production by providing a service, eg maintenance and stores

Allocation – where the whole of an overhead has been incurred by one cost centre, so it is charged in full to that cost centre

Apportionment – where overheads are shared, on a fair basis amongst the cost centres that jointly incurred the cost

Reapportionment – apportionment of service cost centre costs to the production cost centres that use their service

Overhead absorption rate – the rate at which overheads are charged to cost units calculated by dividing budgeted overheads by the budgeted level of activity

Over-absorption – more overheads are absorbed into production than have actually been incurred

Under-absorption – fewer overheads are absorbed into production than were actually incurred

TEST YOUR LEARNING

Test 1

Overhead apportionment is used to (tick the correct answer):

- [ ] Charge whole items of costs to cost centres
- [ ] Charge cost units with an appropriate share of overheads
- [ ] Charge whole items of costs to cost units
- [ ] Spread common costs over cost centres
- [ ] Ensure budgeted overheads are not exceeded

Test 2

Bramble Fabrications Limited has three production departments: the machine shop, assembly and painting. There is one service department which usually spends 40% of its time servicing the machine shop, and the rest of the time equally in the other two production departments. Budgeted overheads to be apportioned between the departments are:

	£
Factory rent, rates and insurance	9,000
Depreciation of machinery	4,000
Supervisor's salary	8,000
Heat and light	2,000

Information for apportionment purposes:

	Machine shop	*Assembly*	*Painting*	*Services*
Floor area (square metres)	500	200	300	200
Value of machinery	£12,000	£4,000	£3,000	£1,000
Number of employees	8	9	5	2

You are required to calculate the final apportionment of budgeted overheads to the three production departments by:

(a) Apportioning the budgeted overheads to the four departments
(b) Reapportioning the service department overheads

Test 3

Vine Limited has two production departments, V and W. There are two service departments, S1 and S2. The budgeted costs of each department, along with overheads which have yet to be allocated or apportioned are listed below, along with details which can be used for allocation and apportionment.

	Total	*V*	*W*	*S1*	*S*
	£	£	£	£	£
Indirect materials	310,000	160,000	120,000	10,000	20,000
Indirect labour	1,125,000	400,000	650,000	40,000	35,000
Buildings depreciation and insurance	100,000				
Cleaning	25,000				
Machinery depreciation and insurance	1,500,000				
Supervision of production	70,000				
Power	250,000				
Heat and light	20,000				

	Total	*V*	*W*	*S1*	*S2*
Volume occupied (cubic metres)	10,000	6,000	3,000	800	200
% of power usage		25%	45%	20%	10%
Supervisor hours worked per week		15	20		
Value of machinery	£1,000,000	£380,000	£600,000		£20,000
% use of department S1		40%	60%		
% use of department S2		40%	50%	10%	
Direct labour hours worked		200,000	500,000		

You are required to calculate:

(a) The total overheads for each department after allocation and apportionment

(b) The overheads in departments V and W after reapportionment of the service departments using the step-down method

(c) Overhead absorption rates based on direct labour hours

Test 4

Overheads apportioned to two production departments have been worked out, along with estimates for labour hours and machine hours expected in the coming budget period. P1 is a labour intensive department, while P2 is highly mechanised with relatively few machine operatives. The budgeted figures are as follows.

	P1	*P2*
Overheads apportioned	£50,000	£60,000
Machine hours	900	4,000
Labour hours	2,500	650

You are required to calculate separate departmental overhead absorption rates for production departments P1 and P2 using an appropriate basis, and explain your choice of basis.

chapter 7: JOB, BATCH AND SERVICE COSTING

chapter coverage

So far we have concentrated on gathering together the costs for individual cost units – the products that a business makes. However there are other costing systems depending upon the type of product or service that a business provides. In the next two chapters we shall consider costing systems other than those that gather costs into the cost of a single cost unit. The topics to be covered in this chapter are:

- Costing systems
- Job costing
- Batch costing
- Service costing
- Service department costing
- Job costing and services

COSTING SYSTEMS

For many organisations the basic system of costing is that which we have considered so far – the collection of direct costs and overheads into the production cost centres in order eventually to absorb these costs into each individual cost unit or product that the business makes. Remember that the UNIT COST is the cost of producing one unit of the organisation's product.

However there are four other types of costing system that are mentioned in the learning outcomes for this unit – job costing, batch costing, service costing and process costing. Each of these will be considered in this or the next chapter. The choice of system is based on the business itself so an oil refinery will use process costing whilst a bridge builder will use job costing. In fact process costing and job costing are the two opposite ends of a spectrum of costing methods that organisations can use. Most choose a mix of the large volume of continuous activity in process costing and the large scale of a single project in job costing.

JOB COSTING

JOB COSTING is used in types of business where the product that is produced is a 'one-off' job for a customer that is different for each individual customer. Typical types of business where job costing is used are engineering, building, painting and decorating, and printing. These are businesses where there is no previously produced product to sell. What is being done for the customer is entirely to the customer's specification.

There are three main areas of job costing that are of concern to the accountant:

- The setting of the price for the job
- The gathering of actual costs for the job
- The control of the job by the monitoring of variances between the expected cost and the actual cost of the job.

Setting the price

The problem with jobbing businesses is that there is no price list as such as there is no standard product. Each individual job will be different with different costs.

When a customer approaches the business requesting a quote for a price for the job they will provide details of the precise requirements they have for this particular job. The business must then decide how much the job is going to cost and how much profit it is to earn on the job and then come up with a price that satisfies this.

It is important to realise that not only must the price of the job cover the direct costs of materials, labour and any direct expenses but it must also cover a portion of the overheads, so that all of the overheads for a period are covered by the prices of the jobs done in that period.

Task 1

What are the three main tasks of the accounting function in a job costing business?

HOW IT WORKS

Brecon Builders have been approached by a potential customer, Petra Jones, who wishes to have a loft conversion. The engineer has visited the site and inspected the loft and taken detailed measurements and drawings. From his estimates the accountant then draws up the following set of estimates for the job on a standard job quote card:

JOB NUMBER 03677
PETRA JONES LOFT CONVERSION

	£
Direct materials	
Plasterboard	1,800.00
Wood and door frames	740.00
Insulation	1,250.00
Electrical fittings	320.00
Staircase	840.00
Windows	720.00
Paint	270.00
Direct labour	
Construction 45 hours @ £13.20	594.00
Electrical 8 hours @ £15.50	124.00
Plastering 16 hours @ £16.00	256.00
Decorating 15 hours @ £11.00	165.00
Direct expenses	
Hire of specialist lathe	240.00
Overheads (based upon direct labour hours)	
84 hours @ £15.00	1,260.00
Total cost	8,579.00
Profit (20% of total cost)	1,715.80
Net price	10,294.80
VAT at 20%	2,058.96
Total price	12,353.76

The important points to note about this job quotation are as follows:

- Each job will be assigned an individual number which will be used when any materials, labour or expense are incurred by the job
- The costs of the direct materials will have come from the stores ledger records for any materials that are already held in inventory and from the purchasing department for any additional materials that are required
- The direct labour costs will be an estimate of the number of hours required for each task and the labour hour rate for each type of employee
- The direct expenses are any specific items of expense that relate to this job only
- The overheads are to be absorbed on a direct labour hour basis. The overhead absorption rate will have been calculated (as we have seen in an earlier chapter) by gathering together all of the budgeted overheads for the period and then dividing by the budgeted number of labour hours for the period
- Once all of the costs of the job have been gathered together, including the absorption of the overheads, then the profit percentage that the business wishes to make over and above the costs is added – this is the net price to the customer
- Finally the VAT (sales tax) must be added in at 20%, if the business is registered for VAT to give the final total price for the job to the customer.

If the customer accepts this price quotation then Brecon Builders will go ahead with the job.

Task 2

Why is it important that overheads are included in the price quoted to a customer for a job?

Actual costs of the job

The next problem with job costing is to ensure that all of the costs of the job are accurately gathered together. This means ensuring that all materials issued to the job are coded and recorded as relating to that particular job and that all of the time of employees who work on that job is coded and recorded as relating to it. Any direct expenses of that job, such as hire of a piece of machinery for the job, must also be recorded.

Finally a portion of the overheads of the business must be apportioned to the job, normally on a basis similar to that used for unit costing such as direct labour hours or direct machine hours.

HOW IT WORKS

Brecon Builders now start work on Petra Jones' loft conversion.

Each time that materials are requisitioned from the stores department for this job a materials requisition form must be completed showing clearly that the materials are required for job number 03677.

For example three wooden doors are required for the entrance to the loft and the wardrobes that are being fitted. The materials requisition must be filled out as follows:

MATERIALS REQUISITION

Material required for: Job 03677		**No.**	**44285**	
		Date.	**4 July**	
Quantity	**Description**	**Code no.**	**Price per unit**	**£**
3	Imperial doors	DI2553	64.00	192.00
Authorised by:	K Finch			

Each materials requisition is passed to the accounts department and they will gather together the cost of the total materials that have been used on Job 03677.

When each employee works on the loft extension they will complete a job card showing the number of hours worked on the job as follows:

<table>
<tr><td colspan="4">JOB CARD</td></tr>
<tr><td colspan="4">Job No 03677
Date 7 July</td></tr>
<tr><td colspan="4">Time allowed 7 hours   Start time 9.00 am
Finish time 5.00 pm</td></tr>
<tr><td>Job description</td><td>Hours</td><td>Rate</td><td>Cost
£</td></tr>
<tr><td>Plastering wall surfaces</td><td>7</td><td></td><td></td></tr>
<tr><td colspan="4">Employee name Melvin Hurd
Employee signature Melvin Hurd
Supervisor's signature John Hunt</td></tr>
</table>

Again each employee's JOB CARD will be sent to the accounts department who will record the correct hourly rate for this employee and gather together all of the labour costs for Job 03677.

When the invoice is received for the hire of the special lathe for the loft conversion this will again be coded for Job 03677 and incorporated into the accounts department's total costs for the job.

Finally, when the job is completed, the number of direct labour hours will be totalled multiplied by the overhead absorption rate of £15.00 per hour and added to the direct costs. In this case the number of hours finally totalled 90 direct labour hours and therefore the overheads absorbed into Job 03677 are £1,350.00 (90 hours × £15.00 per hour).

Monitoring of variances

Once the job has been completed and all of the costs have been gathered together, the actual costs must be compared to the original costs used to price the job and variances will be calculated. This serves as a control over the costs of the actual job itself and over the initial pricing process.

HOW IT WORKS

Petra Jones' loft conversion was completed in early August 20X6 and by 15 August the accounts department had gathered together all of the costs of the job and produced the following variance schedule (FAV = favourable variance ie actual cost was lower than budget; ADV = adverse variance ie actual cost was higher than budget).

JOB NUMBER 03677
PETRA JONES LOFT CONVERSION

	Budget	*Actual*	*Variance*
	£	£	£
Direct materials			
Plasterboard	1,800.00	1,750.00	50.00 FAV
Wood & door frames	740.00	800.00	60.00 ADV
Insulation	1,250.00	1,340.00	90.00 ADV
Electrical fittings	320.00	300.00	20.00 FAV
Staircase	840.00	840.00	–
Windows	720.00	760.00	40.00 ADV
Paint	270.00	250.00	20.00 FAV
Direct labour			
Construction	594.00	641.00	47.00 ADV
Electrical	124.00	160.00	36.00 ADV
Plastering	256.00	250.00	6.00 FAV
Decorating	165.00	205.00	40.00 ADV
Direct expenses			
Hire of specialist lathe	240.00	240.00	–
Overheads (based upon direct labour hours)			
84/90 hours @ £15.00	1,260.00	1,350.00	90.00 ADV
Total cost	8,579.00	8,886.00	307.00 ADV
Profit	1,715.80	1,408.80	
Net price	10,294.80	10,294.80	
VAT at 20%	2,058.96	2,058.96	
Total price	12,353.76	12,353.76	

In total this shows that the business has made £307.00 less profit on the job than expected as the net variances total an adverse variance of £307.00 and the price of the job is fixed.

This shows the importance of ensuring that the very best estimates are made when the initial price is quoted to the customer.

Task 3

A furniture-making business manufactures quality furniture to customers' orders. A piece of furniture is to be manufactured for a customer (job H) and the direct costs are as follows.

	Job H
Direct material	£154
Direct labour	20 hours in department A

The overhead absorption rate is £12.86 per direct labour hour and the labour rate is £3.80 per hour. Calculate the total cost of the job.

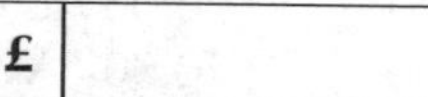

BATCH COSTING

BATCH COSTING is used in manufacturing businesses that make batches of different products rather than single products. For example a shoe manufacturer may make a batch of 400 shoes of one style in size 4 and then a batch of 300 shoes of a different style in size 7. Similarly a food manufacturer may make a batch of 500 portions of chicken tikka followed by a batch of 200 portions of prawn korma.

Batch costing is a costing system whereby all of the costs of making the entire batch are gathered together. This will be the direct materials, direct labour and any direct expenses, together with the overheads that are absorbed into that batch. We have already seen how overheads are absorbed into individual units.

Once all of the costs of the batch have been determined the cost of each individual unit of product in that batch can be found as follows:

$$\text{Cost per unit} = \frac{\text{Cost of the batch}}{\text{Number of units in the batch}}$$

Task 4

The costs to a clothing manufacturer of producing a batch of 450 men's leather jackets was £38,925. What is the cost of each jacket?

SERVICE COSTING

SERVICE COSTING is cost accounting adapted for services or functions, eg canteens, maintenance, payroll. These may be known variously as service centres, departments or functions.

You may remember from your previous studies that service organisations do not make or sell tangible goods. They can be either profit-making or non-profit making organisations. Profit-making service organisations include accountancy firms, law firms, management consultants, transport companies, banks, insurance companies and hotels. Almost all non-profit organisations – hospitals, schools, libraries and so on – are also service organisations.

Service costing differs from other costing methods (product costing methods) for a number of reasons.

(a) With many services, the cost of direct materials consumed will be relatively small compared to the labour, direct expenses and overheads cost. In product costing the direct materials are often a greater proportion of the total cost.

(b) Because of the difficulty of identifying costs with specific cost units in service costing, the indirect costs tend to represent a higher proportion of total cost compared with product costing.

(c) The output of most service organisations is often **intangible** (you can't touch it) and hence difficult to define. A unit cost is therefore difficult to calculate.

(d) The service industry includes such a wide range of organisations which provide such different services and have such different cost structures that costing will vary considerably from one service to another.

A particular problem with service costing is the difficulty in defining a realistic COST UNIT that represents a suitable measure of the service provided. Frequently, a COMPOSITE COST UNIT may be deemed more appropriate if the service combines more than one activity. Hotels, for example, may use the **'occupied bed-night'** as an appropriate unit for cost ascertainment and control.

A company operating a fleet of delivery vehicles may use the **'tonne/kilometre'** as a cost unit. This involves recording and monitoring the cost of carrying one tonne for one kilometre. The cost per tonne/kilometre is comparable regardless of the length of the journey and provides a valid cost unit for control purposes. The construction of this composite cost unit is demonstrated later in the chapter.

Typical cost units used by companies operating in a service industry are shown below.

Service	Cost unit
Road, rail and air transport services	Passenger/kilometre, tonne/kilometre
Hotels	Occupied bed-night
Education	Full-time student
Hospitals	Patient-day
Catering establishments	Meal served

Each organisation will need to work out the most suitable cost unit for its activities. If a number of organisations within an industry use a common cost unit, valuable **comparisons** can be made between similar establishments. This is particularly applicable to hospitals, educational establishments and local authorities. Unit costs are also useful control measures as we shall see in the examples that follow.

Whatever cost unit is decided upon, the calculation of a cost per unit is as follows.

$$\text{Cost per service unit} = \frac{\text{Total costs for period}}{\text{Number of service units in the period}}$$

The following example will illustrate the principles involved in service industry costing and the further considerations to bear in mind when costing services.

HOW IT WORKS

Carry operates a small fleet of delivery vehicles. Expected costs are as follows.

Loading	1 hour per tonne loaded
Loading costs:	
Labour (casual)	£2 per hour
Equipment depreciation	£80 per week
Loading supervision	£80 per week
Drivers' wages (fixed)	£100 per man per week
Petrol	10p per kilometre
Repairs	5p per kilometre
Depreciation	£80 per week per vehicle
Supervision	£120 per week
Other general expenses (fixed)	£200 per week

There are two drivers and two vehicles in the fleet.

During a slack week, only six journeys were made.

Journey	*Tonnes carried (one way)*	*One-way distance of journey Kilometres*
1	5	100
2	8	20
3	2	60
4	4	50
5	6	200
6	5	300

As the management accountant you have been asked to calculate the expected average full cost per tonne/kilometre for the week.

Variable costs

Journey	*1*	*2*	*3*	*4*	*5*	*6*
	£	£	£	£	£	£
Loading labour	10	16	4	8	12	10
Petrol (both ways)	20	4	12	10	40	60
Repairs (both ways)	10	2	6	5	20	30
	40	22	22	23	72	100

Total costs

	£
Variable costs (total for journeys 1 to 6)	279
Loading equipment depreciation	80
Loading supervision	80
Drivers' wages	200
Vehicles depreciation	160
Drivers' supervision	120
Other costs	200
	1,119

Journey	Tonnes	*One-way distance* Kilometres	Tonne-kilometres
1	5	100	500
2	8	20	160
3	2	60	120
4	4	50	200
5	6	200	1,200
6	5	300	1,500
			3,680

$$\text{Cost per tonne/kilometre } \frac{£1,119}{3,680} = £0.304$$

Note that the large element of fixed costs may distort this measure but that a variable cost per tonne/kilometre of £279/3,680 = £0.076 may be useful for budgetary control.

Task 5

Briefly describe cost units that are appropriate to a transport business.

Task 6

Explain why service costing differs from other costing methods.

SERVICE DEPARTMENT COSTING

Service department costing is used to establish a specific cost for an **'internal service'** which is a service provided by one department for another, rather than sold externally to customers. Examples of some internal service departments include the following.

- Canteen
- Data processing
- Maintenance

The costing of internal services has two basic purposes.

(a) **To control the costs and efficiency in the service department.** If we establish a distribution cost per tonne/km, a canteen cost per employee, a maintenance cost per machine hour, job cost per repair, or a mainframe computer operating cost per hour, we can do the following in order to establish control measures.

  (i) Compare actual costs against a target or standard

  (ii) Compare actual costs in the current period against actual costs in previous periods

(b) **To control the costs of the user departments, and prevent the unnecessary use of services.** If the costs of services are charged to the user departments in such a way that the charges reflect the use actually made by each user department of the service department's services then the following will occur.

  (i) The overhead costs of user departments will be established more accurately. Some service department variable costs might be identified as costs that are directly attributable to the user department.

(ii) If the service department's charges for a user department are high, the user department might be encouraged to consider whether it is making an excessively costly and wasteful use of the service department's service.

(iii) The user department might decide that it can obtain a similar service at a lower cost from an external service company and so the service department will have priced itself out of the market. This is clearly not satisfactory from the point of view of the organisation as a whole.

Service costing also provides a **fairer basis** for charging service costs to user departments, instead of charging service costs as overheads on a broad direct labour hour basis, or similar arbitrary apportionment basis. This is because service costs are related more directly to **use**.

Some examples of situations where the costing of internal services would be useful are as follows.

(a) If repair costs in a factory are costed as jobs with each bit of repair work being given a job number and costed accordingly, repair costs can be charged to the departments on the basis of repair jobs actually undertaken, instead of on a more generalised basis, such as apportionment according to machine hour capacity in each department. Departments with high repair costs could then consider their high incidence of repairs, the age and reliability of their machines, or the skills of the machine operators.

(b) If mainframe computer costs are charged to a user department on the basis of a cost per hour, the user department would make the following assessment.

   (i) Whether it was getting good value from its use of the mainframe computer.

   (ii) Whether it might be better to hire the service of a computer bureau, or perhaps install a stand alone microcomputer system in the department.

HOW IT WORKS

The maintenance department of FA charges user departments for its services as follows.

- A predetermined hourly rate for labour hours worked on maintenance jobs
- Specifically identifiable materials are charged at actual cost

The budgeted maintenance labour hours for the latest period were 800 hours, during which maintenance costs of £8,400 were budgeted to be incurred.

During the period, 22 maintenance hours were worked in production department 1, and materials costing £18 were used on these maintenance jobs.

The correct charge to production department 1 for its use of the maintenance service department during the period is

A £28.50 B £231.00 C £249.00 D £399.82

Predetermined labour hour rate for maintenance = £8,400/800
= £10.50 per hour

∴ Charge to production department 1:

	£
Maintenance labour (22 hours × £10.50)	231
Materials	18
	249

Therefore the correct answer is C.

Task 7

Can you think of examples of cost units for internal services such as canteens, distribution and maintenance?

JOB COSTING AND SERVICES

Service costing is one of the subdivisions of **continuous operation costing** and as such should theoretically be applied when the services result from a sequence of continuous or repetitive operations or processes. Service costing is therefore ideal for catering establishments, road, rail and air transport services and hotels. However, just because an organisation provides a service, it does not mean that service costing should automatically be applied.

Remember that job costing applies where work is undertaken to customers' special requirements. An organisation may therefore be working in the service sector but may supply one-off services that meet 'particular customers' special requirements; in such a situation job costing may be more appropriate than service costing. For example, a consultancy business, although part of the service sector, could use job costing.

(a) Each job could be given a separate number.

(b) Time sheets could be used to record and analyse consultants' time.

(c) The time spent against each job number would be shown as well as, for example, travelling time and mileage.

(d) Other costs such as stationery could be charged direct to each job as necessary.

Task 8

A university with annual running costs of £792,000 has the following students.

	Number	*Attendance weeks per annum*	*Hours per week*
Undergraduates	2,700	30	14
Post graduates	1,500	30	10

There are two different types of students, undergraduate and post graduate so we cannot use a 'student' as the cost unit.

Calculate a cost per attendance hour for the university.

£	

CHAPTER OVERVIEW

- Job costing is a costing system that is used in a business that provides individual 'one-off' products for customers.
- In a job costing system the accounting function must first produce a schedule of the expected costs of the product that the customer wants – this schedule must include not only the direct costs of producing the product but also any overheads that need to be absorbed into the job to ensure that all of the overheads of the business for the period are eventually covered by the prices set for the jobs done.
- The price of the job must also include the profit element for the business and the VAT if the business is registered for VAT.
- Once the price has been agreed and the job is started all of the costs of the job must be gathered together by the accounting function – any materials requisitions must quote the job number and all job cards for employees' hours must also show which job was worked on.
- The accounting function will then absorb overheads into the job according to the organisation's policies.
- Once the job has been completed the accounting function will prepare a comparison of the actual costs of the job with those quoted initially to the customer – showing any variances from the original estimated costs.
- Batch costing is used in businesses where instead of there being production runs of identical products there are a number of production runs of batches of different products.
- The purpose of batch costing is to find the cost of an entire batch of a product and then to divide that cost by the number of units produced in the batch – this will then give the unit cost of each unit of that product.
- Service costing is used in service businesses where services are provided rather than goods made. The measurement of activity often involves more than one activity as a composite cost unit.

Keywords

Job costing – costing system that allocates costs to individual 'one-off' jobs for customers

Job card – an individual employee's record of the time spent on each job

Batch costing – a costing system that gathers together the costs of production of an entire batch of a similar product in order to find the cost of each individual item in that batch

Service costing – is cost accounting adapted for services or functions

Unit cost – the cost of producing one unit of the organisation's product

Composite cost unit – cost unit where the service combines more than one activity

Cost per service unit – total costs for the period/number of service units for the period

TEST YOUR LEARNING

Test 1

A curtain manufacturer has been asked to give a quote for the making of a set of curtains for a large, square bay window. It is estimated that the cost of the curtain fabric will be £590 and the lining materials £175. The job is estimated to take 27 hours at a rate of £7.70 per hour. The business absorbs overheads at the rate of £8.70 per hour.

(a) What is the estimated cost of the production of these curtains?

(b) If the business aims to achieve a profit of 15% per job and is also registered for VAT (payable at 20%), what is the final quote to the customer?

Test 2

A kitchen manufacturer has been asked to supply a kitchen to a customer. The estimates of costs are given below:

Materials for manufacturing the units – £12,500

Direct labour for fitting the units – 23 hours @ £8.60 per hour

Direct labour for redecorating – 5 hours @ £6.50 per hour

Overheads are absorbed on the basis of £12.40 per direct labour hour.

Profit on each job is taken at 25% of total costs

VAT is charged at 20%

Prepare a job costing schedule showing how much the kitchen will cost the customer.

Test 3

A pie factory operates on a batch production system. The latest batch to have been produced is 1,200 cheese and mushroom pies. The costs of this batch are:

Ingredients	£840.00
Labour 7 hours @ £6.50	

Overheads are absorbed on the basis of £1.20 per labour hour.

What is the cost of each pie?

Test 4

Which of the following are characteristics of service costing?

(i) High levels of indirect costs as a proportion of total costs
(ii) Use of composite cost units
(iii) Use of equivalent units

A (i) only
B (i) and (ii) only
C (ii) only
D (ii) and (iii) only

Test 5

Which of the following would be appropriate cost units for a transport business?

(i) Cost per tonne-kilometre
(ii) Fixed cost per kilometre
(iii) Maintenance cost of each vehicle per kilometre

A (i) only
B (i) and (ii) only
C (i) and (iii) only
D All of them

Test 6

Which of the following organisations should *not* be advised to use service costing?

A Distribution service
B Hospital
C Maintenance division of a manufacturing company
D An engineering company

chapter 8: PROCESS COSTING

chapter coverage

In the last chapter we considered costing systems which are useful for small-scale, and discrete goods and services. In this chapter we shall consider process costing which is used to cost large-scale manufacturing processes. The topics to be covered are:

- Process costing
- Normal process losses
- Abnormal losses and gains

PROCESS COSTING

In many manufacturing businesses the product is made in a process whereby materials are input to the process, work is carried out on the materials, overheads are incurred by the process and finally a number of completed, identical products appear out of the process. Examples include the brewing industry, oil refining and paint manufacture.

A specific type of costing system is needed in order to cost the final product in such circumstances, known as PROCESS COSTING. The aim of process costing is to gather together all of the costs incurred in a process in a period and divide these costs by the number of units produced in the period. As each of the units is identical what we are effectively doing is finding the average cost for each unit produced in the period.

HOW IT WORKS

Nuneaton Enterprises is a food processing manufacturer which makes a number of different types of product in a number of different processes. The following information is available for Process VF1 for the month of May:

Materials input into the process 120,000 kg	£38,000
Labour hours spent on the process	1,200 @ £9 per hour
Overheads to be absorbed into the process	£11,200
Units produced from the process	120,000 kg

The costs of the process are first totalled:

	£
Direct materials	38,000
Direct labour (1,200 × £9)	10,800
Overheads absorbed	11,200
Total process cost	60,000

The cost per unit produced is the total process cost divided by the number of units produced:

$$\text{Cost per unit} = \frac{£60,000}{120,000 \text{ kg}}$$

$$= 50 \text{ pence per kg}$$

The costs and the production are normally shown in a process account. The process account for process VF1 for May would be made up as follows:

- The materials input into the process in both kilograms and value are debited to the process account.

Process VF1

	kg	£		£
Materials	120,000	38,000		

- The labour and overhead costs are also debited to the account (sometimes these two costs are given together and called the conversion costs).

Process VF1

	kg	£		£
Materials	120,000	38,000		
Labour		10,800		
Overheads		11,200		

- The output is shown on the credit side as 120,000 kgs each valued at 50 pence therefore totalling £60,000 and the process account is balanced.

Process VF1

	kg	£		kg	£
Materials	120,000	38,000			
Labour		10,800			
Overheads		11,200	Output	120,000	60,000
	120,000	60,000		120,000	60,000

NORMAL PROCESS LOSSES

In many processes the quantity of material put into the process is not the same as the quantity that is produced from the process as the process has losses during the processing time, for example due to evaporation or defective units. Over time an organisation will be able to judge what is the normal level of loss from a process. The normal loss is the amount of loss that is expected from a process. This is normally expressed as a percentage of the materials input to the process.

As the normal loss is part of the normal manufacturing process no value is given to the normal loss units; instead the process costs are averaged out over the good units of production.

Task 1

During week 3, 17,000 kg of material were added to a process. The process has a normal loss of 5%. Calculate the expected output.

HOW IT WORKS

Another of Nuneaton's processes is the GS3. There is a normal loss of 10% of materials input into this process. The costs incurred in this process and the output achieved for the month of May are:

Direct materials	50,000 kg	£22,500
Direct labour		£16,500
Overheads		£6,000
Output		45,000 kg

The steps to follow are:

Step 1 Calculate the number of normal loss units:

50,000 kg × 10% = 5,000 kg

Step 2 Calculate the expected output from the process:

50,000 kg – 5,000 kg = 45,000 kg

Step 3 Total the process costs:

£22,500 + £16,500 + £6,000 = £45,000

Step 4 Calculate the cost per unit of expected output

$$\frac{£45,000}{45,000\text{ kg}} = £1 \text{ per kg}$$

This can then all be written up in the process account:

Process GS3

	kg	£		kg	£
Materials	50,000	22,500	Normal loss	5,000	–
Labour		16,500	Output	45,000	45,000
Overheads		6,000			
	50,000	45,000		50,000	45,000

Both the kgs and the value columns must balance. No value has been assigned to the normal loss units, all of the process costs have been shared between the expected output units.

Task 2

During week 26 16,000 litres of material costing £108,000 were added to a process. The process has a normal loss of 5%. The conversion costs for the process were £22,720 for the week. Output from the process during the week was 15,200 litres.

(a) What is the cost per litre of good output?

(b) Write up the process account.

ABNORMAL LOSSES AND GAINS

In many processes the **actual** process loss will differ from the **expected** or normal loss. If the actual loss is greater than the expected loss the difference is known as an ABNORMAL LOSS. If the actual loss is less than the expected loss the difference is known as an ABNORMAL GAIN.

Whereas the normal loss units are expected and unavoidable any abnormal losses or gains are not expected and are considered avoidable therefore the accounting treatment of abnormal losses and gains is different from that of the normal loss. The normal loss units were assigned no value; however, any abnormal loss units are valued in the same way as the good output.

HOW IT WORKS

The normal loss for another of Nuneaton's processes PE7 is 5%. The inputs, costs and output of this process in May are given below.

Direct materials	20,000 kg	£15,400
Direct labour		£6,200
Overheads		£1,200
Output		18,400 kg

Step 1 Calculate the number of normal loss units:

20,000 kg × 5% = 1,000 kg

Step 2 Calculate the expected output from the process:

20,000 kg – 1,000 kg = 19,000 kg

Step 3 Total the process costs:

£15,400 + £6,200 + £1,200 = £22,800

Step 4 Calculate the cost per unit of expected output

$$\frac{£22{,}800}{19{,}000 \text{ kg}} = £1.20 \text{ per kg}$$

The process account is now written up - this is where the units column becomes important. Our expected output was 19,000 kg but in fact only 18,400 kg were produced so there is an abnormal loss of 600 kg which are valued at the same value as the good output, £1.20 per kg, so £720 in total. The good output of 18,400 kg is also valued at £1.20 per kg totalling £22,080 and both the unit columns and value columns balance.

Process PE7

	kg	£		kg	£
Materials	20,000	15,400	Normal loss	1,000	–
Labour		6,200	Abnormal loss	600	720
Overheads		1,200	Output	18,400	22,080
	20,000	22,800		20,000	22,800

The abnormal loss has been credited to the process account and must be debited to an abnormal loss account:

Abnormal loss account

	kg	£		kg	£
Process PE7	600	720			

At the period end, the abnormal loss account is cleared to the statement of profit or loss. In this case it will be an expense of £720. In your assessment you will only need to deal with the process account T account but we have shown you the abnormal loss account just to help your understanding.

Task 3

During the month of March 110,000 kgs of materials with a cost of £526,000 were entered into a process which has a normal loss of 6%. Labour costs for the month for the process were £128,300 and overheads were £110,860. The actual output for the period was 100,400 kgs.

(a) What is the cost per kg?

(b) Write up the process account for the month.

Abnormal gain

The treatment of an abnormal gain is exactly the same as an abnormal loss but the double entry is the other way around.

HOW IT WORKS

Process RD4 in Nuneaton Enterprises has a normal loss of 10%. The inputs, costs and outputs for the month of May are given below:

Direct materials	10,000 kg	£11,200
Direct labour		£9,400
Overheads		£6,400
Output		9,350 kg

Step 1 Calculate the number of normal loss units:

10,000 kg × 10% = 1,000 kg

Step 2 Calculate the expected output from the process:

10,000 kg – 1,000 kg = 9,000 kg

Step 3 Total the process costs:

£11,200 + £9,400 + £6,400 = £27,000

Step 4 Calculate the cost per unit of expected output

$$\frac{£27,000}{9,000 \text{ kg}} = £3 \text{ per kg}$$

Now we can write up the ledger accounts. In this case there is an abnormal gain as actual output is 350 kg more than the expected output. The abnormal gain units are debited to the process account and valued at the cost per unit of £3. The normal loss as usual has no value assigned to it and the output of 9,350 kg is also valued at £3.

Process RD4

	kg	£		kg	£
Materials	10,000	11,200	Normal loss	1,000	–
Labour		9,400	Output	9,350	28,050
Overheads		6,400			
Abnormal gain	350	1,050			
	10,350	28,050		10,350	28,050

The abnormal gain has been debited in the process account and therefore must be credited in an abnormal gain account.

Abnormal gain

	kg	£		kg	£
			Process RD4	350	1,050

This amount is then credited to the statement of profit or loss as an abnormal gain. Again, you will only need to worry about the process T account in your assessment.

Task 4

48,000 litres of material were input to a process at the start of the week at a cost of £164,200. Conversion costs for the week were £56,120. The process has a normal loss of 10% and the output for the week was 44,000 litres.

(a) What is the cost per litre?
(b) Write up the process account to record this.

Losses with a scrap value

In some instances the loss units are defective units or waste materials that can be sold for a scrap value. This has a number of effects on our calculations and accounting entries:

- The most common treatment for the normal loss units is to treat their scrap value as a deduction from the process costs
- In the process account the normal loss is then valued at its scrap value
- The abnormal loss is still valued at its full process cost and transferred to the abnormal loss account at that value
- (The scrap value is then credited to the abnormal loss account to reduce the charge to the statement of profit or loss but you don't need to worry about this for your assessment)

HOW IT WORKS

We will return to Nuneaton's Process PE7 with normal loss of 5%. This time however all loss units can be sold for 38 pence per kg. The inputs, costs and output of this process in May are given below.

Direct materials	20,000 kg	£15,400
Direct labour		£6,200
Overheads		£1,200
Output		18,400 kg

Step 1 Calculate the number of normal loss units:

20,000 kg × 5% = 1,000 kg

Step 2 Calculate the expected output from the process:

20,000 kg – 1,000 kg = 19,000 kg

Step 3 Total the process costs but deduct the scrap value of the normal loss:

(£15,400 + £6,200 + £1,200) – (1,000 × £0.38) = £22,420

Step 4 Calculate the cost per unit of expected output:

$$\frac{£22,420}{19,000 \text{ kg}} = £1.18 \text{ per kg}$$

Now we will write up the process account:

- The normal loss will be given a value of £380 (1,000 × £0.38)
- The output and abnormal loss will be valued at the process cost of £1.18 per kg

Process PE7

	kg	£		kg	£
Materials	20,000	15,400	Normal loss	1,000	380
Labour		6,200	Abnormal loss	600	708
Overheads		1,200	Output	18,400	21,712
	20,000	22,800		20,000	22,800

Task 5

During the month of April 10,000 kg of material were input to a process at a cost of £98,000. The process has a normal loss of 5% and any loss units can be sold for £1.40 per kg. Labour costs were £36,000 for the month and overheads totalled £9,200. Output for the month of April was 9,100 kg.

(a) What is the cost per kg?

(b) Write up the process account to record the process for the month.

Work in progress

At the end of a period in which a process has been carried out it is entirely possible that not only have there been a number of units completed in the process, but there are also a number of partially completed units remaining within the process. These partially completed units are known as CLOSING WORK IN PROGRESS.

At the beginning of a period the work in progress will be OPENING WORK IN PROGRESS

As some work has been carried out on these units they must have some cost assigned to them. However as they are not complete they cannot be given the same cost value as the completed units of output from the process. For instance, units of work in progress are unlikely to have all overheads charged to them until they are completed. The method that is used to cost this closing work in progress is to use EQUIVALENT UNITS. For example, suppose that there are 100 units of work in progress at the end of a period that are judged to be half complete. These units are treated as equivalent to 50 completed units.

HOW IT WORKS

Zed Co makes a product Emm which goes through several processes. The following information is available for the month of June.

	Kg
Opening WIP	5,200
Input	58,300
Normal loss	400
Transferred to finished goods	63,400

What was the abnormal gain in June?

A 260 kg
B 300 kg
C 400 kg
D 560 kg

B

Process account

	Debit £		Credit £
Opening WIP	5,200	Credit	63,400
Input	58,300	Output	400
Abnormal gain		Normal loss	
	63,800		63,800

The abnormal gain is the balancing figure. 63,800 – 5,200 – 58,300 = 300

HOW IT WORKS

Nuneaton Enterprises has another process, SL4. During the month of May the costs of that process were £21,000 and the output was 10,000 completed units and 1,000 units that were half completed. How do we value each of the units of completed output and work in progress? We use equivalent units.

	Equivalent units
Completed production	10,000
Work in progress (1,000 × 1/2)	500
	10,500

Therefore during the period the equivalent of 10,500 completed units have passed through the process. The cost per equivalent unit (EU) can now be found.

$$\text{Cost per equivalent unit} = \frac{\text{£}21{,}000}{10{,}500 \text{ EU}}$$

$$= \text{£}2 \text{ per equivalent unit}$$

In the process account the completed production will be valued at:

Completed production 10,000 × £2 = £20,000

The closing work in progress will be valued at £2 for each equivalent unit:

Closing work in progress 500 × £2 = £1,000

The process account will appear as follows:

Process account

	£		£
Input costs	21,000	Completed production	20,000
		Closing work in progress	1,000
	21,000		21,000

Later on we will look at two ways of calculating opening work in progress. Before that we will finish off looking at equivalent units where costs are incurred at different stages of the process.

Different stages of completion

Remember that in a process we not only have materials input to the process, but also labour costs and overheads. In practice it is common for the materials, labour and overheads to be incurred at different stages of the process. Therefore at the end of the period the closing work in progress may have had all of its material input but only half of the labour input. The method of dealing with this is to split out the costs into their different categories – materials and labour/overheads, and to calculate equivalent units of completion for each category of cost.

HOW IT WORKS

Another of Nuneaton Enterprises processes is the KS2. The costs incurred in this process for the month of May are as follows:

Materials	£23,760
Labour and overheads	£10,200

At the end of the period there were 8,000 units of completed output and 1,000 units of closing work in progress. The work in progress has had 80% of its material input and 50% of the labour and overheads input.

We must now calculate the cost per equivalent unit for materials and labour/overheads.

	Units	*Materials*		*Labour/overheads*	
		Proportion complete	*Equivalent units*	*Proportion complete*	*Equivalent units*
Completed	8,000	100%	8,000	100%	8,000
Work in progress	1,000	80%	800	50%	500
Total equivalent units			8,800		8,500
Cost per equivalent unit		=	£23,760 / 8,800	=	£10,200 / 8,500
		= £2.70 per EU		= £1.20 per EU	

Finally, we can find values for the completed output and the closing work in progress.

	£
Completed output	
Materials (8,000 × £2.70)	21,600
Labour/overhead (8,000 × £1.20)	9,600
	31,200
Work in progress	
Materials (800 × £2.70)	2,160
Labour/overhead (500 × £1.20)	600
	2,760

This can all then be entered into the process account.

Process account

	£		£
Materials	23,760	Completed output	31,200
Labour/overhead	10,200	Closing work in progress	2,760
	33,960		33,960

Opening WIP using FIFO and AVCO methods

The closing WIP from one accounting period will become the opening WIP in the next. There are two methods that we can use when there is opening WIP.

(a) FIFO

- Assumes that opening WIP is completed first;
- Spreads costs incurred in the period over work done in that period;

  ie (i) Finished goods/output (started and finished)
  (ii) Opening WIP (finished)
  (iii) Closing WIP (started)

  and then add on the opening WIP costs to the sum of (i) and (ii) to give the total costs of finished output.

(b) Weighted average

- All items are equally likely to be completed;
- Spread all costs (including those b/fwd in opening WIP) over all units.

HOW IT WORKS

Alpha Ltd has the following costs in a period:

Raw materials 2,050 units	£22,550
Labour	£16,304
Overheads	£8,212

Opening WIP: 50 units with a value of £610. It was 100% complete for materials, 60% for labour and 30% for overheads.

The split of the £610 is:

Materials	£400
Labour	£180
Overheads	£30
	£610

Output from this Process: 2,020 units

Closing WIP: 80 units with a value of £1,456. It was also complete as below

Raw materials	100%	complete
Labour	60%	complete
Overheads	60%	complete

There were no losses.

Required

Prepare a Process ledger account using (a) FIFO and (b) weighted average methods.

(a) **FIFO**

Unit calculation:

Opening WIP + Input Units = Good output + Closing WIP

Note: In the assessment you will not have to deal with WIP and losses at the same time. (If it did, the unit calculation would have to include losses and gains.)

Step 1 Prepare a statement of equivalent units

	Actual Units	*Equivalent Units*		
		Materials	*Labour*	*Overheads*
Opening WIP W1	50	–	20	35
Goods started and finished (=output – opening WIP)	1,970	1,970	1,970	1,970
Good output	2,020	1,970	1,990	2,005
Closing WIP W2	80	80	48	48
Equivalent units	2,100	2,050	2,038	2,053

Step 2 Prepare a statement of cost per equivalent unit

	£	£	£
Input costs	22,550	16,304	8,212
Cost per equivalent unit = Input costs/Equivalent units	11.00	8.00	4.00

Step 3 Value the units

		£
Value of good output =	Costs b/f in opening WIP =	610
	Materials 1,970 × £11	21,670
	Labour 1,990 × £8	15,920
	Overheads 2,005 × £4	8,020
		46,220

Value of Closing WIP = 80 × £11 + 48 × £8 + 48 × £4 = £1,456

Step 4 Prepare the process account

Process

	Units	£		Units	£
Opening WIP b/f	50	610	Good output	2,020	46,220
Raw Materials	2,050	22,550	(see st of equiv units)		
Labour		16,304	Closing WIP W2	80	1,456
Overheads		8,212			
	2,100	47,676		2,100	47,676

Workings

1 Opening WIP is 100% complete for materials but 60% for labour and 30% for overheads.

To complete – labour(100 – 60)% = 40% × 50 = 20

– Overheads (100 – 30)% = 70% × 50 = 35

2 Closing WIP – 100% complete for materials so 100% × 80 = 80

– 60% complete for labour so 60% × 80 = 48

– 60% complete for overheads so 60% × 80 = 48

(b) **Weighted average**

Step 1 Statement of equivalent units

	Actual units	*Equivalent units* Materials	*Labour*	*Overheads*
Good output	2,020	2,020	2,020	2,020
Closing WIP	80	80	48	48
Equivalent units	2,100	2,100	2,068	2,068

Step 2 Costs

	£	£	£
Costs b/f (£610) (from the example)	400	180	30
Input costs	22,550	16,304	8,212
	22,950	16,484	8,242
Cost per equivalent unit = Input costs/Equivalent units	10.93	7.97	3.99
		Total £22.89	

Step 3 Value the units

Value of good output = £22.89 × 2,020 = £46,238

Value of Closing WIP = 80 × £10.93 + 48 × £7.97 + 48 × £3.99 = £1,448

Step 4 Prepare the process account

Note: You can do the calculations for number of units and costs of the process easily as these are the same as the FIFO method.

Process

	Units	£		Units	£
Opening WIP b/f	50	610	Output W1	2,020	46,238
Raw Materials	2,050	22,550	Closing WIP c/d W2	80	1,448
Labour		16,304			
Overheads		8,212	Rounding		(10)
	2,100	47,676		2,100	47,676

Task 6

During the month of June the following inputs were made to a process:

	£
Materials	15,575
Labour and overheads	8,480

The output from the process for the month consisted of 4,000 completed units and 600 units of closing work in progress. The closing work in progress was 75% complete as to material input but only 40% complete as to labour and overheads.

What is the value of the completed units and the closing work in progress?

Tutor's Note

For this unit you will not have to deal with opening and closing work in progress together (only individually) nor will you have to deal with a combination of work in progress and process losses.

Summary

We've now come to the end of costing systems. We covered job costing, batch costing, service costing and process costing. Make sure that you understand when each type of costing system will be used. For example, a civil engineering company will probably use job costing whereas a petrol refinery will probably use process costing.

CHAPTER OVERVIEW

- Where identical products are produced in a continuous process then a process costing system will be in operation.
- The costs of the process are divided by the expected output from the process to find the cost per unit of the good output – any normal losses are not assigned any value.
- Abnormal losses or gains are also valued at the full process cost per unit.
- Any scrap value for normal loss units is deducted from the process cost – the normal loss units are valued at that scrap value – the abnormal losses, gains and good output are valued at the full process unit cost.
- At the end of the period there may be some partially completed units, or closing work in progress.
- In order to value the completed units and the closing work in progress the total number of equivalent units must be calculated and the cost per unit determined.
- If the closing work in progress has different stages of completion for the different elements of input, materials and labour/overheads, then a cost per equivalent unit must be calculated for each element of the input.

Keywords

Process costing – a costing system where the unit cost is determined by averaging the periodic costs of the process over the expected good output from the process

Conversion costs – labour and overhead costs of the process

Normal loss – the expected loss from the process

Abnormal loss – any actual loss units in excess of the normal loss units

Abnormal gain – any actual loss units that are less than the normal loss units

Opening work in progress – partially completed units brought forward at the beginning of the period

Closing work in progress – partially completed units from a process at the end of the period

Equivalent units – the number of complete units to which the work in progress is equivalent

TEST YOUR LEARNING

Test 1

In a process account, abnormal losses are valued: (please tick)

- [ ] At their scrap value
- [ ] At the same rate as good production
- [ ] At the cost of raw materials
- [ ] At good production cost less scrap value

Test 2

In process costing an equivalent unit is: (please tick)

- [ ] A notional whole unit representing incomplete work
- [ ] A unit made at standard performance
- [ ] A unit which is identical to a competitor's product
- [ ] A unit being currently made which is the same as previously manufactured
- [ ] A unit made in more than one process cost centre

Test 3

Sometimes materials are lost during processing and the materials may be scrapped; sometimes scrap may have a value. If this is the case, the accounting treatment for the scrap value of normal loss is:

Debit [ ] account

Credit [ ] account

Test 4

Given below are the details for a process for the month of January:

Direct materials	50,000 kg	£350,000
Direct labour		£125,000
Overheads		£57,000
Normal loss		5%
Output		46,000 kg

Write up the process account to record the process results for the month.

Test 5

Given below are the details for a process for week 18:

Direct materials	6,000 litres	£14,300
Direct labour		£7,200
Overheads		£11,980

The normal loss from the process is 10% and the output for the week was 5,600 litres.

Write up the process account to reflect the process costs for the week.

Test 6

Given below are the details of a process for the month of March. Any loss units can be sold for scrap for £1.00 per kg.

Direct materials	40,000 kgs	£158,200
Direct labour		£ 63,500
Overheads		£ 31,740
Normal loss		8%
Output		35,000 kg

Write up the process account to reflect the process results for the month.

Test 7

A process has the following inputs for the month of July:

	£
Materials	8,960
Labour/overheads	4,290

The output from the process consists of 2,000 completed units and 400 units of closing work in progress. The work in progress is 60% complete as to materials but only 50% complete for labour and overheads.

Calculate the value of the completed output and the closing work in progress, and prepare the process account for the month.

chapter 9: BUDGETING: FIXED AND FLEXED BUDGETS

chapter coverage 🕮

In this chapter, we look at budgeting and how budgets are put together. We also learn how to calculate fixed and flexible budgets. In the following chapter we can then work out variances. The topics covered in this chapter are:

- Fixed and flexible budgets

FIXED AND FLEXIBLE BUDGETS

Budgeting plays a part in the management functions of planning and control. However, budgets set in different ways are more suitable than others for each of these functions.

Fixed budgets

A FIXED BUDGET is a budget that is set in advance of a period and its purpose is to provide a single achievable target for the entire organisation to work to. This target level of activity means that all areas of the business will be coordinated towards achieving this goal.

The purpose of the fixed budget is to aid in the planning processes of the business. The budget will set out the resources that are required in order to achieve that target. Once the sales budget has been set the production budget required to provide the necessary products for sale is then produced. From this production budget the materials and labour necessary to meet this target can be identified from the materials usage budget and labour usage budget. You will look at this at Level 4.

The control element of the budgeting system is in the comparison of the actual results for a period to the budgeted figures. However if the actual activity levels turn out to be significantly different from the target set in the fixed budget then comparison of the actual results to the fixed budget will be fairly meaningless as we will not be comparing like with like.

HOW IT WORKS

Martin Engineering prepares detailed budgets for each quarter of the year. The budget for Quarter 4 of 20X8 was set as follows:

	Quarter 4 budget
	£
Sales 1,000 units	40,000
Material	(10,000)
Labour	(12,000)
Production overhead	(3,000)
Gross profit	15,000
Overheads	(8,000)
Operating profit	7,000

This budget was set on the basis of both production and sales of 1,000 units and no opening or closing inventory.

It is now the first week in January 20X9 and the actual results for Quarter 4 are being compared to the budget:

	Quarter 4 budget		Quarter 4 actual
	£		£
Sales 1,000 units	40,000	1,200 units	45,600
Material	(10,000)		(12,480)
Labour	(12,000)		(13,800)
Production overhead	(3,000)		(3,200)
Gross profit	15,000		16,120
Overheads	(8,000)		(9,080)
Operating profit	7,000		7,040

As part of the process of control, the management accountant of Martin Engineering now prepares a report showing the variances between the budget and the actual results (remember from your earlier studies that variances will be described either as adverse or favourable).

Variance report

	Quarter 4 budget	*Units*	*Quarter 4 actual*	*Variance*
	£		£	£
Sales 1,000 units	40,000	1,200	45,600	5,600 Fav
Material	(10,000)		(12,480)	2,480 Adv
Labour	(12,000)		(13,800)	1,800 Adv
Production overhead	(3,000)		(3,200)	200 Adv
Gross profit	15,000		16,120	1,120 Fav
Overheads	(8,000)		(9,080)	1,080 Adv
Operating profit	7,000		7,040	40 Fav

It would appear that there are a mixture of variances with favourable variances for sales and profit but adverse variances for all of the costs.

The problem however is that the budget and the actual figures are not strictly comparable: the budget was based upon sales and production of 1,000 units whereas the actual activity level was production and sales of 1,200 units.

Flexed budgets

A FLEXED BUDGET is a budget that is prepared at the actual activity level that was achieved in the period, in order to show what the budget costs should have been at that activity level. When these costs are then compared to the actual costs meaningful variances can be calculated.

You will recall from our earlier studies of variance analysis that actual costs were always compared with the budget costs for **actual production** – ie with a **flexed budget**.

The comparison of the flexed budget to the actual figures is therefore part of the control process.

Variable costs and fixed costs

When a budget is being flexed to the actual activity level, care must be taken with the distinction between fixed and variable costs. The variable costs or variable element of a cost will increase as the activity level increases whereas the fixed element of any cost should remain the same whatever the activity level.

HOW IT WORKS

Given below again is the Quarter 4 budget for Martin Engineering:

	Quarter 4 budget
	£
Sales 1,000 units	40,000
Material	(10,000)
Labour	(12,000)
Production overhead	(3,000)
Gross profit	15,000
Overheads	(8,000)
Operating profit	7,000

The details of the cost behaviour of each of the costs is given below:

Materials	the materials cost is totally variable
Labour	each operative can only produce 250 units each quarter – the cost of each operative is £3,000 each quarter
Production overhead	the production overhead is a totally fixed cost
Overheads	the general expenses are made up of a budgeted fixed cost of £8,000

We will now flex the budget to the actual activity level of 1,200 units.

Sales

Budgeted selling price	=	£40,000/1,000 units
	=	£40 per unit

Therefore the budgeted sales revenue for 1,200 units is:

Sales	=	1,200 × £40
	=	£48,000

Materials are totally variable

Budgeted materials per unit	=	£10,000/1,000 units
	=	£10 per unit
Budgeted materials cost for 1,200 units	=	1,200 × £10
	=	£12,000

Labour is a stepped cost

One operative is required for each 250 units, therefore for 1,200 units five operatives will be required. For 1,000 units, 4 operatives would be used. So the cost per operative = £12,000/4 = £3,000.

Budgeted labour cost	=	5 × £3,000
	=	£15,000

Production overheads is a fixed cost

Budgeted cost for 1,200 units	=	£3,000
General overheads is a fixed cost	=	£8,000

The flexed budget will appear as follows:

	Quarter 4 flexed budget
	£
Sales 1,200 units	48,000
Materials	(12,000)
Labour	(15,000)
Production overhead	(3,000)
Gross profit	18,000
Overheads	(8,000)
Operating profit	10,000

The flexed budget can then be compared to the actual figures in the form of an OPERATING STATEMENT and the true variances calculated.

Martin Engineering: Quarter 4 Operating Statement

	Budget	*Units*	*Actual*	*Variance*
	£		£	£
Sales 1,200 units	48,000	1,200	45,600	2,400 Adv
Material	(12,000)		(12,480)	480 Adv
Labour	(15,000)		(13,800)	1,200 Fav
Production overhead	(3,000)		(3,200)	200 Adv
Gross profit	18,000		16,120	1,880 Adv
General expenses	(8,000)		(9,080)	1,080 Adv
Operating profit	10,000		7,040	2,960 Adv

We can now see that instead of an overall favourable profit variance being reported there is in fact a significant adverse profit variance with all the variances other than the labour variance being adverse. This is quite a different picture to the variances calculated using the fixed budget.

Task 1

The budget for production supervisors' costs for a period for a business at an activity level of 120,000 units is £12,000. One production supervisor is required for every 50,000 units of production. If actual production is 180,000 units, what figure would appear in the flexed budget for production supervisors' costs?

Semi-variable cost and flexed budgets

In your assessment you will not be asked to calculate semi-variable costs when flexing budgets. They are still useful elsewhere, for example, in batch costing.

Task 2

The budgeted fixed production overhead cost for a period for a business at an activity level of 120,000 units is £15,000. If actual production is 160,000 units, what figure would appear in the flexed budget for the fixed production overhead cost?

CHAPTER OVERVIEW

- A budgeted costing system which allows the budgeted cost of production to be compared to the actual costs and variances calculated can help management perform their three main roles of decision making, planning and control.
- A fixed budget is set in advance of a budgeting period as a pre-determined plan of activity for all areas of a business.
- A flexed budget is used in the control aspect of the budgetary system as the actual results are compared to the flexed budget in order to determine any variances.
- In order to flex a budget a distinction must be drawn between variable costs and fixed costs. The variable elements of cost will increase or decrease with changes in activity level whereas the fixed elements of cost do not vary with changes in activity levels.

Keywords

Budgeted costing system – a system that assigns budgeted costs to each cost unit and allows a comparison of budgeted costs to actual costs and the calculation of variances

Variances – the difference between the budgeted costs and the actual costs for a period

Fixed budget – a budget set in advance of a period in order to act as a plan of action for the whole organisation

Flexed budget – a budget prepared for the actual activity level for the period

Operating statement – report allowing actual figures to be compared with budget figures and variances calculated.

TEST YOUR LEARNING

Test 1

The budget for a production company for the month of December and the actual results for the month are given below:

	Budget *4,000 units*	*Actual* *3,600 units*
	£	£
Sales	96,000	90,000
Materials	18,000	15,120
Labour	27,200	25,200
Production overhead	5,700	5,900
Gross profit	45,100	43,780
General expenses	35,200	32,880
Operating profit	9,900	10,900

The materials and labour costs are variable costs, the production overhead is a fixed cost and the general expenses are fixed.

(a) Calculate variances between the fixed budget and the actual results.

(b) Prepare a flexed budget for the actual activity level and show the variances for each of the figures.

(c) Comment on the differences shown by the two sets of variances.

Test 2

Vanquish Ltd has the following original budget and actual performance for its product zephyr for the year ending 31 December.

	Budget	Actual
Volume sold	50,000	72,000
	£000	£000
Sales revenue	1,000	1,800
Less costs:		
Direct materials	175	265
Direct labour	200	240
Overheads	350	630
Operating profit	275	665

Both direct materials and direct labour are variable costs, but the overheads are fixed.

Complete the table below to show a flexed budget and the resulting variances against this budget for the year. Show the actual variance amount, for sales and each cost, in the column headed 'Variance' and indicate

whether this is Favourable or Adverse by entering F or A in the final column. If neither F nor A enter 0.

	Flexed Budget	Actual	Variance	Favourable F or Adverse A
Volume sold		72,000		
	£'000	£'000	£'000	
Sales revenue		1,800		
Less costs:				
Direct materials		265		
Direct labour		240		
Overheads		630		
Operating profit		665		

chapter 10: VARIANCE ANALYSIS

chapter coverage

In this chapter, we consider the calculation of the basic variances for materials, labour, overheads and sales. Then we will explain the meaning and significance of the variances. First of all we will run through budgets briefly as variances are calculated by comparing budget figures to actual figures. We will look at fixed and flexed budgets. The topics we shall cover are:

- Fixed budgets and budgetary control
- Reconciling actual and budgeted costs and revenues
- Direct material variance
- Direct labour variance
- Flexed budgets and variances
- Fixed overhead variance
- Sales variance
- Reasons for variances
- Interdependence of variances

Variances to be calculated

The variances to be calculated for this unit are set out in the diagram below:

Direct materials	Direct labour	Fixed overheads	Sales

Budgets

We looked at budgets in the previous chapter and learnt about the differences between fixed and flexible budgets. This chapter goes on from there to calculate variances for direct materials, direct labour, fixed overheads and sales based on the difference between budget and actual costs and revenues. The learning outcomes for the Unit expect students to be able to reconcile budgeted and actual costs and revenues from both fixed and flexed budgets.

FIXED BUDGETS AND BUDGETARY CONTROL

Penny manufactures a single product, the Darcy. Budgeted results and actual results for May are as follows. Calculate the variances arising from a comparison between the fixed budget and actual results.

	Fixed budget	*Actual*	*Variance*
Production and sales of the Darcy (units)	7,500	8,200	
	£	£	
Sales revenue	75,000	81,000	
Direct materials	22,500	23,500	
Direct labour	15,000	15,500	
Production overhead	22,500	22,800	
Administration overhead	10,000	11,000	
	70,000	72,800	
Profit	5,000	8,200	

	Fixed budget	*Actual*	*Variance*
Production and sales of the Darcy (units)	7,500	8,200	
	£	£	£
Sales revenue	75,000	81,000	6,000 (F)
Direct materials	22,500	23,500	1,000 (A)
Direct labour	15,000	15,500	500 (A)
Production overhead	22,500	22,800	300 (A)
Administration overhead	10,000	11,000	1,000 (A)
	70,000	72,800	2,800 (A)
Profit	5,000	8,200	3,200 (F)

Note. (F) denotes a favourable variance and (A) an unfavourable or adverse variance.

The variances are simply the difference between the budget and actual.

However, as you know from Chapter 9, the variances are meaningless for the purposes of control. Any comparison between budget and actual needs to take into account the activity level to make a proper like with like comparison.

Otherwise, it is not possible to tell how much of the increase is due to **poor cost control** and how much is due to the **increase in activity**.

Similarly it is not possible to tell how much of the increase in sales revenue is due to the increase in activity. Some of the difference may be due to a difference between budgeted and actual selling price but we are unable to tell from the analysis above.

For control purposes we need to know the answers to questions such as the following.

- Were actual costs higher than they should have been to produce and sell 8,200 Darcys?
- Was actual revenue satisfactory from the sale of 8,200 Darcys?

Instead of comparing actual results with a fixed budget which is based on a different level of activity to that actually achieved, the correct approach to budgetary control is to compare actual results with a budget that has been **flexed** to the actual activity level achieved.

Suppose that we have the following estimates of the behaviour of Penny's costs.

(a) Direct materials and direct labour are variable costs.

(b) Production overhead is a semi-variable cost, the budgeted cost for an activity level of 10,000 units being £25,000. We show you how to work out the variable and fixed elements of this cost using the high-low method. However in your assessment for this Unit you will not need to do this but you will in later studies.

(c) Administration overhead is a fixed cost.

(d) Selling prices are constant at all levels of sales.

The **budgetary control analysis** should therefore be as follows.

	Fixed budget	*Flexible budget*	*Actual results*	*Variance*	*Working*
Production and sales (units)	7,500	8,200	8,200		
	£	£	£	£	
Sales revenue	75,000	82,000	81,000	1,000 (A)	1
Direct materials	22,500	24,600	23,500	1,100 (F)	2
Direct labour	15,000	16,400	15,500	900 (F)	3
Production overhead	22,500	23,200	22,800	400 (F)	4
Administration overhead	10,000	10,000	11,000	1,000 (A)	5
	70,000	74,200	72,800	1,400 (F)	
Profit	5,000	7,800	8,200	400 (F)	

Workings

(1) Selling price per unit = £75,000 ÷ 7,500 = £10 per unit

Flexible budget sales revenue = £10 × 8,200 = £82,000

(2) Direct materials cost per unit = £22,500 ÷ 7,500 = £3

Budget cost allowance = £3 × 8,200 = £24,600

(3) Direct labour cost per unit = £15,000 ÷ 7,500 = £2

Budget cost allowance = £2 × 8,200 = £16,400

(4) Variable production overhead cost per unit = £(25,000 – 22,500)/(10,000 – 7,500)= £2,500/2,500 = £1 per unit

∴Fixed production overhead cost = £22,500 – (7,500 × £1) = £15,000

∴Budget cost allowance = £15,000 + (8,200 × £1) = £23,200

(5) Administration overhead is a fixed cost and hence budget cost allowance = £10,000

Comment

(a) In selling 8,200 units, the expected profit should have been, not the fixed budget profit of £5,000, but the flexible budget profit of £7,800. Instead actual profit was £8,200 ie £400 more than we should have expected.

One of the reasons for this improvement is that, given output and sales of 8,200 units, the cost of resources (material, labour etc) was £1,400 lower than expected. (A comparison of the fixed budget and the actual costs in the first example appeared to indicate that costs were not being controlled since all of the variances were adverse.)

Total cost variances can be analysed to reveal how much of the variance is due to lower resource prices and how much is due to efficient resource usage.

(b) The sales revenue was, however, £1,000 less than expected because a lower price was charged than budgeted.

We know this because flexing the budget has eliminated the effect of changes in the volume sold, which is the only other factor that can affect sales revenue. You have probably already realised that this variance of £1,000 (A) is a selling price variance.

The lower selling price could have been caused by the increase in the volume sold (to sell the additional 700 units the selling price had to fall below £10 per unit). We do not know if this is the case but without flexing the budget we could not know that a different selling price from that budgeted had been charged. Our initial analysis above had appeared to indicate that sales revenue was ahead of budget.

The difference of £400 between the flexible budget profit of £7,800 at a production level of 8,200 units and the actual profit of £8,200 is due to the net effect of cost savings of £1,400 and lower than expected sales revenue (by £1,000).

The difference between the original budgeted profit of £5,000 and the actual profit of £8,200 is the total of the following.

(a) The savings in resource costs/lower than expected sales revenue (a net total of £400 as indicated by the difference between the flexible budget and the actual results).

(b) The effect of producing and selling 8,200 units instead of 7,500 units (a gain of £2,800 as indicated by the difference between the fixed budget and the flexible budget). This is the **sales volume contribution variance**.

RECONCILING ACTUAL AND BUDGETED COSTS AND REVENUES

A full variance analysis statement using a fixed budget would be as follows.

	£	£
Fixed budget profit		5,000
Variances		
Sales volume	2,800 (F)	
Selling price	1,000 (A)	
Direct materials cost	1,100 (F)	
Direct labour cost	900 (F)	
Production overhead cost	400 (F)	
Administration overhead cost	1,000 (A)	
		3,200 (F)
Actual profit		8,200

If management believes that any of the variances are large enough to justify it, they will investigate the reasons for their occurrence to see whether any corrective action is necessary.

Task 1

Flower budgeted to sell 200 units and produced the following budget.

	£	£
Sales		71,400
Variable costs		
Labour	31,600	
Material	12,600	
		44,200
Contribution		27,200
Fixed costs		18,900
Profit		8,300

Actual sales turned out to be 230 units, which were sold for £69,000. Actual expenditure on labour was £27,000 and on material £24,000. Fixed costs totalled £10,000.

Prepare a flexible budget that will be useful for management control purposes

DIRECT MATERIAL VARIANCE

The TOTAL DIRECT MATERIAL VARIANCE is the difference between the actual cost of the materials used in the production and the budgeted cost for the actual level of production.

Note that we are using the budgeted cost for the actual level of production as our comparison for the actual costs of production even if the actual level of production is different to that which was budgeted. This is an example of flexing a budget.

Let's just re-cap. Suppose that 1,000 units were budgeted to be produced with a total budgeted material cost of £1,000. If 1,500 units were produced with a total material cost of £1,400 it would be meaningless to compare £1,400 to £1,000 as they are for a different numbers of units. Only by flexing the budget to show the budgeted cost of the actual production of 1,500 units at £1,500 can a meaningful comparison be made.

The total direct material variance can be either favourable or adverse. If the actual cost of the materials is more than the budgeted cost for that level of production then there will be an ADVERSE VARIANCE as the production has cost more than anticipated. However if the actual cost of the materials is less than the budgeted cost for that level of production then the variance will be a FAVOURABLE VARIANCE. In our earlier illustration as the budgeted material cost for 1,500 units of production is £1,500 and the actual cost was £1,400 this is a favourable variance of £100.

The total direct material variance can then be split into the material price variance and the material usage variance. This is beyond the scope of the guide so we won't go into any detail on these variances.

HOW IT WORKS

The unit cost card for one of Lawson Ltd's products, the George, is shown below:

	£
Direct materials 4 kg @ £2.00 per kg	8.00
Direct labour 2 hours @ £7.00 per hour	14.00
Fixed overheads 2 hours @ £3.00 per hour	6.00
Total budget cost	28.00

The budget details for the George are in the table. We will complete the table at the end but do the calculations as we go along.

	Fixed budget	*Flexible budget*	*Actual results*	*Variance*
Production and sales (units)	20,000			
	£	£	£	£
Sales revenue	700,000			
Direct materials	160,000			
Direct labour	280,000			
Fixed overhead	120,000			
Total costs	560,000			
Profit	140,000			

The budgeted level of production for July was 20,000 units but in fact only 18,000 units were produced. This means we will need to flex the budget.

The total cost of the materials was £142,800.

We will now determine the direct materials cost variance.

Total direct materials variance

	£
Budgeted materials cost for actual production 18,000 units × 4 kg × £2.00	144,000
Actual materials cost	142,800
Total materials cost variance	1,200 (F)

As the actual cost is less than the budget cost the variance is favourable.

Task 2

A product has a budgeted usage of 12 litres of material at a budgeted cost of £20.50 per litre. The production of the product during the last month was 24,000 units for which 312,000 litres were used at a total cost of £6,240,000.

What is the total direct materials variance?

DIRECT LABOUR VARIANCE

The TOTAL DIRECT LABOUR VARIANCE is the difference between the actual cost of labour for the period and the budgeted cost of labour for the actual production in the period. Note again, that as with the materials cost, we are comparing the actual cost to the budgeted cost for the actual quantity of production.

HOW IT WORKS

Remember that the actual production was 18,000 units rather than the 20,000 units budgeted for.

The total cost of the labour for the month was £254,600 for 38,000 hours.

Total direct labour variance

	£	
Budget labour cost for actual production 18,000 × 2 hours × £7.00	252,000	
Actual labour cost	254,600	
Total labour cost variance	2,600	(Adv)

As the actual cost is greater than the budget total cost the variance is adverse.

Task 3

A product has a budgeted requirement of 4 hours of direct labour per unit at a budgeted hourly rate of £6.50. During the last month production was 12,000 units using 45,000 hours at a total cost of £306,000.

What is the total direct labour variance?

FLEXED BUDGETS AND VARIANCES

You need to know how to flex a budget and show the resulting variances.

HOW IT WORKS

Vanquish Ltd has the following original budget and actual performance for product ZT4 for the year ending 31 December.

	Budget	*Actual*
Volume sold	100,000	144,000
	£000	£000
Sales revenue	2,000	3,600
Less costs:		
Direct materials	350	530
Direct labour	400	480
Overheads	980	980
Operating profit	270	1,610

Both direct materials and direct labour are variable costs, but the overheads are fixed.

Complete the table below to show a flexed budget and the resulting variances against this budget for the year. Show the actual variance amount, for sales and each cost, in the column headed 'Variance' and indicate whether this is Favourable or Adverse by entering F or A in the final column. If neither F nor A enter 0.

	Flexed Budget	Actual	Variance	Favourable F or Adverse A
Volume sold		144,000		
	£'000	£'000	£'000	
Sales revenue		3,600		
Less costs:				
Direct materials		530		
Direct labour		480		
Overheads		980		
Operating profit		1,610		

	Flexed Budget	Actual	Variance	Favourable F or Adverse A
Volume sold	144,000	144,000		
	£'000	£'000	£'000	
Sales revenue	2,880	3,600	720	F
Less costs:				
Direct materials	504	530	26	A
Direct labour	576	480	96	F
Overheads	980	980	0	0
Operating profit	820	1,610	790	F

FIXED OVERHEAD VARIANCE

Tutor note

The assessor for this unit has confirmed that the fixed overhead variance is the difference between actual and budgeted fixed overheads only. It will not be calculated as a difference arising from under or over absorption.

If the question states that overheads are fixed as in the sample assessment this will mean there is no fixed overhead variance.

Background

Under an absorption costing system fixed overheads are absorbed into the actual units of production on the basis of a pre-determined overhead absorption rate. This absorption rate may be expressed as an amount per unit or as an amount per direct labour hour or direct machine hour.

However the absorption rate is expressed the following figures will always be compared:

Fixed overheads incurred	v	Fixed overheads absorbed

If the total fixed overheads incurred are exactly as budgeted and the units of production or hours worked are also exactly as budgeted then these two figures will be equal.

However in practice, it is likely that one of three situations may occur:

(a) The fixed overheads are greater or smaller than the budgeted amount

(b) The actual production or the hours worked are more or less than budgeted; or

(c) There is a combination of both of the first two situations.

When any of these occur then the fixed overheads incurred and the fixed overheads absorbed will be different. We only concern ourselves with (a) in this Unit.

HOW IT WORKS

Using our example of Lawson Ltd's production of the George for the month of July.

The budget cost card for the George is given below:

	£
Direct materials 4 kg @ £2.00 per kg	8.00
Direct labour 2 hours @ £7.00 per hour	14.00
Fixed overheads 2 hours @ £3.00 per hour	6.00
Total budgeted absorption cost	28.00

The budgeted production was 20,000 units and the actual fixed overhead incurred in the period was £115,000.

Total fixed overhead variance

	£
Budgeted fixed overhead (20,000 units × £6.00)	120,000
Fixed overhead incurred	115,000
Overhead variance	5,000 Fav

Task 4

During the month of September a business incurred fixed overheads of £26,000. Budgeted production had been for 2,400 units each requiring two direct labour hours. Fixed overheads are absorbed on the basis of £5.00 per direct labour hour.

You are required to calculate the following:

(a) the budgeted fixed overhead
(b) the total fixed overhead variance

SALES VARIANCE

The SALES VARIANCE can arise due to a difference in budgeted sales volume or a difference in budgeted selling price, or both. The budgeted selling price of the George is £35. Actual sales in the year were 18,000 units at £35.30 per unit.

Let's complete our table. The flexed budget costs have been calculated based on actual activity and compared with the actual costs. We can calculate the variances by comparing like with like.

	Fixed budget	*Flexible budget*	*Actual results*	*Variance*
Production and sales (units)	20,000	18,000		
	£	£	£	£
Sales revenue	700,000	630,000	635,400	5,400 (F)
Direct materials	160,000	144,000	142,800	1,200 (F)
Direct labour	280,000	252,000	254,600	2,600 (A)
Fixed overhead	120,000	108,000	115,000	7,000 (A)
Total costs	560,000	504,000	512,400	8,400 (A)
Profit	140,000	126,000	123,000	3,000 (A)

REASONS FOR VARIANCES

When reporting variances to management a simple table is a useful starting point. However management will also wish to know the reasons for the variances. Before we look at a specific example we will consider some of the possible reasons for each type of variance. In this Unit we only look at total material, labour, fixed overhead and sales variances. These variances are usually refined into more detailed sub-variances for management, to identify the likely causes of the variance. Therefore we have listed these sub-variances under each total variance to show you what the likely causes of a variance are.

Direct materials variance

The total direct materials variance is often divided further into a price variance and a usage variance. Here are some of the main reasons why a variance might arise and what management can do to resolve variances.

Materials price variance – adverse

- An unexpected price increase from a supplier
- Loss of a previous trade or bulk buying discount from a supplier
- Purchase of a higher grade of materials
- A deterioration in the sterling exchange rate where goods are bought from another country

Materials price variance – favourable

- Negotiation of a better price from a supplier
- Negotiation of a trade or bulk purchase discount from a supplier
- Purchase of a lower grade of materials
- An improvement in the sterling exchange rate where goods are bought from another country

Materials usage variance – adverse

- Greater wastage due to a lower grade of material
- Greater wastage due to use of a lower grade of labour
- Problems with machinery

Materials usage variance – favourable

- Use of a higher grade of material which led to less wastage
- Use of more skilled labour leading to less wastage than normal
- New machinery that provides greater efficiency

Direct labour variance

The total direct labour variance is also analysed further to look at the cost of the labour (labour rate) and the efficiency of the labour used. You do not need to know these variances for this Unit but the reasons listed here will enable you to give management some good ideas on why a variance has occurred.

Labour rate variance – adverse

- Unexpected increase in labour costs (wages)
- Use of a higher grade of labour than anticipated
- Unexpectedly high levels of overtime

Labour rate variance – favourable

- Use of a lower grade of labour than budgeted for
- Less overtime than budgeted for

Labour efficiency variance – adverse

- Use of a less skilled grade of labour
- Use of a lower grade of material which takes longer to work on
- More idle time than budgeted
- Poor supervision of the workforce
- Problems with machinery

Labour efficiency variance – favourable

- Use of a more skilled grade of labour
- Use of a higher grade of material which takes less time to work on
- Less idle time than budgeted
- Use of new more efficient machinery

Total fixed overhead variance

The total fixed overhead variance may be subdivided into four variances which look at cost, volume, efficiency and capacity. Although you are not expected to know these variances for this Unit, it is useful to understand how the variances arise and give management some idea of what actions to take to remedy the variances.

Fixed overhead expenditure variance – adverse or favourable

- An unexpected increase or decrease in the cost of any element of fixed overheads

Fixed overhead volume variance – adverse or favourable

- An unexpected increase or decrease in production volume. If absorption is done on the basis of labour or machine hours, analysis of the volume variance into the efficiency and capacity variances can help to find reasons for the volume variance.

Fixed overhead efficiency variance – adverse or favourable

- If the absorption basis is that of labour hours then the fixed overhead efficiency variance will be due to the same causes as the labour efficiency variance

- If the absorption basis is that of machine hours then the fixed overhead efficiency variance will reflect how efficiently the machinery has been used to produce the cost units

Fixed overhead capacity variance – adverse or favourable

- If the absorption basis is that of labour hours this variance measures whether more or fewer hours were worked than budgeted

- If the absorption basis is that of machine hours the capacity variance measures whether more or fewer machine hours were operated than budgeted

Sales variance

The sales variance is often divided further into a price variance and a volume variance. Here are some of the main reasons why a variance might arise.

Sales price variance – adverse

- Lower price per unit charged due to competition

Sales price variance – favourable

- Units sold at a higher selling price

Sales volume variance – adverse

- Demand has fallen (eg due to better product available in the market)

Sales volume variance – favourable

- More units sold than budgeted due to increase in demand

INTERDEPENDENCE OF VARIANCES

You may have noticed from some of the possible causes of variances given above that many of these are likely to be inter-related. This is known as the INTERDEPENDENCE OF VARIANCES.

For example, a favourable material price variance that is caused by purchasing a lower grade of material may lead directly to an adverse materials usage variance, as the lower grade of material means that there is greater wastage.

A further example might be the use of a lower grade of labour on a job than budgeted, leading to a favourable labour rate variance but an adverse materials usage variance, as the less skilled labour cause more materials wastage.

Responsibility for variances

Investigating the causes of variances and determining any interdependence between the variances is an important aspect of management control, as in a system of responsibility accounting the managers responsible for various elements of the business will be held accountable for the relevant variances.

Take the example of a favourable material price variance caused by purchasing a lower grade of material which leads directly to an adverse materials usage variance. The initial reaction might be to praise the purchasing manager for the favourable variance and to lay blame for the adverse usage variance on the production manager. However, the true picture is that, in the absence of any further reasons for the variance, the responsibility for both variances lies with the purchasing manager.

Other reasons for variances

Further causes of variances may be one-off events such as a power cut, breakdown of machinery or annual staff holidays.

CHAPTER OVERVIEW

- A costing system that allows the budgeted cost of production to be compared to the actual costs and variances to be calculated can help management perform their three main roles of decision making, planning and control.
- The total direct materials variance is the difference between the actual cost of materials used in production and the budgeted cost for the actual level of production.
- The total direct labour variance is the difference between the actual cost of labour for the period and the budgeted cost of labour for the actual production in the period.
- The total fixed overhead cost variance is the difference between the actual fixed overhead and the budgeted fixed overhead.
- Management like to know the causes of variances as well as see the numbers. This helps them understand why variances have arisen and how they might avoid them in the future.

Keywords

Variances – the difference between the budgeted costs and the actual costs for a period

Adverse variance – where the actual cost is greater than the budgeted cost

Favourable variance – where the actual cost is less than the budgeted cost

Total direct materials variance – the difference between the budgeted materials cost for the actual production and the actual cost

Total direct labour variance – the difference between the budgeted labour cost for the actual production and the actual cost

Total fixed overhead variance – the difference between the budgeted and actual fixed overhead for the period

Interdependence of variances – causes of variances are often inter-related. This is called the interdependence of variances.

TEST YOUR LEARNING

Test 1

A business budgeted to produce 1,600 units of one of its products, the YG, during the month of October. The YG uses 7 kg of raw material with a budgeted cost of £6.00 per kg. During the month the actual production was 1,800 units of YG using 12,000 kg of raw materials costing £70,800.

Calculate the total direct materials variance.

Test 2

Production of product FFD for the month of December in a manufacturing business was 15,400 units using 41,000 hours of direct labour costing £265,200. The unit cost card shows that the expected input for a unit of FFD is 2.5 hours at a rate of £6.80 per hour.

Calculate the total direct labour variance.

Test 3

A business incurred fixed overheads of £56,000 in the month of May. The fixed overheads are absorbed into units of production at the rate of £2.50 per direct labour hour and the budget provided for 7,000 units. The budgeted labour cost for the production is 3 hours per unit.

You are to calculate:

(a) The budgeted fixed overhead for the month
(b) The total fixed overhead variance

chapter 11: COST BOOKKEEPING

chapter coverage

In previous chapters we have looked at the bookkeeping for each aspect of costing, materials, labour and overheads. In this chapter we will bring it all together with a reminder of how the individual elements of the bookkeeping work and then a comprehensive example of how it all ties in together. The topics covered are:

- The basic requirements for cost bookkeeping
- Control accounts used in bookkeeping
- The integrated bookkeeping system

THE BASIC REQUIREMENTS FOR COST BOOKKEEPING

The preceding chapters have described the basic information that is needed for cost accounting. It is plain, therefore, that a cost bookkeeping system will need to be able to cope with a great deal of detail. For example, it will be insufficient to record all items purchased as 'purchases'; there will need to be distinctions made between direct and indirect items, and each type of material will need its own record. Similarly, each product, batch, job or process will need its own account to record the materials, labour and production overheads incurred on it. To help organise the information into a manageable system there are two important techniques with which you must be familiar:

- Use of control accounts
- Use of an integrated bookkeeping system

CONTROL ACCOUNTS USED IN BOOKKEEPING

You will be familiar with the idea of a cash control account in the main ledger that summarises the detail recorded in the cash book, and the receivables and payables control accounts that summarise the total of transactions in the individual receivable and payable accounts in the receivables and payables ledgers. In a cost bookkeeping system, control accounts can be used to summarise the information in separately maintained detailed accounts, for example

- MATERIALS OR STORES CONTROL ACCOUNT will record the total purchases of materials and issues to WIP, summarising the individual materials or stores ledger accounts;
- WAGES CONTROL ACCOUNT will record the total payroll costs, and the total direct labour charged to each individual product, job, batch or process in WIP, and indirect labour charged to appropriate cost centres;
- PRODUCTION OVERHEAD CONTROL ACCOUNT will record the total production overheads incurred by different cost centres, and the total charged to each individual product, job, batch or process in WIP; and
- WORK IN PROGRESS CONTROL ACCOUNT will summarise each individual product, job, batch or process in WIP, recording the total costs of direct materials, direct labour and production overheads that have been charged and the transfer of items to finished goods.

As with the receivables and payables control accounts, these control accounts will need to be reconciled with the more detailed, individual accounts to help to ensure that the information recorded is accurate.

THE INTEGRATED BOOKKEEPING SYSTEM

There are two main systems of cost bookkeeping.

- The INTEGRATED SYSTEM combines the cost accounting and financial accounting functions into one system of ledger accounts. This gives a saving in terms of time and cost. However, it has the disadvantage of trying to fulfil two purposes with one set of accounts, and in Chapter 1 we looked at the different needs of cost and financial accounting.
- The INTERLOCKING SYSTEM keeps separate ledgers for the cost accounting function (the cost ledger) and the financial accounting function (the financial ledger). The cost ledger will include a cost ledger control account which is essentially there to provide a place for items of a financial nature. For example, when an invoice is received for materials, the materials account is debited, and as the cost ledger does not record payables, the cost ledger control account is credited. A financial ledger control account is used to maintain the integrity of the double entry system in the financial ledger. These two ledgers will need reconciling on a regular basis to ensure that they are in agreement.

The integrated system is much more common, especially in computerised systems, and this is the system on which we are going to concentrate. In this system, the main ledger will contain the cost ledger accounts as well as the usual ledger accounts for cash, capital, non-current assets etc. The double entries are performed as usual; this system must balance to produce a set of financial statements as well as costing information. The table and the diagram below take a general look at how the double entries are recorded, and how the statement of profit or loss is built up. Note that absorption costing is used.

Task 1

How does an integrated system of cost bookkeeping work?

Summary of cost bookkeeping double entries in an integrated system

(read in conjunction with the diagram on the next page)

1 Production costs are recorded	Debit: Materials Debit: Wages Debit: Production ohds	Credit: Cash/payables Credit: Cash/HMRC Credit: Cash/payables
2 Direct costs issued to production	Debit: WIP Debit: WIP	Credit: Materials Credit: Wages
3 Indirect labour transferred to production overheads	Debit: Production ohds	Credit: Wages
4 Production overheads absorbed into production	Debit: WIP	Credit: Production ohds
5 Completed WIP transferred to finished goods	Debit: Finished goods	Credit: WIP
6 Finished goods are sold	Debit: Cost of sales Debit: Cash/receivables Debit: Sales	Credit: Finished goods Credit: Sales Credit: St of profit or loss
7 Non production overheads charged to St of profit or loss	Debit: Non production overheads Debit: St of profit or loss	Credit: Payables /cash Credit: Non production overheads

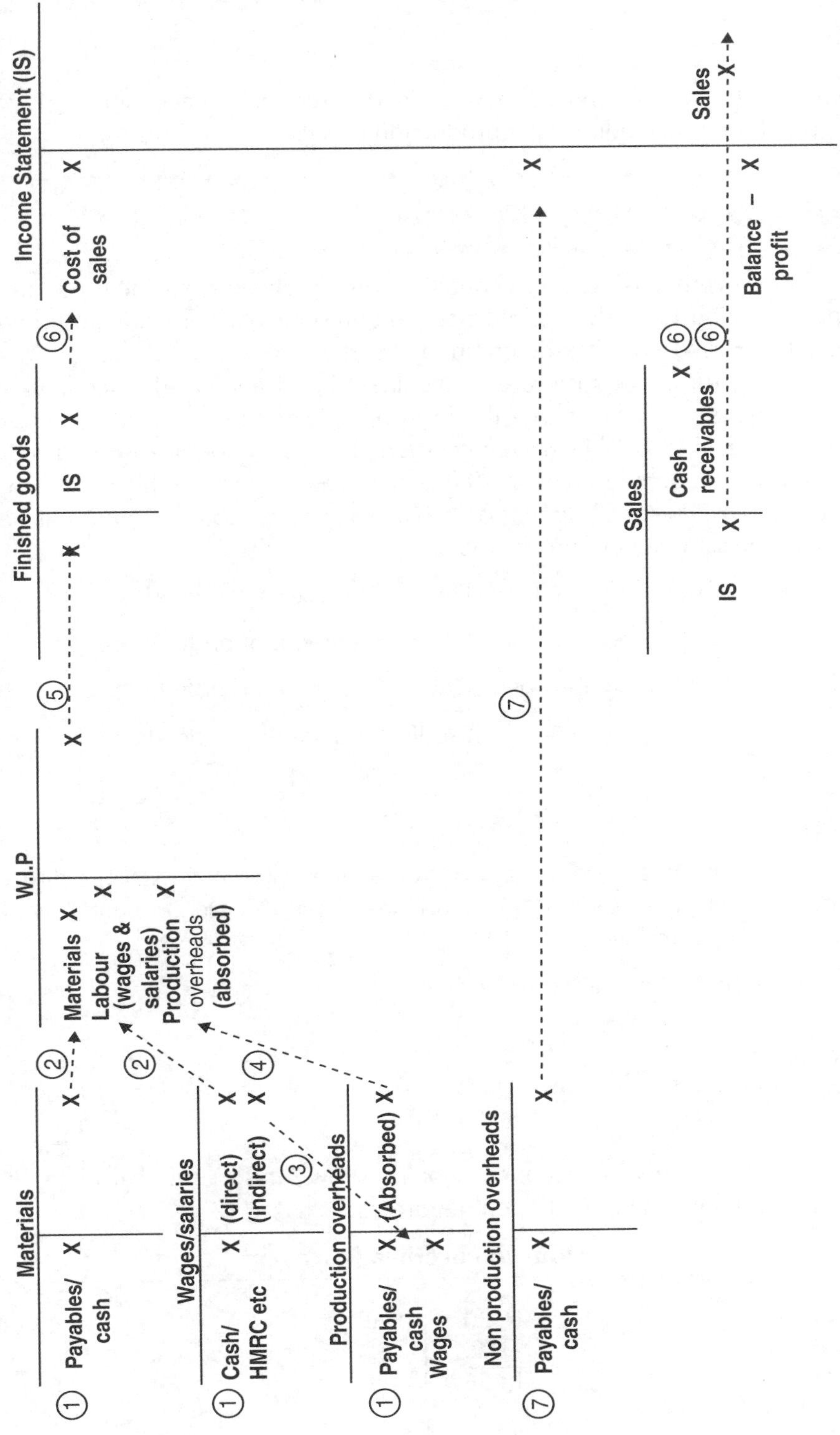

Materials
① Payables/cash X
X ②
Wages/salaries
① Cash/HMRC etc X
(direct) X ②
(indirect) X ③
Production overheads
① Payables/cash X
Wages X
(Absorbed) X ④
Non production overheads
⑦ Payables/cash X
X ⑦
W.I.P
Materials X
Labour (wages & salaries) X
Production overheads (absorbed) X
X ⑤
Finished goods
X
IS X ⑥
Income Statement (IS)
Cost of sales X
X
Balance – profit X
Sales X
Sales
IS X
Cash receivables X ⑥

Task 2

What would be the double entry in an integrated system of cost accounting for materials purchased on credit for the production process?

Under- and over-absorption of overheads

The production overheads account is debited with overhead costs incurred, and if absorption costing is used, credited with the amount of overheads absorbed into production based on a pre-determined absorption rate. As we stressed in a previous chapter, the absorption rate is calculated in advance of the accounting period and is based on estimates of the level of activity and the overhead cost; the estimates are likely to be inaccurate such that the amount absorbed into production will not be the same as the actual cost incurred. The overheads under- or over-absorbed will appear as a balance on the account, and will be transferred to the statement of profit or loss.

Over-absorbed	Absorbed > incurred	Debit:	Production overheads
		Credit:	Statement of profit or loss
Under-absorbed	Incurred > absorbed	Debit:	Statement of profit or loss
		Credit:	Production overheads

Illustration

Cranefly Limited absorbs production overheads at a rate of £2.40 per direct labour hour. During June, 690 labour hours are worked in Department X, and actual overheads incurred were £1,530.

There is an over-absorption of overheads here:

	£
Actual overheads	1,530
Absorbed overheads (690 × £2.40)	1,656
Over-absorbed	126

The production overheads account would show this, and calculate it automatically, as long as all the other entries are correct.

Production overheads account

	£		£
Cash/payables	1,530	WIP	1,656
Over-absorption	126		
	1,656		1,656

Task 3

The overhead absorption rate for a factory is £3.24 per direct labour hour. During the month of July 20X1 the number of direct labour hours worked was 1,050 and the overheads incurred were £3,690.

Write up the production overheads account and explain the accounting treatment of any under- or over-absorption.

HOW IT WORKS: INTEGRATED ACCOUNTS

The information below relates to Shieldbug Limited for the month of April 20X6. (Note that VAT has been ignored for the purpose of this example.)

Opening trial balance at 1 April 20X6

Account	*Debit* £	*Credit* £
Inventory:		
Raw materials	150	
Work in progress	380	
Finished goods	600	
Receivables	937	
Payables		502
HMRC (PAYE and NIC owing)		250
Cash at bank	1,634	
Plant and equipment	3,000	
Allowance for depreciation of plant and equipment		500
Share capital		2,000
Retained earnings		3,449
	6,701	6,701

Transactions in April
Summary of bank transactions

Receivables cheques received	3,000	
Cheques paid to payables		1,900
Wages paid		810
HM Revenue and Customs		250
Pension scheme		50
Production overheads		660
Administration overheads		140
Selling overheads		120
Total	3,000	3,930

Other information	*Debit*	*Credit*
	£	£
Invoices for materials received		1,840
Materials requisitions:		
Production		1,790
Administration		95
Payroll:		
Net	810	
PAYE & NIC	186	
Pension scheme contributions	50	
Total		1,046
Payroll analysis:		
Direct labour (100 hours)	920	
Indirect: production salaries	100	
Indirect: admin salaries	26	
		1,046
Sales invoices issued		3,170
Production transferred to finished goods in the period		2,100
Value of closing inventory of finished goods		200
Overhead absorption rate per direct labour hour		10.50
Depreciation of plant and equipment for the month (factory plant: £80, office equipment: £25)		

Record the above information in appropriate T-accounts, and drawing up an statement of profit or loss. Then prepare an opening trial balance at 1 May.

Solution

Work through the accounts below, checking that you understand each double entry. You may find it useful to begin by checking the opening balances from the trial balance, and then working down the transactions as listed. Finally, follow the amounts transferred to the trading and statement of profit or loss, and any balances left on accounts should appear in the opening trial balance for May.

Note that you will not be required to use T accounts in the assessment. You will have to prepare journal entries instead. We have written up the T accounts to make it easier for you to follow the entries.

Raw materials account

	£		£
Balance b/d	150	WIP (direct materials)	1,790
Payables	1,840	Administration overheads	95
		Balance c/d	105
	1,990		1,990
Balance b/d	105		

Wages and salaries account

	£		£
Cash at bank	810	WIP (direct labour)	920
HMRC	186	Production overheads	100
Pension scheme Contributions	50	Administrative overheads	26
	1,046		1,046

Production overheads account

	£		£
Wages and salaries	100	WIP (absorbed: 100 h @ £10.50)	1,050
Plant depreciation	80		
Cash at bank	660		
Statement of profit or loss (over-absorbed)	210		
	1,050		1,050

WIP account

	£		£
Balance b/d	380	Finished goods	2,100
Raw materials	1,790		
Wages and salaries	920		
Production overheads	1,050	Balance c/d	2,040
	4,140		4,140
Balance b/d	2,040		

Finished goods account

	£		£
Balance b/d	600	St of profit or loss:	
WIP	2,100	cost of sales	2,500
		Balance c/d	200
	2,700		2,700
Balance b/d	200		

Administration overheads account

	£		£
Materials	95	Statement of profit or loss	286
Wages and salaries	26		
Equipment depreciation	25		
Cash at bank	140		
	286		286

Selling overheads account

	£		£
Cash at bank	120	St of profit or loss	120
	120		120

Sales account

	£		£
Statement of profit or loss	3,170	Receivables	3,170
	3,170		3,170

Statement of profit or loss for April

	£		£
Cost of sales	2,500	Sales revenue	3,170
Administration overheads	286	Over-absorbed overheads	210
Selling overheads	120		
Net profit (transfer to retained earnings)	474		
	3,380		3,380

Cash at bank account

	£		£
Balance b/d	1,634	Payables	1,900
Receivables	3,000	Wages and salaries	810
		HMRC	250
		Pension scheme	50
		Production overheads	660
		Administration overheads	140
		Selling overheads	120
		Balance c/d	704
	4,634		4,634
Balance b/d	704		

Receivables account

	£		£
Balance b/d	937	Cash at bank	3,000
Sales	3,170	Balance c/d	1,107
	4,107		4,107
Balance b/d	1,107		

Payables account

	£		£
Cash at bank	1,900	Balance b/d	502
Balance c/d	442	Raw materials	1,840
	2,342		2,342
		Balance b/d	442

HMRC payables account

	£		£
Cash at bank	250	Balance b/d	250
Balance c/d	186	Wages and salaries for April	186
	436		436
		Balance b/d	186

Pension scheme payables

	£		£
Cash at bank	50	Wages and salaries for April	50
	50		50

Plant and equipment account

	£		£
Balance b/d	3,000	Balance c/d	3,000
	3,000		3,000
Balance b/d	3,000		

Allowance for depreciation of plant and equipment account

	£		£
		Balance b/d	500
		Production overhead (plant depn)	80
Balance c/d	605	Administration overheads (office equipment depn)	25
	605		605
		Balance b/d	605

Share capital account

	£		£
Balance c/d	2,000	Balance b/d	2,000
	2,000		2,000
		Balance b/d	2,000

Retained earnings account

	£		£
		Balance b/d	3,449
		Profit for April (transferred from st of profit or loss for the month)	474
Balance c/d	3,923		3,923
	3,923	Balance b/d	3,923

Opening trial balance at 1 May 20X6

Account	*Debit* £	*Credit* £
Inventory:		
Raw materials	105	
Work in progress	2,040	
Finished goods	200	
Receivables	1,107	
Payables		442
HMRC (PAYE and NIC owing)		186
Cash at bank	704	
Plant and equipment	3,000	
Allowance for depreciation of plant and equipment		605
Share capital		2,000
Retained earnings		3,923
	7,156	7,156

The trading and statement of profit or loss T-account could have been presented more formally, if required.

Cranefly Limited
Statement of profit or loss for April 20X6

	£
Sales revenue	3,170
Cost of goods sold	(2,500)
Gross profit	670
Administration overheads	(286)
Selling overheads	(120)
Over-absorption of overheads	210
Profit for the year	474

Task 4

At 1 July 20X6 the Work in Progress ledger account for a business had a balance of £730. During the month of July the following transactions took place:

Materials requisitions for the factory	£2,460
Direct factory labour	£1,070
Production overheads	140 hours @ £2.10 per hour
Production transferred to finished goods	£4,100

Write up the work in progress ledger account.

CHAPTER OVERVIEW

- Control accounts are used in a cost bookkeeping system in order to summarise information about the major elements of production – materials purchased and issued, wages, production overheads and work in progress.
- Each cost incurred must be correctly coded to ensure that it is posted to the correct account in the cost bookkeeping ledger.
- An integrated cost bookkeeping system is one that combines both the entries required for the financial accounting function and the cost accounting function.
- An interlocking system is one where a separate cost accounting ledger is kept – a cost ledger control account is kept for all of the entries that relate to the financial accounting function such as cash, receivables and payables.
- The production overheads account is debited with the overheads actually incurred in the period and credited with the overheads that are to be absorbed into the work in progress for the period – any balance on the account is an under or over absorption of overheads and is taken to the statement of profit or loss.

Keywords

Materials control account – records all purchases of materials and issues to WIP

Wages control account – records the total payroll costs and the transfers of direct labour to WIP and indirect labour to overheads

Production overhead control account – records the actual overhead incurred, the amount of overhead absorbed into WIP and any under- or over- absorption

Work in progress control account – records the total direct materials, direct labour and production overhead used in the production process in the period

Integrated system – a cost bookkeeping system that combines the cost accounting and financial accounting functions

Interlocking system – cost bookkeeping system where a separate ledger is kept for the cost accounting function

TEST YOUR LEARNING

Test 1

A manufacturing business has the following transactions for the week ending 17 August 20X6:

Materials purchased on credit		£4,380
Materials requisitions from the factory		£4,190
Total payroll costs	– direct factory labour	£3,200
	– indirect factory labour	£940
Production overheads incurred		£1,200
Production overheads to be absorbed		480 hours @ 3.10 per hour
Transfer of production to finished goods		£7,900

Write up the following ledger accounts in an integrated cost bookkeeping system to reflect these transactions, showing clearly in which account the other side of the entry would be found. You do not need to balance the accounts in this question.

- Materials control account
- Wages control account
- Production overhead control account
- Work in progress control account

Test 2

A manufacturing business absorbs production overheads into work in progress at a rate of £6.80 per direct labour hour. In the month of June 20X6 the overheads incurred totalled £3,800 and the direct labour hours worked were 550.

Write up the production overhead control account. Explain the accounting treatment of any balance on the account.

Test 3

Given below are extracts from the trial balance of a business at 1 July 20X6:

	Debit	*Credit*
	£	£
Inventory:		
Raw materials	550	
Work in progress	680	
Finished goods	1,040	
Receivables	3,700	
Payables		2,100
Cash at bank	2,090	

You are also given a summary of some of the transactions of the business for the month of July:

Materials purchased on credit	£5,300
Materials requisitions	
– factory	£4,670
– administration	£760
Wages cost	
– direct factory labour (360 hours)	£2,520
– indirect factory labour	£640
Sales invoices issued	£12,000
Cheques received from receivables	£11,000
Cheques paid to payables	£5,140
Production transferred to finished goods	£10,000
Production overheads paid by cheque	£2,700
Administration overheads paid by cheque	£1,580
Closing inventory of finished goods	£2,010

Production overheads are absorbed at the budgeted overhead absorption rate of £7.80 per direct labour hour.

You are required to write up the following ledger accounts to reflect these transactions and to balance each of the accounts at the end of the month:

Materials control account

	£		£

Wages control account

Production overhead control account

	£		£

Work in progress control account

	£		£

Finished goods control account

	£		£

Receivables control account

	£		£

Payables control account

	£		£

Cash at bank account

	£		£

Administration overheads account

	£		£

Sales account

	£		£

Test 4

Returning to the previous question, prepare the statement of profit or loss for the period.

chapter 12: MARGINAL COSTING

chapter coverage

In an earlier chapter we looked at absorption costing and how this works in organisations. Now we will consider this alongside marginal costing – and the effects of both on costing and for reporting purposes. The topics that are covered are:

- Methods of costing
- Absorption versus marginal costing - effect on profit
- The choice between absorption and marginal costing

METHODS OF COSTING

In an earlier chapter we saw how all of the production overheads were allocated, apportioned and then absorbed into the cost of the product giving a total production cost for each cost unit. This is known as ABSORPTION COSTING (or full costing). However there is a different method of costing known as MARGINAL COSTING (or variable costing), which may be preferred by some organisations and can be more useful for some reporting purposes.

Under a marginal costing system the cost unit is valued at just the variable (or marginal) cost of production. The fixed production costs for the period are charged to the statement of profit or loss as an expense for the period rather than being included as part of the cost of the cost unit.

HOW IT WORKS

Graham Associates produce just one product in their factory. The factory has two production departments, assembly and packaging. The anticipated production for the next month, March, is 50,000 units and the expected costs are as follows:

Direct materials	£20 per unit
Direct labour	3 hours assembly at £8 per hour
	1 hour packaging at £6 per hour
Assembly variable overheads	£240,000
Assembly fixed overheads	£120,000
Packaging variable overheads	£100,000
Packaging fixed overheads	£40,000

Overheads are absorbed on the basis of labour hours.

We will start by calculating the cost of each cost unit using absorption costing.

Absorption costing

		Assembly	*Packaging*
Total overhead (variable + fixed)		£360,000	£140,000
Total labour hours	50,000 × 3	150,000	
	50,000 × 1		50,000
Overhead absorption rate		$\frac{£360,000}{150,000}$	$\frac{£140,000}{50,000}$
Total overhead/Total labour hours	=	£2.40 per labour hour	£2.80 per labour hour

Unit cost

		£
Direct materials		20.00
Direct labour	assembly 3 hours × £8	24.00
	packaging 1 hour × £6	6.00
Overheads	assembly 3 hours × £2.40	7.20
	packaging 1 hour × £2.80	2.80
Total unit cost		60.00

Marginal costing

Now we will calculate the same unit cost using marginal costing and therefore only including the variable costs which are direct materials, direct labour and variable overheads.

	Assembly	*Packaging*
Variable overhead	£240,000	£100,000
Total labour hours	150,000	50,000
Variable overhead cost per hour	£240,000 / 150,000	£100,000 / 50,000
=	£1.60 per labour hour	£2.00 per labour hour

Unit cost

		£
Direct materials		20.00
Direct labour	assembly	24.00
	packaging	6.00
Variable overhead	assembly 3 hours × £1.60	4.80
	packaging 1 hour × £2.00	2.00
Prime cost		56.80

Task 1

A factory produces a single product with the following budgeted costs:

Direct materials	£3.40
Direct labour	£6.80
Variable overheads	£1.20
Fixed overheads	£340,000

Overheads are absorbed on the machine hour basis and it is estimated that in the next accounting period machine hours will total 100,000. Each unit requires two hours of machine time.

What is the cost per unit using:

(a) Absorption costing
(b) Marginal costing?

ABSORPTION VERSUS MARGINAL COSTING – EFFECT ON PROFIT

We can now have a look at what effect the two different accounting methods have on the profits that are reported. Under absorption costing the full PRODUCTION COST of the units actually sold in the period is charged as part of cost of sales. The only other entry may be some adjustment for under- or over-absorption of overheads.

However, under marginal costing the lower, variable, cost per unit is charged as part of cost of sales and deducted from sales. This resulting figure is called contribution – it is sales minus variable costs of production and is the contribution towards the fixed costs and any profit. The fixed overheads are then charged to the statement of profit or loss as a PERIOD COST.

In the long run, total profit for a company will be the same whether marginal costing or absorption costing is used. Different accounting conventions merely affect the profit of individual accounting periods.

HOW IT WORKS

Returning to Graham Associates the budgeted sales and production for each of the next three months, March, April and May are 50,000 units. The budgeted cost figures for each month remain the same at:

Direct materials	£20 per unit
Direct labour	3 hours assembly at £8 per hour
	1 hour packaging at £6 per hour
Assembly variable overheads	£240,000
Assembly fixed overheads	£120,000
Packaging variable overheads	£100,000
Packaging fixed overheads	£40,000

The actual production and sales for each of the three months turned out to be:

	March	*April*	*May*
Sales	50,000	45,000	52,000
Production	50,000	50,000	50,000

There were no inventories of the product at the beginning of March. In each month both variable and fixed overheads were exactly as budgeted. Sales were at a selling price of £70 per unit.

Remember that the cost per unit for absorption costing is £60.00 and for marginal costing is £56.80.

March – statement of profit or loss

Absorption costing

	£'000	£'000
Sales (50,000 × £70)		3,500
Less: cost of goods sold		
Opening inventory	–	
Cost of production (50,000 × £60)	3,000	
	3,000	
Less: closing inventory	–	
		3,000
Profit		500

Marginal costing

	£'000	£'000
Sales		3,500
Less: cost of goods sold		
Opening inventory	–	
Cost of production (50,000 × 56.80)	2,840	
	2,840	
Less: closing inventory	–	
		2,840
Contribution		660
Less: fixed costs (120,000 + 40,000)		160
Profit		500

In this month the profits under absorption costing and under marginal costing are exactly the same. The reason for this is that there has been no change in inventory levels. There were no opening inventories and as production and sales were for equal amounts there is also no closing inventory. **When opening and closing inventory amounts are equal then absorption costing profit and marginal costing profit will be equal.**

April – statement of profit or loss

In April sales were 45,000 units and production was 50,000 units leaving closing inventories of 5,000 units.

Absorption costing

	£'000	£'000
Sales (45,000 × £70)		3,150
Less: cost of goods sold		
Opening inventory	–	
Cost of production (50,000 × £60)	3,000	
	3,000	
Less: closing inventory (5,000 × £60)	300	
		2,700
Profit		450

Marginal costing

	£'000	£'000
Sales		3,150
Less: cost of goods sold		
Opening inventory	–	
Cost of production (50,000 × 56.80)	2,840	
	2,840	
Less: closing inventory (5,000 × 56.80)	284	
		2,556
Contribution		594
Less: fixed costs (120,000 + 40,000)		160
Profit		434

In this month there is a difference in profit:

	£'000
Absorption costing profit	450
Marginal costing profit	434
Difference	16

The difference in reported profit under the two costing methods is due to the fixed overheads absorbed into inventory. Under marginal costing the entire fixed overhead for the month is charged to the statement of profit or loss. However, under absorption costing the fixed overhead is included in the cost per unit and therefore any fixed overhead in the closing inventory is carried forward to the next period rather than being charged in this period.

As inventory levels have risen from zero opening inventory to 5,000 units of closing inventory this means that the fixed overhead amount included in the inventory valuation for those 5,000 units has been deducted from this month's cost of sales and carried forward to the next month. This has not happened under marginal costing therefore the absorption costing profit is higher.

The two profit figures can be reconciled as **the difference is due solely to the increase in inventories and the fixed overhead included in that inventory valuation.**

$$\text{Fixed overheads per unit} = \frac{£120{,}000 + £40{,}000}{50{,}000} = £3.20$$

Remember that the difference in profit was £16,000 – this has been caused by:

Fixed overhead included in increase in inventory

(5,000 units × £3.20) £16,000

May – statement of profit or loss

Absorption costing

	£'000	£'000
Sales (52,000 × £70)		3,640
Less: cost of goods sold		
Opening inventory (5,000 × £60)	300	
Cost of production (50,000 × £60)	3,000	
	3,300	
Less: closing inventory (3,000 × £60)	180	
		3,120
Profit		520

Marginal costing	£'000	£'000
Sales		3,640
Less: cost of goods sold		
Opening inventory (5,000 × 56.80)	284	
Cost of production (50,000 × 56.80)	2,840	
	3,124	
Less: closing inventory (3,000 × 56.80)	170.4	
		2,953.6
Contribution		686.4
Less: fixed costs (120,000 + 40,000)		160.0
Profit		526.4

In May the marginal cost profit is £6,400 higher than the absorption cost profit as in this month inventory levels have decreased from 5,000 units to 3,000 units. Therefore under absorption costing more of the brought forward fixed costs have been charged to the statement of profit or loss in the month than have been carried forward to the following month in closing inventory.

The difference is made up of:

Fixed overhead in inventory decrease 2,000 × £3.20 = £6,400

THE CHOICE BETWEEN ABSORPTION AND MARGINAL COSTING

Absorption costing has the advantage of allowing managers to see whether the sales of their products are covering all of the production costs of those products. However, owing to the different nature of fixed costs from that of variable costs it is argued that CONTRIBUTION is a much more useful figure for management than a profit figure after production overheads have been apportioned. We will see later in this Text that for decision making purposes contribution is certainly the figure that must be used.

A further argument for the use of marginal costing rather than absorption costing for cost reporting purposes is to do with the profit differences and inventory levels. Under absorption costing we have seen that it is possible to report a higher profit figure by increasing the closing inventory levels. If a manager is assessed and possibly remunerated on the basis of the figure that he or she reports for profit then the profit can be manipulated by over producing and building up inventory levels. Although this will increase absorption costing profit it may not be in the best interests of the organisation. This type of manipulation of profit cannot take place if marginal costing is used. So generally speaking, **marginal costing** is **more appropriate for short-term decision-making**.

It **is argued, however, that absorption costing is preferable** to marginal costing in management accounting, **in order to be consistent with the requirement of current accounting standards and financial reporting**. This argument might be especially relevant when a firm has an integrated or combined accounting system for its financial and management accounts. It is, however, important to appreciate that the differences in reported profits occur only in the short run, ie in reporting the profit of individual accounting periods. This is because, in the long run, total costs will be the same by either method of accounting. Short-term differences are the results of changes in the level of inventory.

Task 2

Given below is budgeted information about the production of a factory's single product for the month of October.

Opening inventory	1,400 units
Production	12,000 units
Sales	11,600 units
Direct materials	£6.40 per unit
Direct labour	2 hours per unit @ £7.50 per hour
Variable overheads	£120,000
Fixed overheads	£360,000

Overheads are absorbed on the basis of labour hours. The selling price of the product is £65 per unit.

Prepare the budgeted statement of profit or loss for October using:

(a) Absorption costing
(b) Marginal costing

CHAPTER OVERVIEW

- Under absorption costing all production overheads are allocated and apportioned to production cost centres and then absorbed into the cost of the products on some suitable basis.
- Under marginal costing the cost of the products is the variable cost of production with all fixed production costs being charged to the statement of profit or loss as a period charge.
- If inventory levels are constant then both absorption costing and marginal costing will report the same profit figure.
- If inventory levels are increasing absorption costing profit will be higher as **more** fixed overheads are carried forward to the following period in closing inventory than those brought forward in opening inventory .
- If inventory levels are falling marginal costing profit will be higher as **less** fixed overheads are carried forward under absorption costing in the closing inventory figure than those brought forward in opening inventory.
- The difference in profit will be the fixed production overhead included in the increase/decrease in inventory levels under absorption costing.
- The contribution figure shown in marginal costing can be argued to be more use to management than the full absorption costing profit figure.
- It is possible to manipulate profit reporting under absorption costing by increasing inventory levels and thereby increasing reported profit. However, differences in reported profits occur only in the short run and in the long run, total costs will be the same by either method of accounting.

Keywords

Absorption (full) costing – both variable and fixed production overheads are included in unit cost

Marginal (variable) costing – unit cost includes only variable production costs

Contribution – sales value less variable cost of the goods sold

Production or product cost – the cost of a finished product built up from its cost elements

Period cost or a cost relating to a time period – usually fixed overheads which aren't affected by changes in production level

TEST YOUR LEARNING

Test 1

Explain how fixed production overheads are treated in an absorption costing system and in a marginal costing system.

Test 2

Given below is the budgeted information about the production of 60,000 units of a single product in a factory for the following quarter:

Direct materials		£12.50 per unit
Direct labour	– assembly	4 hours @ £8.40 per hour
	– finishing	1 hour @ £6.60 per hour
Assembly production overheads		£336,000
Finishing production overheads		£84,000

It is estimated that 60% of the assembly overhead is variable and that 75% of the finishing overhead is variable.

What is the budgeted cost of the product using:

(a) Absorption costing
(b) Marginal costing?

Test 3

Given below are the budgeted figures for production and sales of a factory's single product for the months of November and December:

	November	*December*
Production	15,000 units	15,000 units
Sales	12,500 units	18,000 units
Direct materials	£12.00 per unit	£12.00 per unit
Direct labour	£8.00 per unit	£8.00 per unit
Variable production cost	£237,000	£237,000
Fixed production cost	£390,000	£390,000

Overheads are absorbed on the basis of the budgeted production and the selling price of the product is £75.

There were 2,000 units of the product in stock at the start of November.

(a) Prepare the budgeted statements of profit or loss for each of the two months using:

(i) Absorption costing
(ii) Marginal costing

(b) Prepare a reconciliation explaining any difference in the two profit figures in each of the two months.

chapter 13: SHORT-TERM DECISION MAKING

chapter coverage

In Chapter 1 we saw that one of the main priorities of management is decision making. In this chapter we will consider a variety of techniques and information that is useful to management in the making of short-term decisions. The topics that are covered are:

- Contribution and profit
- Relevant and irrelevant costs
- Avoidable and unavoidable costs
- Cost-volume-profit analysis
  - Break-even point
  - Target profit
  - Margin of safety
  - Profit volume ratio
- Charts
- Limiting factor analysis

CONTRIBUTION AND PROFIT

In the chapter on marginal costing we defined CONTRIBUTION as sales revenue less variable costs. We can look at contribution in total, as we did in marginal costing, or at contribution per unit.

Provided that the selling price and variable costs remain constant at different levels of activity then contribution per unit will also be a constant figure at each level of activity. However, when we considered fixed costs, we saw that as activity levels increase, although the fixed costs themselves remain constant, the fixed cost per unit falls as the fixed costs are spread over more units. This means that even though contribution per unit will remain constant with increasing levels of activity, profit per unit will increase.

HOW IT WORKS

J R Grantham & Partners are considering expanding their business from its current production and sales of 100,000 units per annum. Market research suggests that it will almost certainly be possible to increase sales to 150,000 and possibly even to 180,000 units per annum.

The single product that the partnership produces sells for £20 and has variable costs of production of £15. The fixed costs are currently £400,000 per annum and are not expected to increase.

We will look at the contribution per unit, cost per unit and profit per unit at each activity level.

	100,000	*150,000*	*180,000*
	£	£	£
Sales	2,000,000	3,000,000	3,600,000
Variable costs	1,500,000	2,250,000	2,700,000
Contribution	500,000	750,000	900,000
Fixed costs	400,000	400,000	400,000
Profit	100,000	350,000	500,000
Contribution per unit	£5	£5	£5
Cost per unit (variable + fixed)			
£15 + £400,000/100,000	£19		
£15 + £400,000/150,000		£17.67	
£15 + £400,000/180,000			£17.22
Profit per unit	£1	£2.33	£2.78

As we can see there is a significant decrease in cost per unit as the activity level rises due to the fixed costs being spread over a larger number of units. This also therefore means that there is a significant increase in profit per unit as the activity level increases. However contribution per unit has remained constant.

This is one of the reasons why, for decision making purposes, contribution per unit is a much more meaningful figure than profit per unit, as the profit per unit figure is simply being affected by the spreading of the fixed costs.

Thus, for decision making purposes, you should always treat total profit as having two distinct elements:

1	Total contribution (= contribution/unit × units)	X
	Less:	
2	Fixed costs	(X)
	Profit	X

Element **1** (contribution) varies proportionately with volume, while element **2** (fixed costs) is a lump-sum period deduction.

Task 1

The manager of a factory making two products believes that one of them is much more profitable than the other and asks for a profit statement to compare them.

Profit statement

	Product A	*Product B*	*Total*
	£'000	£'000	£'000
Sales revenue	100	120	220
Less: direct (variable) costs	(40)	(70)	(110)
Less: fixed production overheads	(20)	(20)	(40)
Gross profit	40	30	70
Less: other fixed expenses	(20)	(40)	(60)
Net profit/(loss)	20	(10)	10

Do you think the company should stop making product B?

The idea of products contributing towards fixed costs is very useful for many decisions and, as we have already said, it is an important concept within a system of marginal costing.

RELEVANT AND IRRELEVANT COSTS

When providing management information for decision making, you must work out which costs and revenues are **relevant** to the decision. If in doubt, always clarify this with the person asking for the information.

In the context of short-term decision making, the RELEVANT COST here is contribution. The fixed costs do not affect the decision made and are IRRELEVANT COSTS.

A RELEVANT COST is a future incremental cash flow arising as a direct consequence of a decision.

Decision making should be based on relevant costs.

(a) **Relevant costs are future costs**. A decision is about the future and it cannot alter what has already been done. Costs that have been incurred in the past are totally irrelevant to any decision that is being made 'now'. Such costs are **past costs** or **sunk costs**.

Costs that have been incurred include not only costs that have already been paid, but also costs that have been **committed**. A **committed cost** is a future cash flow that will be incurred anyway, regardless of the decision taken now.

(b) **Relevant costs are cash flows**. Only cash flow information is required. This means that costs or charges that do not reflect **additional cash spending** (such as depreciation and notional costs) should be ignored for the purpose of decision making.

(c) **Relevant costs are incremental costs**. For example, if an employee is expected to have no other work to do during the next week, but will be paid his basic wage (of, say, £100 per week) for attending work and doing nothing, his manager might decide to give him a job that earns the organisation £40. The net gain is £40 and the £100 is irrelevant to the decision because although it is a future cash flow, it will be incurred anyway whether or not the employee is given work.

AVOIDABLE AND UNAVOIDABLE COSTS

Relevant costs are also known as avoidable costs. AVOIDABLE COSTS are costs that would not be incurred if the activity to which they relate did not exist.

One of the situations in which it is necessary to identify the avoidable costs is in deciding whether or not to **discontinue a product**. The only costs that would be saved are the **avoidable costs** which are usually the variable costs and sometimes some specific costs. Costs that would be incurred whether or not the product is discontinued are known as UNAVOIDABLE COSTS.

The principle underlying decision accounting is that management decisions can only affect the future. In decision making, managers therefore require information about **future costs and revenues** which would be affected by the decision under review. They must not be misled by events, costs and revenues in the past, about which they can do nothing.

As a general rule of thumb, you may assume the following.

- Variable costs will be relevant costs
- Fixed costs are irrelevant to a decision

This is not always the case, however, and you should analyse variable and fixed cost data carefully. Do not forget that 'fixed' costs may only be fixed in the short term.

Non-relevant variable costs

There might be occasions when a variable cost is a **non-relevant variable cost**. For example, suppose that a company has some units of raw material in inventory. They have been paid for already, and originally cost £2,000. They are now obsolete and are no longer used in regular production, and they have no scrap value. However, they could be used in a special job that the company is trying to decide whether to undertake. The special job is a 'one off' customer order, and would use up all these materials in inventory.

(a) In deciding whether the job should be undertaken, the relevant cost of the materials to the special job is nil. Their original cost of £2,000 is a **sunk cost**, which means it has already been spent and should be ignored in the decision.

(b) However, if the materials did have a scrap value of, say, £300, then their relevant cost to the job would be the revenue lost by opting to use them in the special job instead of selling them for scrap, ie £300.

Attributable fixed costs

There might be occasions when a fixed cost is a relevant cost. Some **fixed costs** are, although fixed within a relevant range of activity level, relevant to a decision for either of the following reasons.

(a) They could increase if certain extra activities were undertaken. For example, it may be necessary to employ an extra supervisor if a particular order is accepted.

(b) They would decrease or be eliminated entirely if a decision were taken either to reduce the scale of operations or shut down entirely.

The relevant cost of materials

The relevant cost of raw materials is generally the cost to replace them, *unless* the materials have already been purchased and would not be replaced once used. In this case the relevant cost of using them is the **higher** of the following.

- Their current resale value
- The value they would obtain if they were put to an alternative use

If the materials have no resale value and no other possible use, then the relevant cost of using them for the opportunity under consideration would be nil.

HOW IT WORKS

O'Reilly Ltd has been approached by a customer who would like a special job to be done for him, and who is willing to pay £22,000 for it. The job would require the following materials.

Material	*Total units required*	*Units already in inventory*	*Book value of units in inventory* £/unit	*Realisable value* £/unit	*Replacement cost* £/unit
A	1,000	0	–	–	6
B	1,000	600	2	2.50	5

Material B is used regularly by O'Reilly Ltd, and if units of B are required for this job, they would need to be replaced to meet other production demand.

Calculate the relevant costs of material for deciding whether or not to accept the contract.

(a) **Material A** is not yet owned. It would have to be bought in full at the replacement cost of £6 per unit.

(b) **Material B** is used regularly by the company. There are existing inventories (600 units) but if these are used on the contract under review a further 600 units would be bought to replace them. Relevant costs are therefore 1,000 units at the replacement cost of £5 per unit.

Summary of relevant costs

	£
Material A (1,000 × £6)	6,000
Material B (1,000 × £5)	5,000
Total	11,000

The relevant cost of labour

The relevant cost of labour, in different situations, is best explained by means of an example.

HOW IT WORKS

LW Co is currently deciding whether to undertake a new contract. 15 hours of labour will be required for the contract. LW Co currently produces product L, the budget cost details of which are shown below.

UNIT COST CARD

PRODUCT L

	£/unit
Direct materials (10kg @ £2)	20
Direct labour (5 hrs @ £6)	30
	50
Selling price	72
Contribution	22

(a) What is the relevant cost of labour if the labour must be hired from outside the organisation?

(b) Where labour must be hired from outside the organisation, the relevant cost of labour will be the variable costs incurred.

Relevant cost of labour on new contract = 15 hours @ £6 = £90

It is important that you should be able to identify the relevant costs that are appropriate to a decision. In many cases, this is a fairly straightforward problem, but there are cases where great care should be taken.

COST-VOLUME-PROFIT ANALYSIS

COST-VOLUME-PROFIT ANALYSIS is the general term for the analysis of the relationship between activity levels, costs and profit. One of the most common areas of this analysis is BREAK-EVEN ANALYSIS whereby the break-even point for a business is determined.

Breakeven point

The BREAK-EVEN POINT is the level of activity where the sales revenue is equal to the total costs of the business, meaning that all costs are covered by sales revenue but no profit is made. This is obviously an important point for managers of a business to be aware of; if the activity level falls below the break-even point then losses will be made.

So the break-even revenue point activity level can be expressed as the point where:

Sales revenue = Variable costs + Fixed costs

Alternatively

Sales revenue - Variable costs = Fixed costs

Remember that sales revenue minus variable costs is equal to contribution. So the relationship is that the break-even point is where:

Contribution = Fixed costs

Contribution per unit × break-even point (units) = Fixed costs

We saw in an earlier example in this chapter that provided that selling price and variable costs remain constant at different levels of activity then contribution per unit will also remain constant. We can therefore use this to calculate the break-even point.

$$\text{Break-even point (in units)} = \frac{\text{Fixed cost}}{\text{Contribution per unit}}$$

HOW IT WORKS

Reardon Enterprises sells a single product with a selling price of £10 per unit. The variable costs of producing the product are £6 per unit and the fixed costs of the business are £200,000.

What is the break-even point in units?

$$\text{Break-even point} = \frac{£200{,}000}{£10 - £6}$$
$$= 50{,}000 \text{ units}$$

We can prove that this is the point where no profit or loss is made.

	£
Sales (50,000 × £10)	500,000
Variable costs (50,000 × £6)	300,000
Contribution	200,000
Fixed costs	(200,000)
Profit	–

Therefore the management of Reardon Enterprises will know that they must ensure that sales volumes exceed 50,000 units per annum in order for the business to cover its total costs and make any profit.

Task 2

A business has a single product that it sells for £28. The variable costs of producing the product are £19 per unit and the fixed costs of the business are £360,000.

What is the break-even point in units?

Target profit

It is also possible to extend the analysis using contribution per unit in order to determine the level of sales that are necessary in order to not only cover all of the costs but also to make a particular amount of profit, the TARGET PROFIT.

Thus we want:

Contribution per unit × target activity level	X
Less: fixed costs	(X)
Target profit	X

To work out target profit units, work back from target profit:

$$\text{Activity level} = \frac{\text{Fixed costs} + \text{target profit}}{\text{Contribution per unit}}$$

HOW IT WORKS

Returning to Reardon Enterprises the managing director, Anna Reardon, would like to ensure a profit of £100,000 for the coming year. What level of sales is required for this profit to be made?

$$\text{Activity level} = \frac{£200{,}000 + £100{,}000}{£10 - £6}$$
$$= 75{,}000 \text{ units}$$

Therefore if the business sells 75,000 units of the product, a profit of £100,000 will be made. Again we can check this:

	£
Sales (75,000 × £10)	750,000
Variable costs (75,000 × £6)	450,000
Contribution	300,000
Fixed costs	200,000
Profit	100,000

Task 3

A business has fixed costs of £250,000. It sells just one product for a price of £80 and the variable costs of production are £60.

How many units of the product must the business sell in order to make a profit of £150,000?

Margin of safety

Another figure that management might be interested in is the MARGIN OF SAFETY. This is the difference between the budgeted or forecast sales or actual current sales and the break-even sales level. This is usually expressed as a percentage of the budgeted, forecast or actual sales. (In the assessment, make sure you express the margin of safety as a percentage of the budgeted, forecast or actual sales, **not** as a percentage of break-even sales.)

HOW IT WORKS

Remember that Reardon Enterprises' break-even sales volume was 50,000 units. If the budgeted sales for the forthcoming year are 70,000 units what is the margin of safety?

Margin of safety in units	=	Budgeted sales volume – breakeven sales volume
	=	70,000 units - 50,000 units
	=	20,000 units

This can be expressed as a percentage of budgeted sales, which should be used as the denominator in calculations.

$$\text{Margin of safety \%} = \frac{\text{Budgeted sales volume - breakeven sales volume}}{\text{Budgeted sales volume}} \times 100\%$$

$$\text{Margin of safety \%} = \frac{20,000}{70,000} \times 100$$

$$= 28.6\%$$

This tells management that sales can drop below the budgeted figure by 28.6% before losses start to be made.

The margin of safety can also be expressed in terms of revenue.

Margin of safety revenue = (Budgeted sales units – breakeven sales units) × sales price per unit

= (70,000 – 50,000) × £10

= £200,000

Task 4

A business has budgeted to sell 75,000 units of its single product in the following year. The product sells for £32 and the variable costs of production are £24. The fixed overheads of the business are £480,000.

What is the margin of safety percentage?

Profit volume ratio

When we were calculating the break-even point above, the figure that was derived using contribution per unit and fixed costs was the number of **units** that were required to be sold in order to break-even. However the break-even point can also be expressed in terms of the sales **revenue** required in order to break-even, by using the profit volume ratio (P/V) which can also be called the CONTRIBUTION TO SALES RATIO (C/S).

$$\text{Profit volume ratio} = \frac{\text{Contribution}}{\text{Sales}} \times 100$$

Thus the P/V ratio measures contribution **per £ sales revenue** rather than per **physical sales unit.**

Thus, at break-even sales revenue

Total contribution (PV ratio × break-even sales revenue)	X
Less: fixed costs	(X)
Profit	0

The break-even point in terms of sales revenue can then be found as:

$$\text{Break-even point (£)} = \frac{\text{Fixed cost}}{\text{Profit volume ratio}}$$

HOW IT WORKS

Reardon Enterprises sell their product for £10 and the variable costs are £6 per unit. Total fixed costs are £200,000.

$$\text{Profit volume ratio} = \frac{£10 - £6}{£10} \times 100$$
$$= 40\%$$

$$\text{Break-even point } (£) = \frac{200,000}{0.40}$$
$$= £500,000$$

(which corresponds to a unit activity level of $\frac{£500,000}{£10}$ = 50,000 as before)

Task 5

A business has a single product that it sells for £36. The variable costs of producing the product are £27 per unit and the fixed costs of the business are £360,000.

What is the break-even point in terms of sales revenue?

CHARTS

Break-even points and activity levels where target profits are made are traditionally illustrated on a number of charts. They all show basically the same information – variable costs, fixed costs, sales revenue, profit – but each one has a slightly different emphasis. The three most common are:

- The break-even chart
- The contribution break-even chart
- The profit-volume chart

HOW IT WORKS

We will use the information for Reardon Enterprises to illustrate these charts.

Selling price per unit	£10
Variable cost per unit	£6
Contribution per unit	£4
Fixed costs	£200,000
Break-even point	50,000 units or £500,000
Budgeted sales	70,000 units

Break-even chart

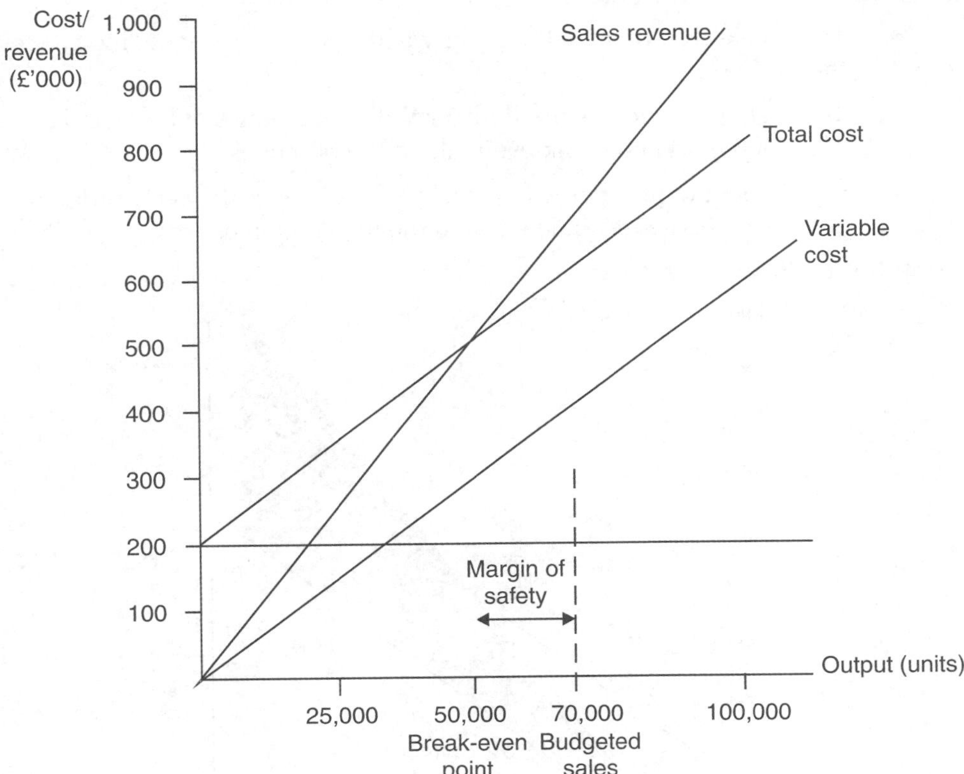

This chart shows variable costs, fixed costs, total costs and sales revenue at various different activity levels.

How to draw it up

- The fixed cost line is a horizontal line at £200,000.
- Variable costs start at the origin – if there are no sales then there are no variable costs. Then plot one further point, for example variable costs at 100,000 units are £600,000 and join this to the origin.
- The total cost line is parallel to the variable cost line but starts at £200,000, the level of the fixed costs.
- Sales revenue again starts at the origin – plot another point such as revenue of £1,000,000 if sales are 100,000 units and join this with a line to the origin.

What does the chart show?

- The break-even point is the point where the sales revenue line crosses the total costs line.
- The margin of safety is the horizontal distance between budgeted sales of 70,000 units and break-even sales of 50,000 units.
- The amount of profit or loss at each activity level is the vertical distance between the sales revenue line and the total cost line.

Contribution break-even chart

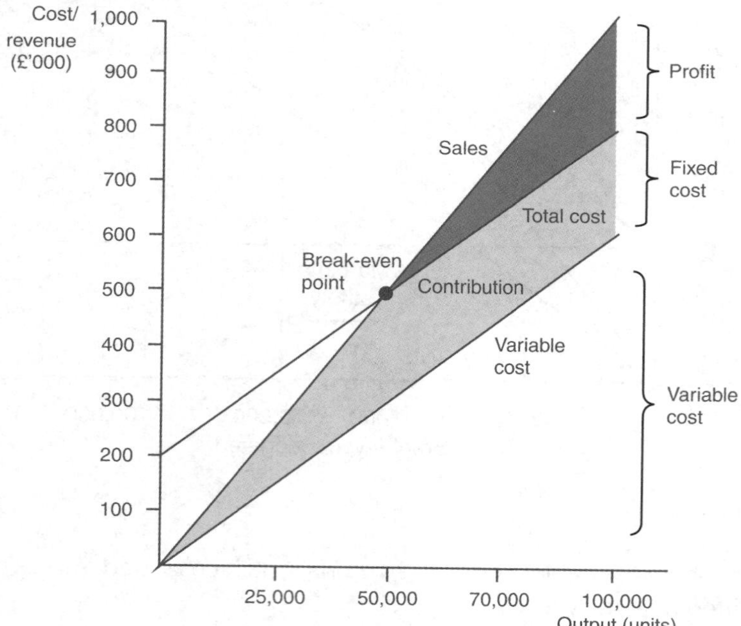

This chart again plots costs and revenue but this time no line for fixed costs.

How to draw it up

- The variable cost line and sales revenue line are drawn up as in the previous chart.
- The total cost line is parallel to the variable cost line but starting at £200,000.

What does the chart show?

- The break-even point is where the sales and total cost line cross.
- The shaded area between the sales line and the variable cost line clearly shows the contribution at each activity level.
- The area between the variable cost line and total cost line is the fixed cost.
- The darker-shaded area between the sales revenue line and the total cost line is the profit.

The only main difference between these first two charts is that in this second one the contribution can be read off more clearly.

Profit-volume chart

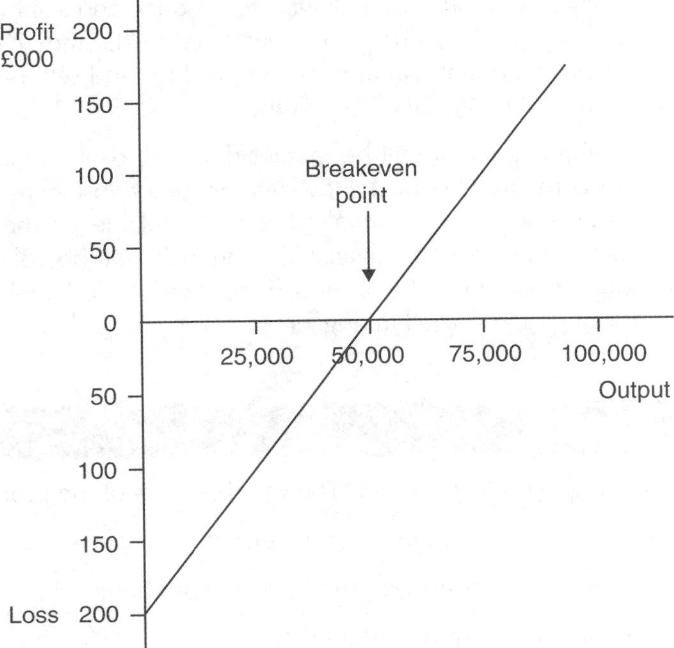

The profit-volume chart simply shows the level of profit or loss at any given level of activity.

How to draw it up

- The vertical axis must range from the profit made at the highest level of activity possible to the loss made when there are zero sales.
- The loss when there are zero sales is equal to the fixed costs, £200,000.
- The profit at the 100,000 units activity level is £200,000.
- Draw a line between these two points.

What does the chart show?

- The profit or loss at any level of activity can be read off the chart.
- The break-even point is where the profit line crosses the horizontal axis – where profit is zero.
- The horizontal axis could alternatively have shown sales revenue rather than activity level.

LIMITING FACTOR ANALYSIS

Obviously the managers of a business will wish to produce and sell more than the break-even number of units in order to cover fixed costs and make a profit. However, in practice, the quantity that they can produce and sell may be limited by one or more factors, the LIMITING FACTOR(S).

In many cases the limiting factor will be market demand, or the amount of units that customers are prepared to buy. However, in other instances the limiting factor might be the amount of materials that are available or the number of machine or labour hours that are available. You will not be asked to make calculations in your assessment but you must understand the principles of limiting factor decision-making for a single limiting factor.

HOW IT WORKS

A business sells a single product for £35. The variable costs of the product are:

Direct materials	3 kg per unit @ £3 per kg
Direct labour	2 hours per unit @ £7.50 per hour

The fixed costs of the business are £800,000.

Materials as limiting factor

If the supply of materials is limited to 360,000 kg, how many units can the business produce and how much profit will be made?

Number of units that can be produced = 360,000kg/3kg per unit
= 120,000 units

	£
Sales (120,000 × £35)	4,200,000
Variable costs (120,000 × (£9 + £15))	2,880,000
Contribution	1,320,000
Fixed costs	800,000
Profit	520,000

Labour hours as limiting factor

If materials are now not restricted, but the business only has 280,000 labour hours available for production, how many units can be made and what is the profit at this production level?

Number of units that can be produced = 280,000 hours/2 hours per unit
= 140,000 units

	£
Sales (140,000 × £35)	4,900,000
Variable costs (140,000 × £24)	3,360,000
Contribution	1,540,000
Fixed costs	800,000
Profit	740,000

MORE THAN ONE PRODUCT

We will now make the position a little more complicated by introducing a business that makes more than one product. If the availability of either materials or labour hours is a limiting factor then it will be necessary to determine the optimum production mix.

In order to make a decision we must determine our criterion for the decision making process. In business the overriding criterion will normally be to make as much profit as possible. As fixed costs in total are assumed to be constant whatever combination of products is made, maximisation of profit will be achieved by maximising **contribution**. So, we want to know how many units of each product to make to obtain maximum contribution.

If a business has more than one product, and only one limiting factor, the technique to use in order to maximise contribution is to determine the contribution per unit of the scarce resource or limiting factor and concentrate upon the production of the product with the highest contribution per limiting factor unit.

HOW IT WORKS

Farnham Engineering makes three products A, B and C. The costs and selling prices of the three products are:

	A	*B*	*C*
	£	£	£
Direct materials @ £4 per kg	8	16	12
Direct labour @ £7 per hour	7	21	14
Variable overheads	3	9	6
	18	46	32
Selling price	22	54	39
Contribution	4	8	7

Sales demand for the coming period is expected to be as follows:

Product A	3,000 units
Product B	7,000 units
Product C	5,000 units

The supply of materials is limited to 50,000 kg during the period and the labour hours available are 28,000.

We have to decide firstly if there is a limiting factor other than sales demand. Consider the materials usage for each product if the maximum sales demand is produced. (You are not given the actual usage of materials of each product but you can work it out – for example, the materials cost for A is £8 and as the materials are £4 per kg, product A must use 2 kg etc.)

	A	*B*	*C*	*Total*
Materials	6,000 kg	28,000 kg	15,000 kg	49,000 kg
Labour	3,000 hours	21,000 hours	10,000 hours	34,000 hours

As 50,000 kg of materials are available for the period and only 49,000 kg are required for the maximum production level, materials are not a limiting factor.

However, only 28,000 labour hours are available whereas in order to produce the maximum demand 34,000 hours are required. Therefore labour hours are the limiting factor.

The next stage is to calculate the contribution per limiting factor unit – so in this case the contribution per labour hour – for each product. Then rank the products according to how high the contribution per labour hour is for each one.

	A	*B*	*C*
Contribution	£4	£8	£7
Labour hours per unit	1 hour	3 hours	2 hours
Contribution per labour hour			
£4/1	£4.00		
£8/3		£2.67	
£7/2			£3.50
Ranking	1	3	2

Therefore in order to maximise contribution we must concentrate first on production of A up to the maximum sales demand, then on C, and finally, if there are any remaining hours available, on B.

The optimal production plan in order to maximise contribution is:

	Units produced	*Labour hours required*
A	3,000	3,000
C	5,000	10,000
B (balance)	5,000	15,000 (balancing figure)
		28,000

The contribution earned from this production plan is:

		£
A	(3,000 × £4)	12,000
B	(5,000 × £8)	40,000
C	(5,000 × £7)	35,000
Total contribution		87,000

Task 6

A business produces four products and the details are:

	P	*Q*	*R*	*S*
Contribution per unit	£12	£15	£9	£14
Materials per unit	3 kg	4 kg	1 kg	2 kg
Labour hours per unit	5hrs	3hrs	1hr	2hrs
Machine hours per unit	3hrs	2hrs	2hrs	4hrs
Maximum demand (units)	2,000	6,000	1,000	4,000

Machine hours are limited to 38,000 hours. Labour hours are limited to 40,000 hours and materials are limited to 30,000 kg. Determine whether any of the resource limits will prevent the maximum demand being produced.

Task 7

Complete the following sentences.

It is assumed in limiting factor analysis that management wishes to maximise profit and that profit will be maximised when (1) [▼] is (2) [▼] .

If a business makes more than one product and there is a limiting factor, then it will be necessary to determine the (3) [▼] .

In a limiting factor situation, contribution will be maximised by earning the biggest possible (4) [▼] .

Picklist (1)	Picklist (2)
contribution	minimised
fixed cost	maximised
variable cost	

Picklist (3)	Picklist (4)
optimum cost per unit of limiting factor	contribution per unit of limiting factor
optimum production mix	profit per unit of limiting factor
optimum limiting factor	

CHAPTER OVERVIEW

- Due to the nature of fixed costs, total unit cost will tend to decrease as activity levels increase as the fixed costs are spread over more units of production – however if selling price and variable costs remain constant then contribution per unit will remain constant as activity levels change.
- In the context of short-term decision making, the relevant cost is contribution. Fixed costs are generally irrelevant. Relevant costs are also known as avoidable costs.
- The break-even point in units is found by dividing the fixed costs by the contribution per unit.
- If a target profit is required the unit sales to achieve this can be found by dividing the fixed costs plus target profit by the contribution per unit.
- The difference between budgeted or actual sales and the break-even point is the margin of safety, which can be expressed as a percentage of budgeted or actual sales.
- The profit volume ratio can be used to find the break-even point in terms of sales revenue.
- Sales revenue, costs, contribution, profit and break-even point can be illustrated by a number of different break-even charts.
- Normally production of products is limited by sales demand however in some instances a factor such as the availability of material, labour hours or machine hours is the limiting factor.
- Where there is more than one product and a limiting factor, overall profit is maximised by concentrating production on the products with the highest contribution per limiting factor unit.

Keywords

Contribution – sales revenue or selling price per unit less variable costs

Relevant cost – is a future incremental cash flow arising as a direct consequence of a decision

Irrelevant cost – is a cost incurred in the past (a past cost or sunk cost) that is irrelevant to any decision being made now; it includes committed costs which are future cash flows that will be incurred anyway, regardless of the decision taken now

Avoidable costs – are costs that would not be incurred if the activity to which they relate did not exist

Unavoidable costs – are costs that would be incurred whether or not the product is discontinued

Cost-volume-profit analysis – analysis of the relationships between activity levels, costs and profits

Break-even analysis – calculations to determine the break-even point

Break-even point – level of sales whereby sales revenue is equal to total costs

Target profit – is a planned level of profit and from this **the target profit units** can be worked out.

Margin of safety – excess of budgeted or actual sales over the break-even point sales

Profit volume (P/V) ratio – ratio of contribution to sales, also known as the **contribution to sales (C/S) ratio**

Limiting factor – a factor of production or sales that limits the amount of a product that can be produced or sold

TEST YOUR LEARNING

Test 1

If selling prices and variable costs remain constant at differing levels of activity explain why unit cost will tend to fall as activity levels increase.

Test 2

A business has budgeted sales of its single product of 38,000 units. The selling price per unit is £57 and the variable costs of production are £45. The fixed costs of the business are £360,000.

Calculate the break-even point in units		units
and the margin of safety (to the nearest whole per cent)		%

Test 3

A business has fixed costs of £910,000. It sells a single product at a selling price of £24 and the variable costs of production and sales are £17 per unit.

How many units of the product must the business sell in order to make a profit of £500,000? [ ]

Test 4

A business sells its single product for £40. The variable costs of this product total £32. The fixed costs of the business are £100,000.

What is the sales revenue required in order to make a profit of £200,000? [ ]

Test 5

In a limiting factor situation where there is more than one product, when is overall profit maximised?

chapter 14: LONG-TERM DECISION MAKING

chapter coverage

In the previous chapter we looked at techniques for making short-term decisions about production and sales. In this chapter we will consider longer-term decisions that have to be made, namely investment decisions. This means comparing initial capital expenditure with the future benefits that are to be received from that expenditure. Do the future benefits give a sufficient return on the initial investment? The topics that are covered are:

- The nature of long-term decisions
- Payback period
- The time value of money
- Net present value
- Net present cost
- Internal rate of return (IRR)
- Advantages and disadvantages of NPV and IRR

THE NATURE OF LONG-TERM DECISIONS

Many decisions that the managers of a business will have to make will affect the business over a fairly long time period. In particular the purchase of buildings, machinery or equipment will be expected to bring benefits to the business over a number of future years. The decisions that managers will have to take are 'should this capital item, which is often a significant amount of expenditure, be purchased?' and 'Are the future benefits from this current expenditure enough to justify the investment?'

The answers to these questions are highly subjective as managers will have to base their decision on estimates of future costs, revenues and performance. However these estimates have to be made and assessed in order to make informed decisions.

The costs and revenues involved in these types of decisions are to be considered over a number of years into the future and there are several techniques that can be used to aid decision-making. For this unit, you need to be able to analyse a project using either the payback period or discounted cash flow techniques. We will start with the payback method.

PAYBACK PERIOD

Suppose a large amount of money is to be spent now on a project, such as the purchase of a major non-current asset. One decision criterion that the management of the business may apply, is keeping the length of time over which the benefits from this asset 'pay back' the original cost within acceptable limits. This is what is meant by the PAYBACK PERIOD.

To find the payback period the initial cost of the project must firstly be known. Then the future cash income or cost savings must be estimated. To calculate the payback period we need to determine how long it will take for this future income or cost saving to pay back the initial expenditure.

HOW IT WORKS

Uckport Industrials is considering investment in major new plant for their factory which will cost £250,000 if purchased now, 1 January 20X6. The benefit of the new plant is that it will provide major cost savings in future production.

The production manager has estimated that the cost savings for each year will be:

20X6	£80,000
20X7	£80,000
20X8	£80,000
20X9	£60,000
20Y0	£40,000

The payback period can be calculated by considering the cumulative cost savings:

Year	*Cost saving*	*Cumulative cost savings*
	£	£
20X6	80,000	80,000
20X7	80,000	160,000
20X8	80,000	240,000
20X9	60,000	300,000

With the initial cost being £250,000 we can see that by the end of 20X8 we have not quite covered that figure but by the end of 20X9 the initial cost has been covered. This is where we must start making assumptions about the timing of these cost savings in order to determine the payback period. There are two options here – either we can assume that the cost savings occur at the end of each year, ie. on 31 December, or that they occur evenly throughout the year.

Assumption – cost savings occur at end of year

If we assume that the cost savings occur at the end of each year then the payback period is four years as the initial cost of £250,000 is not totally paid back until 31 December 20X9.

Assumption – cost savings occur evenly throughout year

If the assumption is made that the cost savings occur evenly throughout the year then we can see that by the end of 20X8 we have almost recovered the cost with cumulative savings of £240,000. In 20X9 the cost savings total £60,000 but in order to payback the initial cost we only need a further £10,000 of this. Therefore the payback period can be calculated as:

Payback period	=	3 years + (£10,000/£60,000 × 12 months)
	=	3 years and 2 months

Read the question carefully to decide which assumption you should make.

How is payback period used?

Once we have calculated the payback period for a project we must then consider how it is to be used in the decision making process. If payback period is used to assess projects then the management will have set a PAYBACK PERIOD LIMIT. This is the time period within which all projects must payback their initial cost if they are to be accepted. In the assessment, if you are not told about the payback limit required by the business, you cannot conclude on the investment purely on the basis of payback.

HOW IT WORKS

Suppose that the management of Uckport Industrials have a payback period limit of four years. In this case this project (under either assumption) does have a payback period that is either four years or less and therefore the project would be accepted.

If Uckport Industrials had a payback period limit of three years, however, then the project would have been rejected.

Task 1

A business is considering investment in new machinery at a cost of £100,000 now, 1 January 20X6. The machinery will be used to make a new product that will provide additional cash inflows as follows:

Year ending	
31 December 20X6	£30,000
31 December 20X7	£40,000
31 December 20X8	£40,000
31 December 20X9	£20,000

The cash inflows occur evenly throughout the year. What is the payback period?

Advantages of payback period

The payback period is one of the most widely used methods of project appraisal. It is a fairly simple calculation to make and is easily understood by management. It also appears to consider the risk of a business being parted from its money as it is considering the time period between the cash outflow for the initial cost and the cash inflow from income or cost savings.

Disadvantages of payback period

It can however be argued that the payback period method is too simple. It does not take account of all of the cash flows associated with the project, only those up to the end of the payback period and it does not take any account of how those cash flows occur over the period. For example, with Uckport Industrials' project, if the same machinery had not had any cost savings in the first three years but £300,000 of cost savings in 20X9 it would still have had a payback period of four years but clearly may not have been acceptable due to the cash flow implications.

Most importantly the payback period fails to take any account of the TIME VALUE OF MONEY.

THE TIME VALUE OF MONEY

The time value of money is all to do with our preference to receive money sooner rather than later. If we are offered £100 now or in a year's time then we would prefer to have the money now rather than wait. There are three main reasons for this:

Risk preference	If the money is received now then it is ours and there is no risk that it might not be paid in one year's time
Consumption preference	If the money is received now then we can spend it now rather than having to wait for a year (when it may be worth less in real terms)
Investment preference	If the money is received now then we can invest it, and earn interest on it so that in one year's time it is worth more than £100

Present values

If we are offered £100 now or £100 in one year's time we are not comparing like with like. If interest rates are, say, 10% per annum then if the £100 were received now, it could be invested for a year at 10% interest. After one year the amount that we would have would be:

£100 × 1.10 = £110

We would therefore definitely prefer the £100 now.

We would only be indifferent if we were offered the option of £100 now or £110 in one year's time. By turning it around we can say that the present value of £110 in one year's time is £100 now (if interest rates are 10%) – the equivalent sum now of that future income. We can calculate the present value (PV) as:

$$PV = \frac{£110}{1.10} = £100$$

Let's now suppose that if we had £100 now we would invest it for two years at 10% interest without removing the interest – this is known as COMPOUND INTEREST.

After one year our investment would be	£100 × 1.10	=	£110
After two years our investment would be	£110 × 1.10	=	£121

This can be simplified to:

Investment after two years	£100 × 1.10 × 1.10	=	£121
OR	£100 × 1.10^2		

We can therefore also say that the present value of £121 arising after two years is £100. This would have been calculated as:

$$\frac{£121}{1.10^2}$$

OR

$$£121 \times \frac{1}{1.10^2}$$

The element that the cash flow is multiplied by, in this case:

$$\frac{1}{1.10^2}$$

is known as the DISCOUNT FACTOR or the PRESENT VALUE FACTOR (PV factor).

In general terms, the present value of a future amount of £y can be expressed as:

$$£y \times \frac{1}{(1+r)^n}$$

where r = the periodic interest rate or **discount rate** (expressed as a decimal)

n = the number of periods before payment/receipt

Fortunately you do not need to remember that formula or to make the long hand calculations as the discount factors will be given to you in the assessment.

Task 2

What is the present value of £115.76 which will be received in three years' time (to 2 dp)?

The present value factors at 5% are

Year 0 1.0000

Year 1 0.9524

Year 2 0.9070

Year 3 0.8638

Timing of cash flows

Using the discount factors you must take care to ensure that you are quite clear which time period you are using. Dates are very important. Today's date is year 0, year 1 is in one year's time, year 2 is in two years' time etc.

Task 3

Calculate the present value of each of the following cash flows and fill in the table. The discount factors are shown in the table.

(a) Cash outflow today of £2,030,000
(b) Cash inflow of £380,000 four years from now
(c) Cash inflow two years from today of £7,100,00

	Year 0	*Year 1*	*Year 2*	*Year 3*	*Year 4*
	£'000	£'000	£'000	£'000	£'000
Cash outflow	2,030,000				
Cash inflows			7,100,000		380,000
Net cash flows					
PV factor	1.0000	0.9346	0.8734	0.8163	0.7629
Discounted cash flows	2,030,000		6,201,140		289,902

NET PRESENT VALUE

The computation of a present value is a DISCOUNTED CASH FLOW (DCF) TECHNIQUE. We are finding the discounted (present) value of each individual cash flow or annuity.

If we are appraising a project then the technique that we can use is to find the NET PRESENT VALUE of all of the cash flows of the project. This involves calculating the present value of each individual cash flow and then totalling them all, remembering that the initial cost of the project is a cash outflow and any income or cost savings are cash inflows. The total of the present value of the inflows minus the outflows is the net present value (NPV).

Take care with the cash flows as we are dealing only with cash inflows or outflows and savings of cash outflows. Therefore any non-cash figures such as depreciation should be ignored.

If the net present value is a positive figure, a positive NPV, then the project should be accepted as this means that even after having taken account of the time value of money the cash inflows from the project exceed the cash outflows. If however the net present value is a negative figure, a negative NPV, then the project should be rejected.

HOW IT WORKS

We will return to Uckport Industrials.

Uckport Industrials is considering investment in major new plant for their factory that will cost £250,000 if purchased now, 1 January 20X6. The benefit of the new plant is that it will provide major cost savings in future production. The production manager has estimated that the cost savings for each calendar year will be:

20X6	£80,000
20X7	£80,000
20X8	£80,000
20X9	£60,000
20Y0	£40,000

The discount rate, or COST OF CAPITAL to be used, is 10%.

We can now use discounted cash flow techniques to determine the net present value of this project. When using DCF techniques we have to be very careful about our assumptions about the timing of cash flows. As we have seen DCF techniques are used for cash flows at specific time intervals.

For this example therefore we will have to assume that the cost savings all occur on the last day of each year, but the investment occurs immediately, now, which we shall call year 0. Therefore the timings are as follows:

1 January 20X6	=	Year 0
31 December 20X6	=	Year 1
31 December 20X7	=	Year 2

and so on.

We can now build up the net present value of these cash flows:

Year	*Cash flow*	*Discount factor*	*Present value*
	£	@ 10%	£
0	(250,000)	1.0000	(250,000)
1	80,000	0.9091	72,728
2	80,000	0.8264	66,112
3	80,000	0.7513	60,104
4	60,000	0.6830	40,980
5	40,000	0.6209	24,836
Net present value			14,760

There are a number of points to note here:

- The initial cost occurs at year 0 or NOW, therefore the discount factor is 1.0000 as £250,000 is the present value of the outflow now.
- Although the cost savings are not actual income they are the saving of an outflow, ie, they are reducing the cash costs of the business, and this is why they are treated as cash inflows.
- The initial cost of the machinery is a cash outflow and is therefore traditionally shown in brackets to distinguish it from the cost savings and cash inflows.

The layout above shows clearly how the net present value is arrived at. An alternative layout, used in the sample assessment for this unit, is as follows:

	Year 0	*Year 1*	*Year 2*	*Year 3*	*Year 4*	*Year 5*
	£'000	£'000	£'000	£'000	£'000	£'000
Capital expenditure	(250)					
Cash inflows		80	80	80	60	40
Net cash flows	(250)	80	80	80	60	40
PV factors	1.0000	0.9091	0.8264	0.7513	0.6830	0.6209
Discounted cash flows	(250.000)	72.728	66.112	60.104	40.980	24.836
Net present value	14.760					

So for Uckport Industrials at their cost of capital or discount rate of 10% the project cash flows have a positive net present value and therefore the project should be accepted.

Task 4

A business is considering investment in new machinery at a cost of £100,000 now, 1 January 20X6. The machinery will be used to make a new product which will provide additional cash inflows as follows:

Year ending	
31 December 20X6	£30,000
31 December 20X7	£40,000
31 December 20X8	£40,000
31 December 20X9	£20,000

The cash inflows occur the end of each year. What is the net present value at the cost of capital of 8%? The discount factors you need are: 0.9259, 0.8573, 0.7938 and 0.7350. Should the investment go ahead?

NET PRESENT COST

The NET PRESENT COST of a project is the sum of the present value of all costs over the period of interest.

If a number of options are being considered then the option with the lowest net present cost will be the most favourable financial option.

The net present cost is similar to the net present value and but excludes any benefits from the project. The calculation is done in the same way but using costs instead of revenues and costs. It is particularly useful for comparing costs, for example, comparing alternative supplier for electricity or gas. The preferred choice is the one with the lowest net present cost.

INTERNAL RATE OF RETURN (IRR)

The INTERNAL RATE OF RETURN is the discount rate or interest rate that will result in a net present value of zero for a set of cash flows.

If the internal rate of return of a project is higher than the organisation's cost of capital or higher than its required return from investments the project should be accepted. If it is lower then it should be rejected.

For this Unit tasks that require the computation of a project's internal rate of return may be set and you should also be aware of its meaning.

HOW IT WORKS

A project might have the following NPVs at the following discount rates.

Discount rate	*NPV*
%	£
5	5,300
10	2,900
15	(1,700)
20	(3,200)

You can see that the NPV changes from a positive value to a negative value somewhere between 10% and 15%. The IRR is the discount rate which gives an NPV of zero. So the IRR is somewhere between 10% and 15%.

It might help you to see this on a graph but just ignore the graph if it is not helpful for you. The important points to note are

- The IRR is the discount rate that gives a zero NPV.
- The IRR must be greater than the organisation's cost of capital for the project to be acceptable.

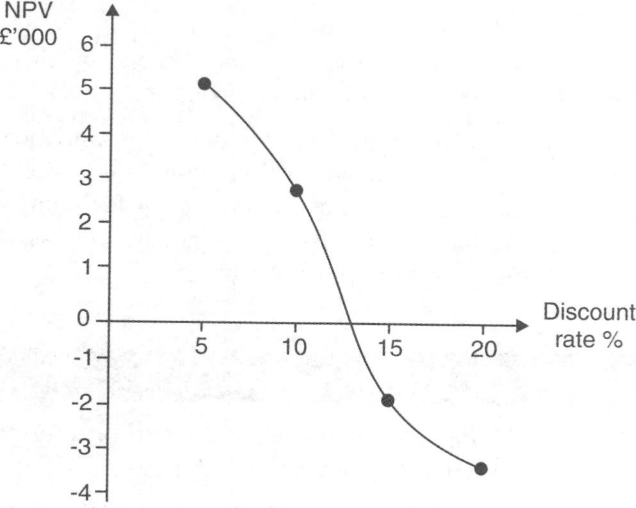

We can estimate an approximate internal rate of return based on the NPVs at particular costs of capital.

HOW IT WORKS

A project has estimated net cash flows as follows. The cost of capital is 13%.

	Year 0	*Year 1*	*Year 2*	*Year 3*	*Year 4*
	£'000	£'000	£'000	£'000	£'000
Net cash flows	-173	75	50	60	40
PV factor	1.000	0.885	0.783	0.693	0.613
Discounted cash flows	-173	66.375	39.150	41.580	24.520
NPV	-1.375				

What is the approximate internal rate of return (IRR) of the project?

A 0% B 11% C 15% D 20%

Generally speaking (although not always), the higher the cost of capital, the lower the NPV will be. We know from the table that at a cost of capital of 13%, the NPV is negative but fairly close to zero. This means that the IRR is fairly close to 13% but needs to be a bit lower to obtain an NPV of zero. The correct estimate is therefore 11%.

Task 5

A project has the following NPVs at the following discount rates.

Discount rate	*NPV*
%	£
9	6,235
11	755
13	-4,430

What is the approximate IRR of the project?

A 0% B 11.3% C 15.5% D 19.5%

Estimating using basic linear interpolation

Another way of estimating the IRR is to use a formula. This is known as interpolation.

$$IRR = A + \left[\frac{a}{a - b} \times (B - A)\right]$$

where A is the discount rate which provides the positive NPV

a is the amount of the positive NPV

B is the discount rate which provides the negative NPV

b is the amount of the negative NPV

As you can see from the formula we need two rates of return.

(a) One at which the NPV is a **small positive value**. The actual IRR will be higher than this rate of return.

(b) One at which the NPV is a **small negative value**. The actual IRR will be lower than this rate of return

HOW IT WORKS

A project has the following NPVs at discount rates of 10% and 20%.

Discount rate	*NPV*
%	£
9	6,235
11	755
13	-4,430

Use linear interpolation to estimate the IRR.

$$\text{IRR} = \text{A} + \left[\frac{\text{a}}{\text{a - b}} \times (\text{B - A})\right]$$

We will use A = 11% and B = 13% (so a = 755 and b = -4,430)

$$\text{IRR} = 11 + \left[\frac{755}{755 - -4,430} \times (13 - 11)\right]$$

Look very carefully at a – b. As b = -4,430 we have two minus signs next to each other. Note the rule of maths that says that two minuses make a plus. So we can re-write the formula as

$$\text{IRR} = 11 + \left[\frac{755}{755 + 4,430} \times (13 - 11)\right]$$

$$\therefore\ \text{IRR} = 11 + \left[\frac{755}{5,185} \times 2\right]$$

$$\therefore\ \text{IRR} = 11.29\%$$

Make sure that you learn the IRR formula.

Task 6

A project has the following NPVs at the following discount rates.

Discount rate	*NPV*
%	£
9	22
10	-4

What is the approximate IRR of the project?

A 9.15% B 9.85% C 10.15% D 10.85%

ADVANTAGES AND DISADVANTAGES OF NPV AND IRR

Here are the advantages and disadvantages of net present value and internal rate of return. We have set these out in two handy tables. The first refers to net present value and the second to internal rate of return.

Advantages of NPV	Disadvantages of NPV
Shareholder wealth is **maximised**.	It can be difficult to identify **an appropriate discount rate**.
It takes into account the **time value of money**.	For simplicity, cash flows are sometimes all assumed to occur at **year ends:** this assumption may be unrealistic.
It is based on **cash flows** which are less subjective than profit.	Some managers are **unfamiliar** with the concept of NPV.
Shareholders will **benefit** if a project with a positive NPV is accepted.	

Advantages of IRR	Disadvantages of IRR
It takes into account the **time value of money**, unlike other approaches such as payback period.	Some **managers** are **unfamiliar** with the IRR method.
Results are expressed as a **simple percentage**, and are more easily understood than some other methods.	It cannot accommodate **changing interest rates**.

Advantages of IRR	Disadvantages of IRR
It indicates how **sensitive** calculations are to changes in interest rates.	It assumes that funds can be **re-invested** at a rate equivalent to the IRR, which may be too high.
	Projects with unconventional cash flows can produce **negative** or **multiple IRRs**.

CHAPTER OVERVIEW

- Long-term decisions are often of the nature of large initial capital expenditure followed by benefits in terms of additional revenue or cost savings.
- The payback period is a method of assessing a project based upon how quickly the inflows from the project repay the initial investment.
- If the payback period for a project is shorter than the organisation's payback period limit then the project will be accepted.
- The main disadvantage of the payback period is that it takes no account of the time value of money – if cash is to be received in the future it must be discounted to take account of the time value of money.
- Present value tables can be used so that individual discount factors do not have to be calculated.
- The net present cost of a project is the sum of the present value of all costs over the period of interest.
- One method of using discounted cash flow techniques for project appraisal is to calculate the net present value of the project cash flows - if the net present value at the organisation's cost of capital is positive then the project should be accepted but if it is negative it should be rejected.
- If the internal rate of return of the project is greater than the organisation's cost of capital the project should be accepted.

Keywords

Payback period – the time it takes for the cash inflows from a project to repay the initial investment cost

Payback period limit – the period set by an organisation within which projects must pay back their initial investment

Time value of money – the fact that money received or paid in the future is worth less than money received or paid now due to risk, consumption and investment preferences

Risk preference – money received sooner rather than later carries less risk of not materialising

Consumption preference – money received sooner rather than later can be used earlier

Investment preference – money received sooner rather than later can be invested to earn interest

Present value – the discounted value of a future cash flow to put it on equivalent terms with cash flows now

Compound interest – a system where interest is accumulated rather than being withdrawn – interest is then paid on the interest

Discount factor – the factor applied to a future cash flow to find its present value

Discount rate – the interest rate used to discount cash flows

Present value tables – tables of pre-calculated discount factors for annual cash flows and annuities

Net present value – the total of the individual present values of the cash flows of a project

Net present cost – the sum of the individual present costs over the project life

Cost of capital – the discount rate used by an organisation to appraise projects

Internal rate of return – the discount rate which when applied to project cash flows gives a zero net present value

TEST YOUR LEARNING

Test 1

A business is considering one of the following two possible investments:

	Investment A	*Investment B*
Cost at 1 July 20X6	£120,000	£100,000
Cash inflow at 30 June 20X7	£43,000	£21,000
Cash inflow at 30 June 20X8	£51,000	£21,000
Cash inflow at 30 June 20X9	£52,000	£21,000
Cash inflow at 30 June 20Y0	£38,000	£21,000
Cash inflow at 30 June 20Y1		£40,000
Cash inflow at 30 June 20Y2		£70,000

All of the cash inflows are spread evenly over the year.

The business has a policy of only investing in projects with a payback period of three years or less.

(a) Which of the two investments, if either, would be accepted?

(b) Using the two investments given, illustrate any problem there may be with using this method of investment appraisal.

Test 2

Today's date is 1 January 20X6. What are the present values of each of the following cash flows?

(a) A receipt of £3,100 on 31 December 20X7 – discount factor 0.7972

(b) A payment of £15,000 on 1 January 20X6 – discount factor 1.0000

(c) A receipt of £1,000 on 31 December 20X6 and 20X7 – discount factors 0.8929 and 0.7972

(d) A payment of £4,400 on 31 December 20X8 – discount factor 0.8734

Test 3

A business is considering investment in new machinery at a cost of £340,000 on 1 April 20X6. This machinery will be used to produce a new product which will give rise to the following net cash inflows:

31 March 20X7	£80,000
31 March 20X8	£70,000
31 March 20X9	£90,000
31 March 20Y0	£120,000
31 March 20Y1	£60,000

The new machinery is to be depreciated at 7% per annum on cost. The discount factors to use are 0.9346, 0.8734, 0.8163, 0.7629 and 0.7130.

What is the net present value of this project?

Test 4

A business is considering investment in new plant and machinery on 1 January 20X6 at a cost of £90,000. The cash cost savings are estimated to be:

31 December 20X6	£23,000
31 December 20X7	£31,000
31 December 20X8	£40,000
31 December 20X9	£18,000

The business has a cost of capital of 11%. The discount factors to use are 0.9009, 0.8116, 0.7312 and 0.6587.

(a) What is the net present value of this project? (Round your present values to the nearest whole pound.)

(b) Advise the business as to whether it should invest in the new plant and machinery and justify your advice.

ANSWERS TO CHAPTER TASKS

CHAPTER 1 Introduction to cost accounting

Task 1 A The component parts are directly attributable to the special bicycle so are a direct cost.

D The paint which is just used on the special bicycle is directly attributable to it so is a direct cost.

E The wages are directly attributable to the special bicycle so are a direct cost.

The other costs are indirect costs because you can't say exactly how much of them relate to the special bicycle.

CHAPTER 2 Cost classification and cost behaviour

Task 1 An extension to a building is an improvement to an existing non-current asset; it is like acquiring another building. It will increase the ability of the business to earn profits and is therefore a capital item. Repairs are treated as revenue expenditure as they only maintain the existing ability to earn profits.

Task 2

(a) Production cost

(b) Administration cost – the Managing Director is involved in co-ordinating all areas of operations of a business

(c) Selling and distribution cost

(d) Administration cost, unless any part of this can be separately identified and attributed to another function

(e) Production cost

(f) Selling and distribution cost

(g) Production cost

Task 3 This is a direct cost as the painter is working directly on the product which the business sells. Painters doing maintenance work in a factory that makes toys would be classified as indirect labour. This emphasises the importance of considering each case on its own merits; the same job is treated differently in two different situations.

Task 4 (a) £5
(b) £2.50
(c) £1.25

As the number of units increases, the fixed cost per unit decreases.

Task 5 The relevant range of a fixed cost is the range of activity within which the cost does not change. Once the relevant range of activity is exceeded the cost will increase.

Task 6 (a) Semi-variable cost
(b) Variable cost
(c) Step-fixed
(d) Fixed cost
(e) Fixed, then semi-variable cost

Task 7

(a)	£800 + (4 × £20)	=	£880
(b)	£800 + (8 × £20)	=	£960
(c)	£800 + (15 × £20)	=	£1,100

Task 8

	Output (units)	*Total cost*
		£
Highest	4,200	54,000
Lowest	2,900	41,000
High-low	1,300	13,000

$$\text{Variable cost per unit} = \frac{\text{High cost} - \text{low cost}}{\text{High output} - \text{low output}}$$

$$= \frac{£13,000}{1,300}$$

$$= £10$$

At 4,200 units

	£
Total cost	54,000
Less: variable cost (4,200 × £10)	42,000
= fixed cost	12,000

Or, at 2,900 units

	£
Total cost	41,000
Less: variable cost (2,900 × £10)	29,000
= fixed cost	12,000

Task 9

Output (units)		*Total cost*
		£
Highest	8,000	115,000
Lowest	6,000	97,000
High-low	2,000	18,000

$$\text{Variable cost per unit} = \frac{\text{High cost} - \text{low cost}}{\text{High output} - \text{low output}}$$

$$= \frac{£18,000}{2,000}$$

$$= £9$$

At 8,000 units

	£
Total cost	115,000
Less: variable cost (8,000 × £9)	72,000
= fixed cost	43,000

So, at 7,500 units	£
Fixed cost	43,000
Variable cost (7,500 × £9)	67,500
Total cost	110,500

CHAPTER 3 Material costs and inventory valuation

Task 1 Leather (upper)
Rubber (sole)
Plastic and card (insole)

Glue and thread (may be included in indirect materials due to their relatively small value)

Cardboard box and tissue (packaging)

Task 2

(a) C £260 × 18 + £270 × 12 – £260 × 10 = £5,320

STORES LEDGER ACCOUNT

Inventory item: Doggy bed — Maximun: 200

Code: D49802 — Minimum: 20

Day	Receipts				Issues				Balance		
	GRN	Qty	Unit price £	£	Req No	Qty	Unit price £	£	Qty	Unit price £	£
1	Bal.								0	0	0
2	G23	18	260	4,680					18	260	4,680
									18	260	4,680
3	G31	12	270	3,240					12	270	3,240
									30		7,920
4					R10	10	260	2,600	8	260	2,080
									12	270	3,240
									20		5,320
6					R15	8	260	2,080			
						6	270	1,620	6	270	1,620

Task 3

JOURNAL

Code	**Debit (£)**	**Credit (£)**
1 Raw materials 500	**1,250**	
Payables 700		**1,250**
2 Work in progress 600	**750**	
Raw materials 500		**750**

Task 4 Reorder level = buffer inventory + (budgeted or maximum usage × maximum lead time)

= (2 × 5,000) + (5,000 × 3)

= 25,000 mands.

Task 5 Maximum inventory level is limited to 520.

520 = 72 + reorder quantity – (2 × 1)

Reorder quantity = 520 – 72 + 2

= 450

The order is placed when inventory falls to 72 units. Two units is the minimum number used in the lead time, so that when the next delivery arrives there will be 70 units still in inventory. Only 450 more can be fitted into the storage space to take the total to 520 units, so the reorder quantity must be limited to 450 units.

Task 6 Perpetual inventory is the term used for the up-to-date record of the amount of each inventory line on hand. The records are updated for every receipt and issue of inventory so that, in theory, they will show the amount of goods on hand at any particular moment.

Continuous inventory counting is a check to ensure that the physical inventory agrees with the perpetual inventory record. It is a system of stocktaking that counts inventory lines on a rotational basis, ensuring that each inventory line is counted at least once a year. Valuable and high-turnover items will be checked more often than this. The physical counts are compared with the inventory records so that any discrepancies can be investigated. Continuous stocktaking is only of use if there is a perpetual inventory kept.

Task 7

(a) Incorrect materials being delivered

(b) Incorrect prices being paid

(c) Deliveries other than at the specified time, causing disruptions

(d) Insufficient control over quality

(e) Invoiced amounts differing from quantities of goods actually received or prices agreed

(f) Stockouts and over-stocking

(g) Misappropriation of inventory

You may, of course, have thought of other equally valid consequences.

CHAPTER 4 Labour costs and expenses

Task 1

		Direct cost	*Indirect cost*
		£	£
Basic pay (37 × £10)		370	
Overtime:	basic (4 × £10)	40	
	premium (4 × £5)		20
Total		410	20

Task 2

	£
First 400 units: 400 × 50p	200.00
Next 100 units: 100 × 70p	70.00
Last 30 units: 30 × 90p	27.00
Gross pay	297.00

Task 3

DEBIT	Wages control account	£30,700	
CREDIT	Bank		£30,700
DEBIT	Wages control account	£16,600	
CREDIT	HMRC payables		£16,600
DEBIT	WIP	£38,050	
CREDIT	Wages control account		£38,050
DEBIT	Production overhead	£9,250	
CREDIT	Wages control account		£9,250

You will not have to prepare a T account in your assessment but we have prepared one here to show you that it balances.

Wages control account

	£		£
June 20X9 Bank	30,700	June 20X9 WIP	38,050
June 20X9 HMRC	16,600	June 20X9 Prod o/h	9,250
	47,300		47,300

CHAPTER 5 Accounting for overheads

Task 1 Overhead absorption rate $= \frac{£75,000}{15,000\text{h}}$ (budgeted direct labour hours)

$= £5$ per direct labour hour

Task 2 (a) Overhead absorption rate $= \frac{£54,000}{60,000\text{h}}$ (budgeted direct labour hours)

$= £0.90$ per direct labour hour

(b)

	£
Actual overheads	47,000
Absorbed overheads (55,000h × £0.90 per h)	49,500
Over absorption	2,500

The amount over absorbed will be an addition to profit.

CHAPTER 6 Absorption costing

Task 1

Overhead	(a) Allocate or apportion?	(b) Cost centre(s) charged?	(c) Basis of apportionment?
Factory light & heat	Apportion	The four factory cost centres	Floor area or volume occupied
Rent	Allocate	Factory office (this is the only cost centre rented)	
Factory rates	Apportion	The four factory cost centres	Floor area
Office stationery	Allocate	Offices	
Cleaning of workers' overalls	Apportion	The four factory cost centres and the warehouse	Number of workers using overalls
Roof repair to warehouse	Allocate	Warehouse	

Task 2

Cost centre		*A*	*B*	*C*	*Total*
	Basis used	£	£	£	£
Electricity	3:2:1	7,500	5,000	2,500	15,000
Rent	6:3:1	7,200	3,600	1,200	12,000
Supervision	1:1:0	2,500	2,500		5,000
Licence	Allocated	–	–	2,000	2,000
		17,200	11,100	5,700	
Reapportion C		2,850	2,850	(5,700)	
Total		20,050	13,950	0	34,000

Task 3 (a) Separate departmental rates per direct labour hour

Department X $= \dfrac{£20{,}000}{4{,}000\text{h}}$

= £5 per direct labour hour

Department Z $= \dfrac{£40{,}000}{16{,}000\text{h}}$

= £2.50 per direct labour hour

(b) Separate departmental rates per machine hour

$$\text{Department X} = \frac{£20{,}000}{12{,}000\text{h}}$$

$$= £1.67 \text{ per machine hour}$$

$$\text{Department Z} = \frac{£40{,}000}{100}$$

$$= £400 \text{ per machine hour}$$

(c) It is obvious from these results that the two departments are very different. Department Z seems to utilise a lot of labour, but very little machinery in its production process, so a direct labour hour rate would be the best overhead absorption rate to use; the machine hour rate looks unreasonably high! Department × uses a lot more machine hours than labour hours, so it may be more meaningful to use a machine hour rate in this department.

CHAPTER 7 Job, batch and service costing

Task 1

- Setting the price for the job
- Gathering the actual costs for the job
- Control of the job by the monitoring of variances between the actual cost and the expected cost of the job

Task 2 If the overheads of the business are not included in the job quote then the overheads will never be covered by the income from jobs. Only by including the overheads before any profit element is added can the business be sure of earning enough to cover its overheads as well as the direct costs.

Task 3 Total cost of job = £487.20.

	Job H
	£
Direct material	154.00
Direct labour (20 hours × £3.80)	76.00
Overhead cost (20 hours × £12.86)	257.20
	487.20

Task 4

$$\text{Cost per jacket} = \frac{£38{,}925}{450}$$

$$= £86.50$$

Task 5

The cost unit is the basic measure of control in an organisation, used to monitor cost and activity levels. The cost unit selected must be measurable and appropriate for the type of cost and activity. Possible cost units that could be suggested are as follows.

Cost per kilometre

- Variable cost per kilometre
- Fixed cost per kilometre

This is not particularly useful for control purposes because it will tend to vary with the kilometres run.

- Total cost of each vehicle per kilometre – this suffers from the same problem as above
- Maintenance cost of each vehicle per kilometre

Cost per tonne kilometre

This can be more useful than a cost per kilometre for control purposes, because it combines the distance travelled and the load carried, both of which affect cost.

Cost per operating hour

Once again, many costs can be related to this cost unit, including the following.

- Total cost of each vehicle per operating hour
- Variable costs per operating hour
- Fixed costs per operating hour

Task 6

Service costing differs from other costing methods (product costing methods) for a number of reasons.

(a) With many services, the cost of direct materials consumed will be relatively small compared to the labour, direct expenses and overheads costs. In product costing the direct materials are often a greater proportion of the total cost.

(b) Because of the difficulty of identifying costs with specific cost units in service costing, the indirect costs tend to represent a higher proportion of total cost compared with product costing.

(c) The output of most service organisations is often **intangible** (you can't touch it) and hence difficult to define. A unit cost is therefore difficult to calculate.

(d) The service industry includes such a wide range of organisations which provide such different services and have such different cost structures that costing will vary considerably from one service to another.

Task 7

Service	**Cost unit**
Canteen	Meal served
Vans and lorries used in distribution	Mile or km, tonne/mile or tonne/km
Maintenance	Man hour

Task 8

We need to calculate the number of units (ie the number of attendance hours.)

	Number	*Attendance weeks per annum*	*Hours per week*	*Total hours per annum*
Undergraduates	2,700	× 30	× 14	1,134,000
Post graduates	1,500	× 30	× 10	450,000
				1,584,000

$$\text{Cost per unit} = \frac{\text{Total cost}}{\text{Number of units}} = \frac{£792,000}{1,584,000} = £0.50$$

CHAPTER 8 Process costing

Task 1 Expected output: 17,000 kg × 95% = 16,150 kg

Or: Expected loss = 17,000 kg × 5% = 850 kg

So expected output = 17,000 kg – 850 kg = 16,150 kg

Task 2 (a) **Step 1** Calculate the number of normal loss units:

16,000 ltr × 5% = 800 ltr

Step 2 Calculate the expected output from the process:

16,000 ltr – 800 ltr = 15,200 ltr

Step 3 Total the process costs:

£108,000 + £22,720 = £130,720

Step 4 Calculate the cost per unit of expected output:

$$\frac{£130,720}{15,200 \text{ ltr}} = £8.60 \text{ per ltr}$$

(b)

Process account

	ltr	£		ltr	£
Materials	16,000	108,000	Normal loss	800	–
Conversion cost		22,720	Output	15,200	130,720
	16,000	130,720		16,000	130,720

Task 3 (a) **Step 1** Calculate the number of normal loss units:

110,000 kg × 6% = 6,600 kg

Step 2 Calculate the expected output from the process:

110,000 kg – 6,600 kg = 103,400 kg

Step 3 Total the process costs:

£526,000 + £128,300 + £110,860 = £765,160

Step 4 Calculate the cost per unit of expected output:

$$\frac{£765,160}{103,400 \text{ kg}} = £7.40 \text{ per kg}$$

(b)

Process account

	kg	£		kg	£
Materials	110,000	526,000	Normal loss	6,600	–
Labour		128,300	Abnormal loss	3,000	22,200
Overheads		110,860	Output	100,400	742,960
	110,000	765,160		110,000	765,160

Task 4 (a) **Step 1** Calculate the number of normal loss units:

48,000 ltr × 10% = 4,800 ltr

Step 2 Calculate the expected output from the process:

48,000 ltr – 4,800 ltr = 43,200 ltr

Step 3 Total the process costs:

£164,200 + £56,120 = £220,320

Step 4 Calculate the cost per unit of expected output:

$$\frac{£220,320}{43,200 \text{ ltr}} = £5.10 \text{ per litre}$$

(b)

Process account

	ltr	£		ltr	£
Materials	48,000	164,200	Normal loss	4,800	–
Labour		56,120	Output	44,000	224,400
Abnormal gain	800	4,080			
	48,800	224,400		48,800	224,400

Task 5 (a) **Step 1** Calculate the number of normal loss units:

10,000 kg × 5% = 500 kg

Step 2 Calculate the expected output from the process:

10,000 kg – 500 kg = 9,500 kg

Step 3 Total the process costs and deduct the scrap value of the normal loss:

(£98,000 + £36,000 + £9,200) – (500 × £1.40) = £142,500

Step 4 Calculate the cost per unit of expected output:

$$\frac{£142{,}500}{9{,}500\text{kg}} = £15 \text{ per kg}$$

(b)

Process account

	kg	£		kg	£
Materials	10,000	98,000	Normal loss	500	700
Labour		36,000	Abnormal loss	400	6,000
Overheads		9,200	Output	9,100	136,500
	10,000	143,200		10,000	143,200

Task 6

		Materials		*Labour/overheads*	
	Units	*Proportion complete*	*Equivalent units*	*Proportion complete*	*Equivalent units*
Completed units	4,000	100%	4,000	100%	4,000
Closing work in progress	600	75%	450	40%	240
Total equivalent units			4,450		4,240
Cost per equivalent unit		£15,575/4,450		£8,480/4,240	
		= £3.50 per EU		= £2 per EU	

Valuation

	£
Completed units	
Materials (4,000 × £3.50)	14,000
Labour/overheads (4,000 × £2)	8,000
	22,000
Closing work in progress	
Materials (450 × £3.50)	1,575
Labour/overheads (240 × £2)	480
	2,055

CHAPTER 9 Budgeting: fixed and flexed budgets

Task 1 At 120,000 units – 3 supervisors required – cost = £12,000/3
= £4,000 each

At 180,000 units – 4 supervisors required – cost = £16,000

Task 2 Remember cost behaviour! Fixed costs remain the same whatever the level of activity. The flexed budget will therefore show £15,000 for the fixed production overhead.

CHAPTER 10 Variance analysis

Task 1

	Budget 200 units	*Budget per unit*	*Flexed budget 230 units*	*Actual 230 units*	*Variance*
	£	£	£	£	£
Sales	71,400	357	82,110	69,000	13,110 (A)
Variable costs					
Labour	31,600	158	36,340	27,000	9,340 (F)
Material	12,600	63	14,490	24,000	9,510 (A)
	44,200	221	50,830	51,000	
Contribution	27,200	136	31,280	18,000	13,280 (A)
Fixed costs	18,900		18,900	10,000	8,900 (F)
Profit	8,300		12,380	8,000	4,380 (A)

Task 2

Total materials variance		£
Budget cost for actual production	24,000 × 12 × £20.50	5,904,000
Actual cost		6,240,000
		336,000(A)

Task 3

Total direct labour variance	£
Budget cost for actual production 12,000 × 4 × £6.50	312,000
Actual cost	306,000
	6,000(F)

Task 4 (a) Budgeted fixed overhead = 2,400 units × 2 hours × £5.00
= £24,000

(b)

Total fixed overhead variance	£
Fixed overhead budgeted	24,000
Fixed overhead incurred	26,000
	2,000 (A)

CHAPTER 11 Cost bookkeeping

Task 1 An integrated cost bookkeeping system is one that combines the cost accounting and financial accounting functions in one system of ledger accounts. This means that there will be ledger accounts that relate to the cost accounting function such as materials control account, wages control account, production overheads control account and Work in Progress control account, as well as financial accounting ledgers such as the cash account and receivables and payables control accounts.

Task 2 DEBIT Materials control account

CREDIT Payables control account

Task 3

Production overheads account

	£		£
Overheads incurred	3,690	Overheads absorbed	3,402
		Under-absorbed overheads	288
	3,690		3,690

The under-absorbed overhead would be debited to the statement of profit or loss as an additional cost for the period.

Task 4

Work in progress ledger account

	£		£
Opening balance	730	Transfer to finished goods	4,100
Direct materials	2,460		
Direct labour	1,070		
Production overhead 140 hours @ £2.10	294	Closing balance	454
	4,554		4,554

CHAPTER 12 Marginal costing

Task 1

(a) **Absorption costing – unit cost**

	£
Direct material	3.40
Direct labour	6.80
Variable overhead	1.20
Prime cost	11.40
Fixed overhead ((£340,000/100,000) × 2)	6.80
Absorption cost	18.20

(b) **Marginal costing – unit cost**

	£
Direct material	3.40
Direct labour	6.80
Variable overhead	1.20
Prime cost or marginal cost	11.40

Task 2

Unit cost

	£
Direct material	6.40
Direct labour	15.00
Variable overhead ((120,000/24,000) × 2)	10.00
Marginal costing unit cost	31.40
Fixed overhead ((360,000/24,000) × 2)	30.00
Absorption costing unit cost	61.40

(a) **Absorption costing – statement of profit or loss**

	£	£
Sales (11,600 × £65)		754,000
Less: cost of goods sold		
Opening inventory (1,400 × £61.40)	85,960	
Production cost (12,000 × £61.40)	736,800	
	822,760	
Less: closing inventory (1,800 × £61.40)	110,520	
		712,240
Profit		41,760

(b) **Marginal costing – statement of profit or loss**

	£	£
Sales		754,000
Less: cost of goods sold		
Opening inventory (1,400 × £31.40)	43,960	
Production cost (12,000 × £31.40)	376,800	
	420,760	
Less: closing inventory (1,800 × £31.40)	56,520	
		364,240
Contribution		389,760
Less: fixed overheads		360,000
Profit		29,760

CHAPTER 13 Short-term decision making

Task 1 The important idea here is that products can contribute towards paying the fixed costs of the business provided their:

Sales revenue is greater than variable costs.

So for example if 1,000 units of a product are sold at £40 per unit and the actual cost of making those units is £25 per unit, then the excess of revenue over costs = 1,000 (40 – 25) = £15,000. This £15,000 is available as a **contribution** to help pay for fixed costs such as insurance.

The idea of products contributing towards fixed costs is very useful for many decisions.

Task 2 Break-even point $= \frac{£360{,}000}{£28 - £19}$

$= 40{,}000$ units

Task 3 Target profit output $= \frac{£250{,}000 + £150{,}000}{£80 - £60}$

$= 20{,}000$ units

Task 4 Break-even point $= \frac{£480{,}000}{£32 - £24}$

$= 60{,}000$ units

Margin of safety $= \frac{£75{,}000 - 60{,}000}{75{,}000} \times 100$

$= 20\%$

Task 5 Profit volume ratio $= \frac{£36 - £27}{£36} \times 100$

$= 25\%$

Break-even point $= \frac{£360,000}{0.25}$

$= £1,440,000$

Task 6

Material requirements = (3kg × 2,000) + (4kg × 6,000) + (1kg × 1,000) + (2kg × 4,000)

= 39,000 kg

but only 30,000kg are available

Labour hour requirements = (5 × 2,000) + (3 × 6,000) + (1 × 1,000) + (2 × 4,000)

= 37,000 hours

and 40,000 hours are available

Machine hour requirements = (3 × 2,000) + (2 × 6,000) + (2 × 1,000) + (4 × 4,000)

= 36,000 hours

and 38,000 hours are available

So only the materials are in short supply.

Task 7

It is assumed in limiting factor analysis that management wishes to maximise profit and that profit will be maximised when **contribution** is **maximised**.

If a business makes more than one product and there is a limiting factor then it will be necessary to determine the **optimum production mix**.

In a limiting factor situation, contribution will be maximised by earning the biggest possible **contribution per unit of limiting factor**.

CHAPTER 14 Long-term decision making

Task 1

1

Time	*Cash flows*	*Cumulative cash flows*
	£	£
31 Dec X6	30,000	30,000
31 Dec X7	40,000	70,000
31 Dec X8	40,000	110,000
31 Dec X9	20,000	130,000

The initial cost of the investment is fully covered after three years; however as the cash inflows occur evenly throughout the year this can be calculated more accurately.

2 years + £30,000/£40,000 × 12 months = 2 years and 9 months

Task 2 £115.76 × 0.8638 = £99.99 (to 2 dp)

Task 3

	Year 0	*Year 1*	*Year 2*	*Year 3*	*Year 4*
	£'000	£'000	£'000	£'000	£'000
Cash outflow	(2,030)				
Cash inflows			7,100		380
Net cash flows	(2,030)		7,100		380
PV factor	1.0000	0.9346	0.8734	0.8163	0.7629
Discounted cash flows	(2,030)		6,201.14		289.90

Task 4

Year	*Cash flows*	*Discount factor*	*Present value*
	£	@ 8%	£
0	(100,000)	1.000	(100,000)
1	30,000	0.9259	27,777
2	40,000	0.8573	34,292
3	40,000	0.7938	31,752
4	20,000	0.7350	14,700
Net present value			8,521

The investment should go ahead because the NPV is positive.

Task 5

IRR = 11.3%

Generally speaking, the higher the cost of capital, the lower the NPV will be. We know from the table that at a cost of capital of 13%, the NPV is negative and at 11% it is positive. This means that the IRR is in between 11% and 13%. The correct estimate is therefore 11.3%.

Task 6

B IRR = 9.85%

$$IRR = A + \left[\frac{a}{a - b} \times (B - A)\right]$$

$$IRR = 9 + \left[\frac{22}{22 - -4} \times (10 - 9)\right]$$

$$IRR = 9 + \left[\frac{22}{22 + 4} \times 1\right]$$

$$\therefore\ IRR = 9 + \left[\frac{22}{26}\right]$$

$\therefore$ IRR = 9.85%

TEST YOUR LEARNING – ANSWERS

CHAPTER 1 Introduction to cost accounting

Test 1 (a) The three main functions of management are *planning*, *control* and *decision making*.

(b) Direct cost are costs that can be directly attributed to a *cost unit*.

(c) Indirect costs are initially allocated and apportioned to *cost centres*.

Test 2 C This is the definition of a cost unit.

In options A and B, the hour of operation and the unit of electricity are both examples of cost units for which costs have been ascertained.

Option D is an example of a particular cost unit which may be used for control purposes. It is not a definition of the term 'cost unit'.

Test 3 C This is the correct definition of a cost centre.

Option A is the definition of a cost unit.

Option B describes the *cost* of an activity or cost centre.

Option D describes a budget centre (which will not be in your assessment). Although a budget centre may also be a cost centre at times, this is not always the case.

Test 4 D It would be appropriate to use the cost per invoice processed and the cost per supplier account for control purposes. Therefore items (ii) and (iii) are suitable cost units and the correct answer is D.

Postage cost, item (i), is an expense of the department, therefore option A is not a suitable cost unit.

If you selected option B or option C you were probably rushing ahead and not taking care to read all the options.

Items (ii) and (iii) *are* suitable cost units, but neither of them are the *only* suitable suggestions.

Test 5 B Prime cost is the total of direct material, direct labour and direct expenses. Therefore the correct answer is B.

Option A describes total production cost, including absorbed production overhead. Option C is only a part of prime cost. Option D is an overhead or indirect cost.

Test 6 A Option A is a part of the cost of direct materials.

Options B and D are production overheads. Option C is a selling and distribution expense.

Test 7 A Special designs, and the hire of tools etc for a particular job can be traced to a specific cost unit. Therefore they are direct expenses and the correct answer is A.

Item (iii) is a selling and distribution overhead and item (iv) describes production overheads.

Test 8 A Depreciation is an indirect cost because it does not relate directly to the number of units produced.

Items (ii) and (iii) can be traced directly to specific cost units therefore they are direct expenses.

CHAPTER 2 Cost classification and cost behaviour

Test 1

	Capital	Revenue
A new telephone system. This will be used within the business for several accounting periods. All the associated costs of installation can be capitalised.	✓	
Depreciation of vehicles. Depreciation can be thought of as the way in which part of a capital cost is converted to a revenue expense.		✓
Salesperson's car. A company car is used by the salesman to obtain benefits for the business in the form of sales.	✓	
Road fund licence for delivery van. Although the van is a capital item, the road fund licence is a revenue expense of running the van.		✓
Telephone bill. The bill for rental and calls on the telephone system is a revenue expense.		✓
Computer software. Another example of something that is used by the business to bring benefits. The software might be used for the main business activity, such as in design of buildings by an architect, or in the processing of information necessary to administer the business	✓	
Repairs to the Managing Director's company car after an accident. This will not improve the earnings capacity of the car; it just restores it to what it was before.		✓

Test 2 (a) Fixed costs

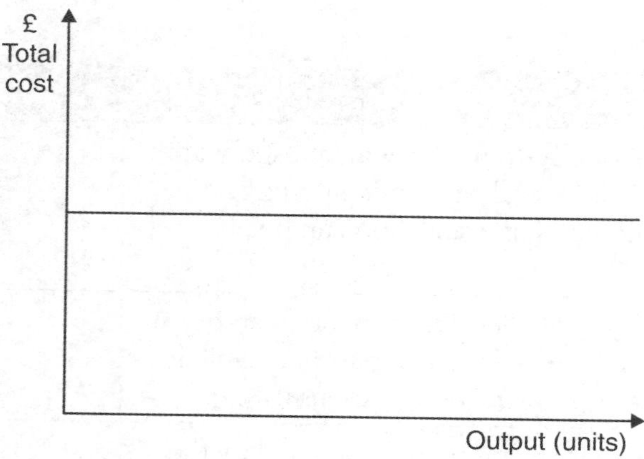

(b) Fixed cost per unit

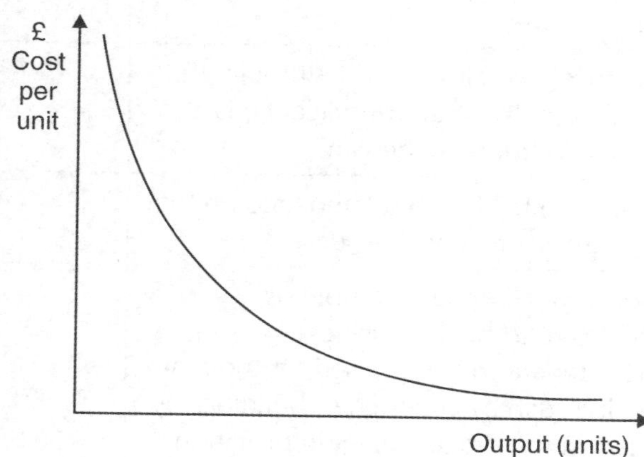

Test 3

		Cost behaviour	
		Does fit the graph shape	**Does not fit the graph shape**
(a)	Plastic used in the manufacture of moulded plastic furniture. A bulk-buying discount is given at point A on the graph.		✓
(b)	Straight-line depreciation of a freehold factory. A new factory is bought at point A.	✓	
(c)	Rent of a warehouse. A further warehouse is rented at point A.	✓	
(d)	Electricity costs that have a standing charge and a cost per unit of power used. At point A the level of production reaches the point where a nightshift is required, which uses electricity at a cheaper rate.		✓

Explanation

(a) This is a variable cost. The bulk purchase discount would give a one-off kink in the graph at point A. The graph would appear as shown below.

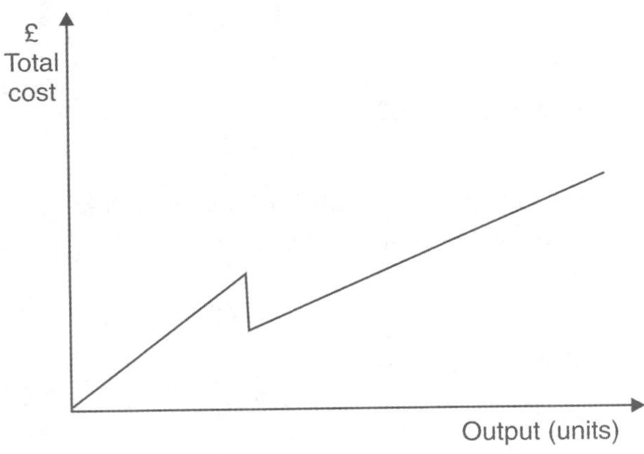

(b) and (c) are both step-fixed costs and will fit the graph shape.

(d) This is a semi-variable cost. At point A, where the cheaper rate of electricity kicks-in, the graph will flatten as each unit of product will cost slightly less in electricity. This is illustrated in the graph below.

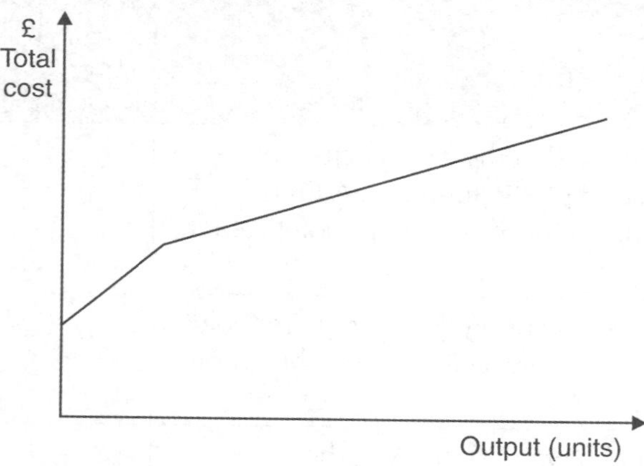

Test 4

Output (units)		*Total cost*
		£
Highest	13,500	31,500
Lowest	6,500	17,500
High-low	7,000	14,000

$$\text{Variable cost per unit} = \frac{\text{High cost} - \text{low cost}}{\text{High output} - \text{low output}}$$

$$= \frac{£14{,}000}{7{,}000}$$

$$= £2$$

At 6,500 units

	£
Total cost	17,500
Less: variable cost (6,500 × £2)	13,000
= fixed cost	4,500

Using the fixed cost of £4,500, and the variable cost of £2 per unit, we can now estimate the total cost at 12,000 units:

	£
Fixed cost	4,500
Add: variable cost (12,000 × £2)	24,000
Total cost	28,500

Test 5

COST CARD: Filing Cabinet	
	£
Direct materials (3.8 + 1.8 + 0.9)	6.50
Direct labour	6.70
Prime cost	13.20
Production overheads (0.3 + 0.2)	0.50
Production cost	13.70
Non-production overheads	
– selling and distribution	3.00
Total cost	16.70

Test 6 A Variable costs are conventionally deemed to increase or decrease in direct proportion to changes in output. Therefore the correct answer is A. Descriptions B and D imply a changing unit rate, which does not comply with this convention. Description C relates to a fixed cost.

Test 7 A The depicted cost has a basic fixed element which is payable even at zero activity. A variable element is then added at a constant rate as activity increases. Therefore the correct answer is A.

Graphs for the other options would look like this.

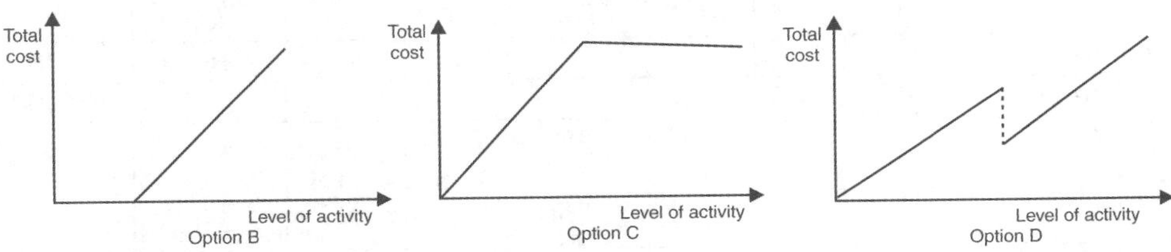

Test 8 B The cost described consists of a fixed amount up to a certain level of activity. This will be represented by a straight horizontal line. At a certain point a variable element is added and the cost line will slope upwards at a constant rate. Graph 2 demonstrates this pattern therefore the correct answer is B.

If you selected option D, graph 4, you had the right idea for the second part of the graph. However, graph 4 depicts zero cost up to a certain level, which is not correct.

Test 9 A The cost described will increase in steps, remaining fixed at each step until another supervisor is required. Graph 1 depicts a step cost therefore the correct answer is A.

Test 10 C The cost described begins as a linear variable cost, increasing at a constant rate in line with activity. At a certain point the cost becomes fixed regardless of the level of activity. Graph 3 demonstrates this behaviour pattern. Therefore the correct answer is C.

Test 11 D The salary is part fixed (£650 per month) and part variable (5 pence per unit). Therefore it is a semi-variable cost and answer D is correct.

If you chose options A or B you were considering only part of the cost.

Option C, a step-fixed cost, involves a cost which remains constant up to a certain level and then increases to a new, higher, constant fixed cost.

CHAPTER 3 Materials costs and inventory valuation

Test 1 (a) **FIFO**

Inventory Record Card								
	Purchases			Requisitions			Balance	
Date	Quantity	Cost	Total cost	Quantity	Cost	Total cost	Quantity	Total cost
	(kg)	£	£	(kg)	£	£	(kg)	£
3 Jan							100	880
16 Jan	400	9.00	3,600				500	4,480
27 Jan				100 150 250	8.80 9.00	880 1,350 2,230	250	2,250
5 Feb				180	9.00	1,620	70	630
9 Feb	400	9.30	3,720				470	4,350
17 Feb				70 350 420	9.00 9.30	630 3,255 3,885	50	465
25 Feb	500	9.35	4,675				550	5,140

Cost of material issues = £2,230 + £1,620 + £3,885
= £7,735

Value of closing inventory = £5,140

(b) **LIFO**

Inventory Record Card								
	Purchases			Requisitions			Balance	
Date	Quantity	Cost	Total cost	Quantity	Cost	Total cost	Quantity	Total cost
	(kg)	£	£	(kg)	£	£	(kg)	£
3 Jan							100	880
16 Jan	400	9.00	3,600				500	4,480
27 Jan				250	9.00	2,250	250	2,230
5 Feb				150	9.00	1,350		
				30	8.80	264		
				180		1,614	70	616
9 Feb	400	9.30	3,720				470	4,336
17 Feb				400	9.30	3,720		
				20	8.80	176		
				420		3,896	50	440
25 Feb	500	9.35	4,675				550	5,115

Cost of material issues = £2,250 + £1,614 + £3,896

= £7,760

Value of closing inventory = £5,115

(c) **AVCO**

Inventory Record Card								
	Purchases			Requisitions			Balance	
Date	Quantity	Cost	Total *cost*	Quantity	Cost	Total *cost*	Quantity	Total *cost*
	(kg)	£	£	(kg)	£	£	(kg)	£
3 Jan							100	880.00
16 Jan	400	9.00	3,600				500	4,480.00
27 Jan				250	8.96	2,240	250	2,240.00
5 Feb				180	8.96	1,612.80	70	627.20
9 Feb	400	9.30	3,720				470	4,347.20
17 Feb				420	9.249	3,884.58	50	462.62
25 Feb	500	9.35	4,675				550	5,137.62

Cost of material issues = £2,240.00 + £1,612.80 + £3,884.58

= £7,737.38

Value of closing inventory = £5,137.62

Test 2 The LIFO method of valuing materials has the advantage of being fairly easy to calculate and understand. Materials issues tend to be at current prices which makes managers more aware of the prevailing prices.

There are several disadvantages of LIFO. Prices charged for issues will constantly change, which makes managers' job of decision-making more difficult. The calculations are sometimes cumbersome, as there may be part-batches of unused old prices that have to be carried forwards for when inventories run low and they are needed. The LIFO cost flow assumption, that the latest deliveries are used first, is rarely the case in practice, and it can therefore be argued that it is not appropriate. HM Revenue & Customs and Accounting Standards do not approve of LIFO for tax or financial reporting purposes.

Test 3

Materials control account

		£			£
1 Mar	Opening balance	12,400	31 Mar	WIP	160,400
31 Mar	Bank/payables	167,200	31 Mar	Production o/h control	8,300
			31 Mar	Closing balance	10,900
		179,600			179,600

Work in progress control account

		£			£
31 Mar	Materials control	160,400			

Production overhead control account

		£			£
31 Mar	Materials control	8,300			

Test 4 Holding costs: warehouse rent, insurance, and cost of capital tied up.

Ordering costs: postage of order, wages for the checkers in the goods inwards department, salary of the clerk dealing with the order.

(**Note.** These are only suggestions. Refer to the section entitled Inventory control for more examples.)

If the reorder quantity were increased, fewer orders would be needed each year to obtain the same overall quantity of inventory, leading to a decrease in ordering costs. However, the amount of inventory stored at any point in time would be greater so holding costs would increase.

Test 5 $$EOQ = \sqrt{\frac{2cd}{h}}$$

$$= \sqrt{\frac{2 \times £50 \times (15 \times 52)}{£19.65}}$$

$$= \sqrt{3,969}$$

$$= 63 \text{ rolls}$$

Test 6 Reorder level = maximum usage × maximum lead time

= 200 litres per day × 8 days

= 1,600 litres

Test 7 Using the FIFO method, the total value of the issues on 30 April is £ 2,765

Date	*Receipts* Units	*Issues* Units	*Balance*		£
1 April			275 @ £3.20		880
8 April	600		600 @ £3.00		1,800
15 April	400		400 @ £3.40		1,360
					4,040
					£
30 April		900			
		275 @ £3.20		=	880
		600 @ £3.00		=	1,800
		25 @ £3.40		=	85
					2,765

Test 8 Using the weighted average price method of inventory valuation, the total value of the components remaining in inventory on 23 March was £ 20,790

Average price of inventory on 23 March:

Units			£
2,400	×	£6	14,400
4,000	×	£6.20	24,800
2,000	×	£6.86	13,720
8,400			52,920

Average price per component = £52,920/8,400 = £6.30

Value of inventory on 23 March = (8,400 – 5,100) × £6.30

= £20,790

Test 9 Using the FIFO method of inventory valuation, the total value of the components issued on 23 March was £ 31,140 (to the nearest £)

The FIFO method uses the price of the oldest batches first:

			£
2,400	×	£6	14,400
2,700	×	£6.20	16,740
5,100			31,140

CHAPTER 4 Labour costs and expenses

Test 1

	J Sparrow	K Finch	M Swallow	B Cuckoo
Total hours	39.5	37.5	38.75	37.5
Basic pay (35 × £7)	£245.00	£245.00	£245.00	£245.00
Time and a half	(1.5 × £10.50)	(2.5 × £10.50)	(1.75 × £10.50)	(0.5 × £10.50)
	= £15.75	= £26.25	= £18.38	= £5.25
Double time	(3 × £14)		(2 × £14)	(2 × £14)
	= £42.00		= £28.00	= £28.00
Total gross pay	£302.75	£271.25	£291.38	£278.25

Test 2 Direct labour cost = 40h × £10 per h = £400

Indirect labour cost = 5h × £4 per h = £20

Alternatively:	£
Direct cost	
Basic pay (35h × £10 per h)	350
Overtime: at basic rate (5h × £10 per h)	50
	400
Indirect cost	
Overtime: premium (5h × £4 per h)	20

Test 3 Rather than paying just a time rate or a salary, an employer can make use of a bonus system to give employees an incentive to increase production. The bonus is paid if output is higher than a target level. The target set might be a certain time taken to do a job or a certain level of profit earned, or it might be judgmental, for example, management makes the decision as to who receives a bonus. Piecework, whereby employees are paid for each good unit of output, is another incentive scheme.

The major problem with these two methods of remuneration is that they reward quantity and not quality. Therefore, whilst output increases, there can be a consequent fall in quality and increased wastage. More inspectors will be needed to offset this problem, but this will add to costs. Other problems can arise from the complexity of the schemes adopted: they often involve more complex calculations and pay negotiations are more complicated. Bonus and piecework systems are not appropriate for all types of employees, and pay will be affected by production problems even when a guaranteed minimum amount is built into a piecework scheme.

Test 4 The hours recorded in the timesheet can be used to calculate M. Rooney's pay for the week.

Employee's weekly timesheet for week ending 5 April

Employee: M Rooney			**Profit Centre:** Widget carving			
Employee number: A450			**Basic pay per hour:** £10.00			
	Hours spent on production	**Hours worked on indirect work**	**Notes**	**Basic pay £**	**Overtime premium £**	**Total pay £**
Monday	6	2	10am–12am Machine calibration	80	10	90
Tuesday	2	4	9am–1pm HR awareness course	60	–	60
Wednesday	8			80	10	90
Thursday	6			60	–	60
Friday	6	1	3pm–4pm Customer care training	70	5	75
Saturday	6			60	20	80
Sunday	3			30	30	60
Total	**37**	**7**		440	75	515

Test 5 D The overtime was not worked on any specific job and is therefore an indirect wages cost to be 'collected' in the overhead control account. The direct wages of £70,800 is debited to the work-in-progress account and the total wages cost is credited to the wages control account.

CHAPTER 5 Accounting for overheads

Test 1 (a)

	£
Actual overheads	1,600
Absorbed overheads (650 units @ £3 per unit)	1,950
Over absorption	350

The over absorption of £350 would be added to profit (a credit) in the statement of profit or loss

(b)

	£
Actual overheads	8,600
Absorbed overheads (590h × £15 per hr)	8,850
Over absorption	250

* Overhead absorption rate $= \dfrac{\text{£9,000}}{\text{600 direct labour hours}} =$ £15 per direct labour hour

The over absorption of £250 would be added to profit (a credit) in the statement of profit or loss

(c)

	£
Actual overheads	3,500
Absorbed overheads (552hr × £5)	2,760
Under absorption	740

The under absorption of £740 would be deducted from profit (a debit) in the statement of profit or loss.

Test 2 A Overhead absorption rates are determined in advance for each period, usually based on budgeted data. Therefore statement (i) is correct and statement (iii) is incorrect. Overhead absorption rates are used in the final stage of overhead analysis, to absorb overheads into product costs. Therefore statement (ii) is correct. Statement (iv) is not correct because overheads are controlled using budgets and other management information. Therefore the correct answer is A.

Test 3 A Description B could lead to under-absorbed overheads if actual overheads far exceeded both budgeted overheads and the overhead absorbed. Description C could lead to under-absorbed overheads if budgeted overhead absorbed does not increase in line with actual overhead incurred. Description D could also lead to under absorption if actual overhead does not decrease in line with absorbed overheads.

Test 4 A Budgeted overhead absorption rate $= \frac{£258,750}{11,250} = £23$ per machine hour

	£
Overhead absorbed = £23 × 10,980 hours	252,540
Overhead incurred	254,692
Under-absorbed overhead	2,152

If you selected option B or C you calculated the difference between the budgeted and actual overheads and interpreted the result as an under or over absorption.

If you selected option D your calculations were correct but you misinterpreted the result as over absorbed.

Test 5 B Overhead absorption rate $= \frac{\text{budgeted overheads}}{\text{budgeted labour hours}} = \frac{£148,750}{8,500}$

$= £17.50$ per hr

If you selected option A you divided the actual overheads by the budgeted labour hours. Option C is based on the actual overheads and actual labour hours. If you selected option D you divided the budgeted overheads by the actual hours.

Test 6 D

	£
Overhead absorbed = £17.50 × 7,928 =	138,740
Overhead incurred=	146,200
Under-absorbed overhead=	7,460

If you selected options A or B you calculated the difference between the budgeted and actual overheads and interpreted it as an under or over absorption. If you selected option C you performed the calculations correctly but misinterpreted the result as an over absorption.

CHAPTER 6 Absorption costing

Test 1 ✓ Spread common costs over cost centres

Overhead apportionment involves sharing overhead costs as fairly as possible over a number of cost centres. Apportionment is used when it is not possible to allocate the whole cost to a single cost centre.

Test 2 (a) **Basis of apportionment**

	Total	*Machine shop*	*Assembly*	*Painting*	*Services*
	£	£	£	£	£
Factory rent, rates and insurance (floor area) 5:2:3:2	9,000	3,750	1,500	2,250	1,500
Depreciation of machinery (value of machinery) 12:4:3:1	4,000	2,400	800	600	200
Supervisor's salary (number of employees) 8:9:5:2	8,000	2,667	3,000	1,667	666
Heat and light (floor area) 5:2:3:2	2,000	833	333	500	334
Apportionment to all departments	23,000	9,650	5,633	5,017	2,700
(b)					
Reapportionment of Services (40:30:30)	–	1,080	810	810	(2,700)
Total after reapportionment	23,000	10,730	6,443	5,827	Nil

Test 3 (a) **Basis of apportionment**

	Total	*V*	*W*	*S1*	*S2*
	£	£	£	£	£
Indirect materials	310,000	160,000	120,000	10,000	20,000
Indirect labour	1,125,000	400,000	650,000	40,000	35,000
Buildings depreciation and insurance (volume occupied) 60:30:8:2	100,000	60,000	30,000	8,000	2,000
Cleaning (volume occupied) 60:30:8:2	25,000	15,000	7,500	2,000	500
Machinery depreciation and insurance (value of machinery) 380:600:0:20	1,500,000	570,000	900,000	–	30,000
Supervision of production (supervisor hours) 15:20:0:0	70,000	30,000	40,000		
Power (% of power usage) 25:45:20:10	250,000	62,500	112,500	50,000	25,000
Heat and light (volume occupied) 60:30:8:2	20,000	12,000	6,000	1,600	400
Total after allocation and apportionment	3,400,000	1,309,500	1,866,000	111,600	112,900

(b) **Reapportionment**

(step-down method) S2 first 40:50:10		45,160	56,450	11,290	(112,900)
				122,890	
S1 next 40:60		49,156	73,734	(122,890)	
Total after reapportionment	3,400,000	1,403,816	1,996,184	nil	nil

(c) **Overhead absorption rates**

	V	*W*
$\frac{\text{Overheads}}{\text{Direct labour hours}} =$	$\frac{1,403,816}{200,000}$	$\frac{1,996,184}{500,000}$
	= £7.02 per direct labour hour	= £3.99 per direct labour hour

Test 4 Department P1 $= \frac{£50,000}{2,500 \text{ h}}$

= £20 per direct labour hour

Department P2 $= \frac{£60,000}{4,000 \text{ h}}$

= £15 per machine hour

Direct labour hours was chosen as the basis for absorption of the overheads of department P1 as this department is labour intensive, and there is likely to be a link between the direct labour hours worked and the overheads incurred. Similarly, with department P2, which is more mechanised and less dependent upon direct labour, the use of the machinery is more likely to be related to overheads in that department.

CHAPTER 7 Job, batch and service costing

Test 1

	£
Direct materials fabric	590.00
– lining	175.00
Labour 27 hours @ £7.70	207.90
Overheads 27 hours @ £8.70	234.90
(a) **Cost of production**	1,207.80
Profit 15% × 1,207.80	181.17
	1,388.97
VAT at 20%	277.79
(b) **Final quote to the customer**	1,666.76

Test 2

Job costing schedule	£
Materials	12,500.00
Direct labour –fitting 23 hours @ £8.60	197.80
– decorating 5 hours @ 6.50	32.50
Overheads 28 hours @ £12.40	347.20
Total costs	13,077.50
Profit 25% × 13,077.50	3,269.38
	16,346.88
VAT at 20%	3,269.38
Cost to the customer	19,616.26

Test 3

	£
Ingredients	840.00
Labour 7 hours @ £6.50	45.50
Overheads 7 hours @ £1.20	8.40
	893.90

$$\text{Cost per pie} = \frac{£893.90}{1{,}200}$$

$$= 74.5 \text{ pence}$$

Test 4 B In service costing it is difficult to identify many attributable direct costs. Many costs must be shared over several cost units, therefore characteristic (i) does apply. Composite cost units such as tonne-mile or room-night are often used, therefore characteristic (ii) does apply. Equivalent units are more often used in costing for tangible products, therefore characteristic (iii) does not apply, so the correct answer is B.

Test 5 C Cost per tonne – kilometre (i) is appropriate for cost control purposes because it combines the distance travelled and the load carried, both of which affect cost.

The fixed cost per kilometre (ii) is not particularly useful for control purposes because it varies with the number of kilometres travelled.

The maintenance cost of each vehicle per kilometre (iii) can be useful for control purposes because it focuses on a particular aspect of the cost of operating each vehicle.

The correct answer is therefore C.

Test 6 D All of the activities identified would use service costing, except the engineering company which will be providing products not services.

CHAPTER 8 Process Costing

Test 1 ✓ At the same rate as good production

Test 2 ✓ A notional whole unit representing incomplete work

Test 3 Debit [Scrap] account

Credit [Process] account

Test 4

Step 1 Calculate the number of normal loss units:

50,000 kg × 5% = 2,500 kg

Step 2 Calculate the expected output from the process:

50,000 kg – 2,500 kg = 47,500 kg

Step 3 Total the process costs:

£350,000 + £125,000 + £57,000 = £532,000

Step 4 Calculate the cost per unit of expected output:

= £11.20 per kg

Process account

	kg	£		kg	£
Materials	50,000	350,000	Normal loss	2,500	–
Labour		125,000	Abnormal loss	1,500	16,800
Overheads		57,000	Output	46,000	515,200
	50,000	532,000		50,000	532,000

Test 5

Step 1 Calculate the number of normal loss units:

6,000 ltr × 10% = 600 ltr

Step 2 Calculate the expected output from the process:

6,000 ltr – 600 ltr = 5,400 ltr

Step 3 Total the process costs:

£14,300 + £7,200 + £11,980 = £33,480

Step 4 Calculate the cost per unit of expected output:

$$\frac{£33,480}{5,400 \text{ ltr}} = £6.20 \text{ per litre}$$

Process account

	ltr	£		ltr	£
Materials	6,000	14,300	Normal loss	600	–
Labour		7,200			
Overheads		11,980			
Abnormal gain	200	1,240	Output	5,600	34,720
	6,200	34,720		6,200	34,720

Test 6 **Step 1** Calculate the number of normal loss units:

40,000 kg × 8% = 3,200 kg

Step 2 Calculate the expected output from the process:

40,000 kg – 3,200 kg = 36,800 kg

Step 3 Total the process costs and deduct the scrap proceeds for the normal loss:

(£158,200 + £63,500 + £31,740) – (3,200 × £1) = £250,240

Step 4 Calculate the cost per unit of expected output:

$$\frac{£250{,}240}{36{,}800 \text{ kg}} = £6.80 \text{ per kg}$$

Process account

	kg	£		kg	£
Materials	40,000	158,200	Normal loss	3,200	3,200
Labour		63,500	Abnormal loss	1,800	12,240
Overheads		31,740	Output	35,000	238,000
	40,000	253,440		40,000	253,440

Test 7

		Materials		*Labour/overheads*	
	Units	*Proportion complete*	*Equivalent units*	*Proportion complete*	*Equivalent units*
Completed units	2,000	100%	2,000	100%	2,000
Closing work in progress	400	60%	240	50%	200
Total equivalent units			2,240		2,200
Cost per equivalent unit		£8,960/2,240		£4,290/2,200	
		= £4.00 per EU		= £1.95 per EU	

Valuation	£
Completed units	
Materials (2,000 × £4.00)	8,000
Labour/overheads (2,000 × £1.95)	3,900
	11,900
Closing work in progress	
Materials (240 × £4.00)	960
Labour/overheads (200 × £1.95)	390
	1,350

Process account

	£		£
Materials	8,960	Completed units	11,900
Labour/overhead	4,290	Closing work in progress	1,350
	13,250		13,250

CHAPTER 9 Budgeting: fixed and flexed budgets

Test 1

(a)

	Budget *4,000 units*	*Actual* *3,600 units*	*Variance*
	£	£	
Sales	96,000	90,000	6,000 Adv
Materials	18,000	15,120	2,880 Fav
Labour	27,200	25,200	2,000 Fav
Production overhead	5,700	5,900	200 Adv
Gross profit	45,100	43,780	1,320 Adv
General expenses	35,200	32,880	2,320 Fav
Operating profit	9,900	10,900	1,000 Fav

(b)

	Flexed budget *3,600 units*	*Actual* *3,600 units*	*Variance*
	£	£	
Sales 3,600 × £24	86,400	90,000	3,600 Fav
Materials 3,600 × £4.50	16,200	15,120	1,080 Fav
Labour 3,600 × £6.80	24,480	25,200	720 Adv
Production overhead	5,700	5,900	200 Adv
Gross profit	40,020	43,780	3,760 Fav
General expenses	35,200	32,880	2,320 Fav
Operating profit	4,820	10,900	6,080 Fav

(c) When the actual results are compared to the fixed budget even though the overall result is a favourable profit variance the comparison is between actual sales and production of 3,600 units and a budget of 4,000 units. In particular this has affected the sales showing an adverse variance of £6,000.

However when the actual results are compared to the flexed budget the sales variance becomes a £3,600 favourable variance and the favourable profit variance has increased.

Test 2

	Flexed Budget	Actual	Variance	Favourable F or Adverse A.
Volume sold	72,000	72,000		
	£000	£000	£000	
Sales revenue	1,440	1,800	360	F
Less costs:				
Direct materials	252	265	13	A
Direct labour	288	240	48	F
Overheads	350	630	280	A
Operating profit	550	665	115	F

CHAPTER 10 Variance analysis

Test 1

	£
Total materials cost variance	
Budget cost of actual production	
1,800 × 7 kg × £6.00	75,600
Actual cost	70,800
	4,800 (Fav)

Test 2

	£
Total labour cost variance	
Budget cost of actual production	
15,400 × 2.5 hours × £6.80	261,800
Actual cost	265,200
	3,400 (Adv)

Test 3

(a) Budgeted fixed overhead = 7,000 units × 3 hours × £2.50
= £52,500

(b) Total fixed overhead variance

	£
Budgeted fixed overhead	52,500
Actual fixed overhead	56,000
	3,500 (Adv)

CHAPTER 11 Cost bookkeeping

Test 1

Materials control account

	£		£
Payables control	4,380	WIP control	4,190

Wages control account

	£		£
Bank	4,140	WIP control	3,200
		Production overhead control	940

Production overhead control account

£	£	£	£
Bank	1,200	WIP control 480 hours @ £3.10	1,488
Wages control	940	Under absorbed overhead	652

Work in progress control account

	£		£
Materials control	4,190	Finished goods	7,900
Wages control	3,200		
Production o/h control	1,488		

Test 2

Production overhead control account

	£		£
Overhead incurred	3,800	Overhead absorbed 550 @ £6.80	3,740
	3,800	Under-absorbed overhead	60
	3,800		3,800

The balance on the account, representing under-absorbed overheads, is debited to the statement of profit or loss.

Test 3

Materials control account

	£		£
Opening balance	550	WIP control	4,670
Payables control	5,300	Administration overhead	760
		Closing balance	420
	5,850		5,850

Wages control account

	£		£
Bank (2,520 + 640)	3,160	WIP control	2,520
		Production overhead control	640
	3,160		3,160

Production overhead control account

	£		£
Wages control	640	WIP control 360 hours @ £7.80	2,808
Bank	2,700	Under-absorbed overhead	532
	3,340		3,340

Work in progress control account

	£		£
Opening balance	680	Finished goods	10,000
Materials control	4,670		
Wages control	2,520		
Production o/h control	2,808	Closing balance	678
	10,678		10,678

Finished goods control account

	£		£
Opening balance	1,040	Cost of sales (bal fig)	9,030
WIP	10,000	Closing inventory	2,010
	11,040		11,040

Receivables control account

	£		£
Opening balance	3,700	Bank	11,000
Sales	12,000	Closing balance	4,700
	15,700		15,700

Payables control account

	£		£
Bank	5,140	Opening balance	2,100
Closing balance	2,260	Materials control	5,300
	7,400		7,400

Cash at bank account

	£		£
Opening balance	2,090	Wages control	3,160
Receivables control	11,000	Payables control	5,140
		Production overhead control	2,700
		Administration overhead control	1,580
		Closing balance	510
	13,090		13,090

Administration overheads account

	£		£
Materials control	760	St of profit or loss	2,340
Bank	1,580		
	2,340		2,340

Sales account

	£		£
		Receivables control	12,000

Test 4 Statement of profit or loss

	£
Sales revenue	12,000
Cost of goods sold	9,030
Gross profit	2,970
Administration overhead	(2,340)
Under-absorbed production overhead	(532)
Profit for the year	98

CHAPTER 12 Marginal costing

Test 1 In an absorption costing system all fixed production overheads are absorbed into the cost of the products and are included in unit cost. In a marginal costing system the fixed production overheads are written off in the statement of profit or loss as a period cost.

Test 2 (a) Absorption costing – unit cost

	£
Direct materials	12.50
Direct labour assembly (4 × £8.40)	33.60
finishing	6.60
Assembly overheads (£336,000/(60,000 × 4) × 4)	5.60
Finishing overheads (£84,000/60,000)	1.40
	59.70

(b) Marginal costing – unit cost

	£
Direct materials	12.50
Direct labour assembly (4 × £8.40)	33.60
finishing	6.60
Assembly overheads $\frac{£336,000 \times 60\%}{240,000} \times 4$	3.36
Finishing overheads $\frac{£84,000 \times 75\%}{60,000}$	1.05
	1.05
	57.11

Test 3 Unit cost

	£
Direct materials	12.00
Direct labour	8.00
Variable overhead (£237,000/15,000)	15.80
Marginal costing unit cost	35.80
Fixed overhead (£390,000/15,000)	26.00
Absorption costing unit cost	61.80

(a) (i) Absorption costing – statement of profit or loss

		November		December
	£	£	£	£
Sales (12,500/18,000 × £75)		937,500		1,350,000
Less: cost of goods sold				
Opening inventory				
(2,000 × £61.80)	123,600			
(4,500 × £61.80)			278,100	
Production costs				
(15,000 × £61.80)	927,000		927,000	
	1,050,600		1,205,100	
Less: closing inventory				
(4,500 × £61.80)	278,100			
(1,500 × £61.80)			92,700	
		772,500		1,112,400
Profit		165,000		237,600

(ii) Marginal costing – statement of profit or loss

		November		December
	£	£	£	£
Sales (12,500/18,000 × £75)		937,500		1,350,000
Less: cost of goods sold				
Opening inventory				
(2,000 × £35.80)	71,600			
(4,500 × £35.80)			161,100	
Production costs				
(15,000 × £35.80)	537,000		537,000	
	608,600		698,100	
Less: closing inventory				
(4,500 × £35.80)	161,100			
(1,500 × £35.80)			53,700	
		447,500		644,400
Contribution		490,000		705,600
Less: fixed overheads		390,000		390,000
Profit		100,000		315,600

(b)

	November	December
	£	£
Absorption costing profit	165,000	237,600
Increase in inventory × fixed cost per unit		
((4,500 – 2,000) × £26)	(65,000)	
Decrease in inventory × fixed cost per unit		
((4,500 – 1,500) × £26)		78,000
Marginal costing profit	100,000	315,600

CHAPTER 13 Short-term decision making

Test 1 As activity levels increase the fixed costs will be split amongst more units, and the amount of fixed cost in a unit cost will get smaller. With no change in selling cost or variable cost the total unit cost will decrease.

Test 2 Break-even point $= \frac{£360,000}{£57 - £45}$

$= \boxed{30,000}$ units

Margin of safety $= \frac{38,000 - 30,000}{38,000}$

$= \boxed{21\%}$

Test 3 Target profit sales $= \frac{£910,000 + £500,000}{£24 - £17}$

$= \boxed{201,429}$ units

Test 4 Profit volume ratio $= \frac{£(40 - 32)}{£40} \times 100$

$= 20\%$

Target profit sales revenue $= \frac{£100,000 + £200,000}{0.20}$

$= \boxed{£1,500,000}$

Test 5 Where there is more than one product and a limiting factor, overall profit is maximised by concentrating production on the products with the highest contribution per limiting factor unit.

CHAPTER 14 Long-term decision making

Test 1

(a) **Payback period – Investment A**

Date	*Cash flow*	*Cumulative cash flow*
	£	£
30 June 20X7	43,000	43,000
30 June 20X8	51,000	94,000
30 June 20X9	52,000	146,000

2 years $+ \frac{£26,000}{£52,000} \times$ 12 months

= 2 years and 6 months

Payback period – Investment B

30 June 20X7	21,000	21,000
30 June 20X8	21,000	42,000
30 June 20X9	21,000	63,000
30 June 20Y0	21,000	84,000
30 June 20Y1	40,000	124,000

$$4 \text{ years} + \frac{£16,000}{£40,000} \times 12 \text{ months}$$

= 4 years and 5 months

Therefore only Investment A would be accepted.

(b) The payback period method is only concerned with how quickly the initial cost of the investment is repaid from cash inflows. It ignores any cash flows after the payback period. In this case only Investment A would be accepted under the payback method; however, overall, Investment B has greater total cash inflows and a lower initial investment than Investment A.

Test 2

(a) £3,100 × 0.7972 = £2,471.32

(b) £15,000 × 1.000 = £15,000.00

(c) £1,000 × 1.6901 = £1,690.10

(d) £4,400 × 0.8734 = £3,842.96

Test 3

Year	*Cash flows*	*Discount factor*	*Present value*
	£	@ 7%	£
0	(340,000)	1.000	(340,000)
1	80,000	0.9346	74,768
2	70,000	0.8734	61,138
3	90,000	0.8163	73,467
4	120,000	0.7629	91,548
5	60,000	0.7130	42,780
Net present value			3,701

Remember that depreciation is not a cash flow and is therefore excluded from the net present value calculations.

Test 4

(a)

Year	Cash flows	Discount factor	Present value
	£	@ 11%	£
0	(90,000)	1.000	(90,000)
1	23,000	0.9009	20,721
2	31,000	0.8116	25,160
3	40,000	0.7312	29,248
4	18,000	0.6587	11,857
Net present values			(3,014)

(b) As the investment in the new plant and machinery has a negative net present value at the cost of capital of 11% then the investment should not take place.

INDEX

BPP
LEARNING MEDIA

Notes

Notes

Notes

Notes

BPP
LEARNING MEDIA

Notes

BPP
LEARNING MEDIA

Notes

Notes

REVIEW FORM

How have you used this Text?
(Tick one box only)

☐ Home study

☐ On a course ____________________

☐ Other ____________________

During the past six months do you recall seeing/receiving either of the following?
(Tick as many boxes as are relevant)

☐ Our advertisement in Accounting Technician

☐ Our Publishing Catalogue

Why did you decide to purchase this Text? *(Tick one box only)*

☐ Have used BPP Texts in the past

☐ Recommendation by friend/colleague

☐ Recommendation by a college lecturer

☐ Saw advertising

☐ Other ____________________

Which (if any) aspects of our advertising do you think are useful?
(Tick as many boxes as are relevant)

☐ Prices and publication dates of new editions

☐ Information on Text content

☐ Details of our free online offering

☐ None of the above

Your ratings, comments and suggestions would be appreciated on the following areas of this Text.

	Very useful	*Useful*	*Not useful*
Introductory section	☐	☐	☐
Quality of explanations	☐	☐	☐
How it works	☐	☐	☐
Chapter tasks	☐	☐	☐
Chapter overviews	☐	☐	☐
Test your learning	☐	☐	☐
Index	☐	☐	☐

	Excellent	*Good*	*Adequate*	*Poor*
Overall opinion of this Text	☐	☐	☐	☐

Do you intend to continue using BPP Products? ☐ Yes ☐ No

Please note any further comments and suggestions/errors on the reverse of this page. The author of this edition can be e-mailed at: ianblackmore@bpp.com

Please return to: Ian Blackmore, AAT Range Manager, BPP Learning Media Ltd, FREEPOST, London, W12 8AA.

REVIEW FORM (continued)

TELL US WHAT YOU THINK

Please note any further comments and suggestions/errors below